Imagining Philadelphia

Imagining Philadelphia

Edmund Bacon and the Future of the City

Edited by
Scott Gabriel Knowles

PENN

University of Pennsylvania Press

Philadelphia

Published by
University of Pennsylvania Press
Philadelphia, Pennsylvania 19104-4112

Printed in the United States of America on acid-free paper
10   9   8   7   6   5   4   3   2   1

Library of Congress Cataloging-in-Publication Data

Imagining Philadelphia : Edmund Bacon and the future of the city / edited by Scott Gabriel Knowles.
    p.   cm.
  Includes bibliographical references and index.
  ISBN 978-0-8122-2078-0 (alk. paper)
  Includes index
  1. City planning—Pennsylvania—Philadelphia—History—20th century.
2. Philadelphia (Pa.)—Forecasting.   3. Bacon, Edmund N.   4. Bacon, Edmund N.—Political and social views.   5. City planners—Pennsylvania—Philadelphia—Biography.
6. Philadelphia City Planning Commission—Biography.   7. City planning—United States—Case studies.   I. Knowles, Scott Gabriel.
HT168.P43E56   2009
307.1'21609748110904—dc22   2009008430

Contents

Introduction: Revisiting Edmund Bacon's Vision for the City

When Philadelphia's iconoclastic City Planning Commission director Edmund Bacon looked into his crystal ball in 1959—imagining his city fifty years in the future—he saw a remarkable vision, Philadelphia transformed into "an unmatched expression of the vitality of American technology and culture." In that year, Bacon painted a word picture in an essay for *Greater Philadelphia Magazine,* "Tomorrow: A Fair Can Pace It," originally titled "Philadelphia in the Year 2009."[1] He saw a vision of a city remade in time to host the 1976 Philadelphia World's Fair—an event that would necessarily take place alongside the national Bicentennial celebration of that year. Basing his optimism on the success of the Better Philadelphia Exhibition of 1947 and his knowledge of previous world's fairs, he was undertaking one of the great sales pitches of his long career: the Bicentennial and a Philadelphia World's Fair as catalysts for a golden age of urban renewal in a major American city. What Bacon did not predict was that Philadelphia was about to enter a long, bitter period of economic decline, population dispersal to the suburbs, and racial confrontation and violence, and that by 1976 the nation would be far less inclined than usual to celebrate, with the memories of Watergate and Vietnam still fresh. As such, Bacon's "2009" essay comes to us as a time capsule, a message from one of the city's most influential and controversial shapers, opening the way to discussions of what might have been and how certain pieces of Bacon's vision have in fact materialized in the intervening half century.

"Philadelphia in the Year 2009" opens with a brief history lesson, a paean to the long-lasting genius of Quaker founder William Penn's grid design for the city. Then Bacon delivers us to the city of the future, the Philadelphia he predicts can and must rise from a post-Depression, postwar inertia—from the old industrial city. Among the many projects he describes in the essay are Washington Square East, "buttressed by a continuous band of good housing extending from the Delaware to the Schuylkill River," and the Delaware River Marina, "a magnet for visitors . . . the point of departure for the launches that take visitors to the Navy

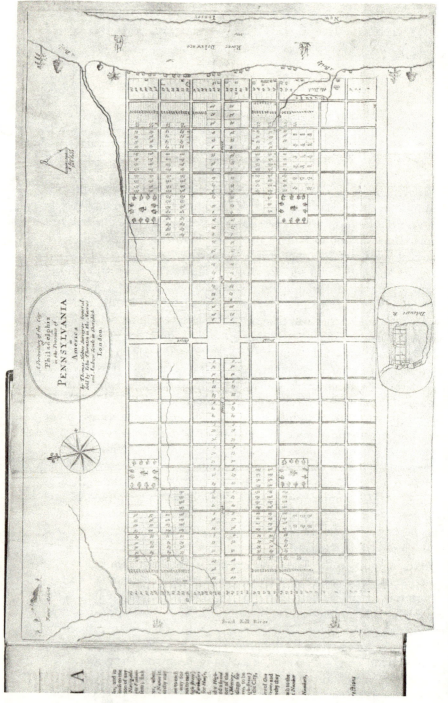

Figure 1. Map of Philadelphia by Thomas Holme and William Penn, 1683. Courtesy of the Rare Book and Manuscript Library, University of Pennsylvania.

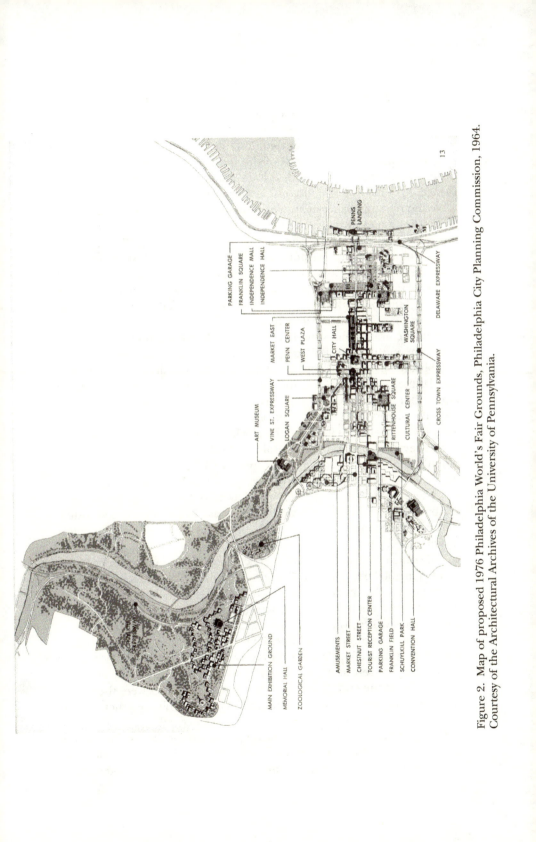

Figure 2. Map of proposed 1976 Philadelphia World's Fair Grounds, Philadelphia City Planning Commission, 1964. Courtesy of the Architectural Archives of the University of Pennsylvania.

PARKING GARAGE
FRANKLIN SQUARE
INDEPENDENCE MALL
INDEPENDENCE HALL

PENNS LANDING

MARKET EAST

PENN CENTER

WEST PLAZA

CITY HALL

WASHINGTON SQUARE

DELAWARE EXPRESSWAY

ART MUSEUM

VINE ST. EXPRESSWAY

LOGAN SQUARE

RITTENHOUSE SQUARE

CULTURAL CENTER

CROSS TOWN EXPRESSWAY

AMUSEMENTS
MARKET STREET
CHESTNUT STREET
TOURIST RECEPTION CENTER
PARKING GARAGE
FRANKLIN FIELD
SCHUYLKILL PARK
CONVENTION HALL

MAIN EXHIBITION GROUND
MEMORIAL HALL
ZOOLOGICAL GARDEN

13

Yard for trips through aircraft carriers and cruisers, and a stop at Old Fort Mifflin." Chestnut Street will be barred to automobile traffic, allowing "open-sided electric cars" to traverse this "Midway . . . [where] stores have removed their front windows and carry on outdoor activities, loggia-like half in and half out of the building." The east bank of the Schuylkill River is redeveloped, as is the area north of the Spring Garden Bridge, for world's fair buildings. Underground streets must be built to serve the parking terminal at Broad Street, with a moving sidewalk, and the East Market Center will "amalgamate the Pennsylvania and Reading commuter railroads into one system"—a project that "involves the rebuilding of much of the north side of Market Street." At the regional level, we can expect a metropolitan transportation authority that will integrate rail, subway, and bus lines, and an expressway system. Heliports must be built on both rivers. Factories must be "well kept and in good surroundings. Industrial Parks have become both a name and a fact." Last, in the area of housing, Bacon sees a rehabilitation of home values down deep into South Philadelphia, while Temple University anchors a revitalized North Philadelphia, just as the "University of Pennsylvania and Drexel Institute of Technology are helping to create a university atmosphere in residential sections of West Philadelphia." Bacon predicts the victory of the well-built brick row house over the "newer but less well built suburbs just over the city line." In fact, he sees suburbanization leveling off and the morale of Philadelphians rising in every neighborhood: "By the year 2009 no part of Philadelphia is ugly or depressed." At the broadest level, he advocates land-use planning that will preserve "Open Country" districts beyond the city limits, with regional parks, and the end of the "road rash" of billboards and other unregulated commercial activities that mar the pristine suburban countryside.

"Of course," Bacon concludes, "I actually know no more about Philadelphia in 2009 than does anyone else." Perhaps. But few people writing in the postwar era anywhere knew more about urban planning, and even fewer knew as much about the political and economic levers that would have to be worked to realize a renewal in Philadelphia along the lines he imagined. Bacon proved himself a tough competitor among a collection of cagy and often brilliant power brokers in postwar Philadelphia; the primary movers and their interactions are described in the chapters that follow. In the end, Bacon believed that strong plans were the beginning of compromises and collaborations that could restructure the metropolis as it moved into the space age and beyond.

Though many of the changes Bacon predicted for the city have come to pass, few of them arrived in the way he imagined. Others are left still on the drawing board. While compelling on its own, the "2009" essay demands context, ways to ask and examine a number of questions, such as why Bacon would have thought such a vision workable and how his own biography brought him to such a place. What were the internal dynamics of Philadelphia's planning, architecture, and real estate communities at the time—that is, how would he work to persuade both colleagues and critics that his ideas were the right ideas? What were the emerging realities of a deindustrializing economy, and how were city officials reacting to economic decline; how was a shrinking industrial base reframing the social struggles embedded in metropolitan life? What historical precedents shaped Bacon's faith in a grand world's fair as an agent of urban redesign and renewal? How did it work to plan a fair amid the incongruous and simultaneously emerging techno-enthusiasm, racial strife, and ethos of community-based planning in the 1960s? Finally, where are we now as "visionaries"? Is it desirable or even possible to employ similarly far-reaching visions to frame contemporary urban planning and economic development debates?

The authors in this volume take on the problem of rethinking Ed Bacon's big ideas in different ways. Biography is critical; otherwise, Bacon might be a floating "great man," out there in a loopy stratosphere with Le Corbusier and Robert Moses. Every chapter in this book argues in its way that Bacon was decidedly *not* "Philadelphia's Robert Moses." He was a planner and an architect, first of all, unlike Moses, and he never displayed the political cunning or the fins of the bureaucratic shark that made Moses swim so fast and (if Robert Caro was right) sink so far to accomplish his aims. Instead, Ed Bacon operated in a middling-powerful municipal body, a planning commission with mostly advisory powers, rising and falling based on its ideas and its willingness to sell the occasional big idea, rather than on raw political power. Beyond this, though, the authors strike off in different directions from Bacon's "2009" essay, and in areas of overlap, they do not always draw the same conclusions from the historical record. The conversation that plays out is a microcosm of what we hope will follow as people reexamine this path-setting time in American urban history.

The local economic situation was in flux throughout Ed Bacon's years in the Philadelphia City Planning Commission. He and his cohort in city government were constantly trying to understand, in real time, trends that we now see with greater clarity. We need to know more about how these urbanists learned—why they asked the questions they did, held up the historical models they found fascinating, forged the alliances they found useful, and set their metrics of success. Philadelphia's historical record tells us little of people like William Rafsky, Oskar Stonorov, or Catherine Susan Leslie, an imbalance we try to correct. By the 1950s, the hundred-year-old model of the industrial city was rusting, badly. Urbanists set their minds in creative ways to the problems unfolding before them, addressing housing, industrial decline, zoning, and crime, as well as stoking urban hope in the face of obvious decline. Ed Bacon was educated in a New Deal-era world of faith in the federal patron, the unlimited possibilities of science and technology, and the dominance of the expert. Make no mistake: Ed Bacon was the ultimate expert, the consummate urban insider. He was the confidant of mayors and genius architects. The 1960s and 1970s, though, were a different sort of education, leaving just about everyone tired and speechless, less impressed with the future than they were in, say, 1959. Access and a big office were not enough to staunch the urban hemorrhage. Ed Bacon tried everything he knew, as we will see in the pages to follow, to save the city he loved. But why did he know what he knew, and how did his trials play out? The buildings left behind are silent on this, but the written record is (thankfully for us) very noisy.

Naturally, it is no accident that this book appears in 2009. With the election of Barack Obama to the presidency and Mayor Michael Nutter's administration now settled into office, our desire is that these chapters will foreground a much-needed set of conversations about some big ideas: about strategies in planning for the city in dynamic times, the critical role of city planning and development among broader national challenges, the ways we frame and learn from the urban present and past, and the historical heritage of all these issues in the city of Philadelphia. Not since the major comprehensive plans undertaken when Ed Bacon directed the Philadelphia City Planning Commission in the early 1960s has there been the promise of comprehensive planning—integrating public and private sectors, thinking regionally, and setting goals that aim to inspire an urban renaissance in Philadelphia. Bacon set forward ideas on each of these work areas in his "2009" essay. It is time to reconsider how they played out, how his work speaks to the challenges of sustainability in the twenty-first-century post-industrial metropolis, as other cities like Philadelphia are now, right now, reengaged in this work. The results will matter, as we know from the urban planning failures of recent decades. Awakening from the joyous suburban-to-exurban daydreams of the last generation, we find ourselves back in a moment of wide-awake, expensive-gasoline, cheap-mortgage-foreclosure, global-warming reality. It also happens to be a moment of profound opportunity. Ed Bacon, in fact, imagined a "post-petroleum city" two decades ago and started working hard on an idea that to many at the time seemed a bit ludicrous—a topic for another book—but a lesson for urbanists who might lose hope from time to time to keep focused on the work ahead. It is always necessary to inject democratic, creative, and human-centered ideas into the urban mix.

Leafing through the pages of Bacon's vision, we see opportunities lost but also possibilities waiting—waterfronts worth visiting, for example; suburbanites returning to the city because of the imperatives of sustainable living and freedom from the car-as-life angst felt by so many Americans today; the real prospect of renewed urban neighborhood life.

Take the ideas as they come, work them over, then free them for a moment or two from their specific time and place to see where they deliver us today. Let us imagine the next Baltimore or St. Louis or Houston. Let us imagine Philadelphia in the year 2059.

Chapter One
Philadelphia in the Year 2009

EDMUND N. BACON

The future of Philadelphia will be determined, not by technological advances but by the character of its leadership and by the strength and quality of the ideas it supports.

Philadelphia and William Penn

This dominance of idea over technology is clearly shown in the history of center city development. When William Penn laid out his plan for Philadelphia in 1682 he could not possibly have foreseen that people would move about his city in electrically-driven vehicles running in tubes under the ground. Yet, when these things actually were built two hundred years later, they followed exactly William Penn's original idea, established in his plan, for one major east-west and one major north-south traffic way intersecting halfway between the two Rivers.

It is precisely this centrality and clarity of form, reinforced by the fact that City Hall was built in "Center Square," just where Penn suggested it should be, that gives downtown Philadelphia much of the character that it has today.

Simple as the idea was, the plan for four squares in the four quadrants of Penn's City has also become a dominant factor in center city. It is significant that these squares have become the focal centers for four important phases of Philadelphia life, Washington Square for historic tradition, Rittenhouse Square for urban living, Logan Square for cultural and scientific values. Franklin Square, hardly representative of the best in Philadelphia today, is soon to become the center of commercial and industrial renewal.

Philadelphia Today Seen from 50 Years Ago

If we take a shorter time span, equal to the one we are dealing with now, and attempt to project Philadelphia of 1959 from a point in time of about fifty years ago, again we will be impressed by the dominance and survival of an idea.

In 1909 the Parkway, just now approaching completion with the building of Park Towne Place, was begun. It was only fifteen years later that Dr. George E. Neitsche [George E. Nitzche] of the University of Pennsylvania first suggested Independence Mall, which still has several years of construction before completion. To be sure the specific agreement between the Pennsylvania Railroad and the city leading to Penn Center was signed in 1925, but there must have been several years of negotiation before that.

None of these ideas would have been brought to realization if the leadership in business and government had not been stimulated to vigorous and dynamic action.

Looking Forward

So, as we look forward over the fifty years ahead, we recognize that the form of city then will be set by the nature of the ideas we generate now and by the degree to which its leadership is stimulated to carry them out.

Philadelphia, among the cities of the nation, now enjoys perhaps top place in recognition for its achievements over the past few years. What caused this spurt of activity is for history to evaluate, but there is one factor on which most people can agree, that the Better Philadelphia Exhibition of 1947 played its part. The fact that 400,000 Philadelphians saw a concrete picture of what their city could become undoubtedly had some effect on what it actually is becoming.

The grave danger is that people will accept the idea that this recent activity is, in fact, a spurt, and that this spurt is more than half spent and that we will sink into a former state of apathy. If this idea is allowed to become dominant we may expect Philadelphia in the year 2009 to be somewhat worse than it is today.

The great need is for a new, clear, concrete objective set for a manageable time in the future, which establishes new, strong ideas and which acts as a continuing stimulant to sustain civic activity.

Such an objective is available, ready made, only waiting to be used, in the form of the 1976 Philadelphia World's Fair.

World's Fair as a Dominant Force in Philadelphia's Development

In order to explain the enormous potential force of the 1976 Exposition, it is necessary to place it against a world background.

Our country is now engaged in a bitter world struggle, one element of which is the survival and acceptance of American values and American culture. The basic concepts and principles first enunciated here in 1776 are even more alive and needed in the world today than they were then.

Our national government, in trying to put forth the best of our national life in the 1958 Brussels World's Fair, chose as an important part of the American exhibition the same downtown model that was the principal feature of the 1947 Better Philadelphia Exhibition, a dream or vision of what we would like a downtown American city to become.

What could be more natural than to establish, as a national policy, the idea that the United States will receive the world in Philadelphia in 1976, and that the location of the Exposition will be downtown Philadelphia? In this way the reconsideration of the ideas of 1776 will occur in the place where they were originally formulated, and the world will determine, by observation, that the vision of Brussels was not a dream, but a driving force that led to the actual reconstruction of Philadelphia as an unmatched expression of the vitality of American technology and culture.

Seen within this framework, the Fair should inspire the Federal Government to lend special support to see to it that the main features of the downtown plan are actually completed by 1976, and completed at a high level of engineering and design, as a part of its world strategy.

Physical Nature of the 1976 Exposition

It is surprising to realize how many of the requirements necessary for the Exposition have already been accomplished or are in the works.

Independence Hall, the central focus of the Exposition, will have a superb setting developed to full richness because of the maturing of the trees on Independence Mall and Independence National Historical Park. The famous spectacle, "Lights of Freedom" performed nightly in Independence Square will thrill visitors by its recounting, through light and sound, the great days of 1776. The evening will end with an illuminated display at the Lewis Fountain. On special days there will be a great pageant on the middle block of Independence Mall.

The Washington Square East redevelopment project, extending from Independence Hall into restored Society Hill, will still be regarded as the finest achievement of American redevelopment, but now will be buttressed by a continuous band of good housing extending from the Delaware to the Schuylkill River, meeting the active business area to the north cleanly, without a layer of blight between.

The Delaware River Marina will be a magnet for visitors, with its historical ships and marine museum, aquarium, swimming pool and restau-

Figure 3. The planner imagines a symbol for the 1976 World's Fair. Artwork by William Barron, 1959. Courtesy of the Architectural Archives of the University of Pennsylvania and *Philadelphia Magazine.*

rants. It will be the point of departure for the launches that take visitors to the Navy Yard for trips through aircraft carriers and cruisers, and for a stop at Old Fort Mifflin.

But the great attraction will be the open-sided electric cars with their striped awnings that go up and down the length of Chestnut Street, which has been relieved of automobiles to provide enough room for the visitors to the Fair. Chestnut Street is the backbone of the Fair, connecting the historic areas with the main part of the Exposition that extends up both banks of the Schuylkill River from Convention Hall to Memorial Hall in Fairmount Park. It has become the Midway where the visitors

spend their money for food, drinks, mementos and all the various neces-
sities and frivolities that go with such an event, rather than in some tem-
porary, soon to be removed bazaar.

Some of the stores have removed their front windows and carry on
outdoor activities, loggia-like half in and half out of the building. Sidewalk cafes and outdoor bazaars add a festive atmosphere.

There are outdoor performances nightly in City Hall Courtyard of the
world famous plays of many nations. Molière, Shakespeare, as well as Jed-
ermann and the Kabuki Dancers. Special exhibits are spread between
the sculpture and flowers of Penn Center esplanade, Reyburn Plaza, and
up the Parkway to the Art Museum.

Much of the area along the East Bank of the Schuylkill River has been
cleared under the process of redevelopment, and the land is being used
for Fair Buildings pending permanent construction. The same is true of
parts of West Philadelphia, particularly the spectacular Knoll just north
of the Spring Garden Bridge, where the symbol of the Exposition would
greet travelers arriving on the Schuylkill Expressway. The railroad tracks
would be covered providing space useful later for civic projects.

As many of the values as possible would be salvaged for the permanent
benefit of the City, including the park along the East Bank of the Schuylkill from the Art Museum to South Street, and the great orientation center introducing the United States to the foreign visitor, which would be
built and maintained by the Federal Government as part of its tourist
promotion program. Chestnut Street would finally become established
as one of the great shopping streets of the world. Many of the other
attractions of the Fair will continue because Philadelphia is bound to
become a world center of tourism.

A new system of underground streets serving a large underground
parking terminal at Broad Street, fed directly by ramps from the crosstown expressway, will help care for the mass of visitors, who are conducted to central points by a brilliantly-lighted moving sidewalk in the
subway concourse. There will be a large parking garage fed by the Vine
Street Expressway between 15th and 16th Streets, and new garages on
the Schuylkill and Delaware Expressways connecting directly with the
Chestnut Street Cars.

East Market Street Transportation Center

The one great additional element that must be built to have downtown
Philadelphia in shape for the Fair is the transportation center on East
Market Street.

Under the stimulus of the World Fair idea, the Federal Government
has at last been persuaded to devote some attention to the transporta-

Figure 4. Philadelphia City Hall in the future. Artwork by William Barron, 1959.
Courtesy of the Architectural Archives of the University of Pennsylvania and
Philadelphia Magazine.

tion side of the traffic problem, and, as a pilot project, has made a loan and provided a subsidy to make possible the great East Market Center.

The basic purpose of the project is to amalgamate the Pennsylvania and Reading commuter railroads into one system, based not on two terminals, but on one continuous underground railroad loop connecting Penn Center and the East Market Street area so that travelers on any line may stop either east or west of Broad Street. The multi-level project involves the rebuilding of much of the north side of Market Street.

Lower level gardens bring light and freshness into the subway, providing a more gracious entrance to center city. At the street level, the new development stretches from City Hall to the Department Store cluster at Eighth Street, with plazas, esplanades and fountains, recognizing that it is here that the great mass of shopping is done. At the level above the street an air conditioned moving sidewalk continues, uninterrupted, into the second floors of the department stores serviced by the bus terminal and the 4,000 car parking garage connected with the Vine Street Expressway by its own ramp system. This finally establishes the prestige of East Market Street as a commercial area, and assures the continued prosperity of the Department Stores bordering on it.

With the completion of this project, plus the rebuilding of the areas adjacent to Independence Mall and some rehabilitation of older structures, the basic plan for center city will be nearing completion. This summary shows, what surely is true, that downtown Philadelphia is well on its way to becoming the most interesting and beautiful center city in the country, and, with a little push, will truly become so.

Significance of the Fair to Philadelphia

For the City of Philadelphia the Fair will have the value of serving as a focal point in a continuing work program which starts now and extends far beyond the 1976 date. It will bring about acceptance of many ideas not otherwise acceptable, and accomplishment of many specific things that otherwise would not get done.

Despite its tremendous natural assets, Philadelphia on the whole has done a miserable job of taking care of the out-of-town visitor. This is short sighted in dollar terms because the tourist could add millions to the income of hotels, restaurants and stores. It is unfortunate in that this creates an attitude toward the city which can, and often does, redound to its disadvantage and, in a subtle way, affects the decisions of many people, including businessmen and industrialists considering locating their enterprises here.

The Fair certainly would correct this, and would include many features that would continue indefinitely after the Fair was over. The stimulus of getting ready for the Fair, plus the prestige and interest in Philadelphia that it would generate, plus its continuing features would help tremendously in all of the other phases of Philadelphia's building program.

Regional Development

The effort toward regionalism will have caught hold. A coordinated mass transit system, operated by a metropolitan authority, will have incorporated commuter rail lines, subways and bus lines into one coordinated unit. Helicopter service will operate regularly from the two heliports—on the Delaware and Schuylkill Rivers at each end of the business district.

The expressway system will connect directly to the centers of the outlying towns, building the larger metropolitan area into one functioning unit.

Great marginal berthing facilities will have been built along the lower Delaware River, with roll-on roll-off handling for rapid interchange of goods. Industrial Parks are developed in many parts of the City, some on open land, some in cleared former slum areas. Finally, it has become recognized that the work hours and the work environment of everyone are as important as the home hours or recreation hours, and, as a general practice, factories are well kept and in good surroundings. Industrial Parks have become both a name and a fact.

So, roughly the first half of our fifty-year period has been spent on economic and technical advances, and on making our downtown the symbol of our region, a symbol that commands world respect.

So, I think, the second half of this period will be a great, concentrated social and human effort. Finally, after all these years of trial and effort, of discussion, thought and shouting, we finally turn our full energies to the job of housing our people.

The Future of Housing in Philadelphia

As a background for considering the future of housing in Philadelphia, we should observe what has been happening over the years from 1960–1976.

The outward push from center city of suburban and newly-formed families deciding to live in town has far exceeded the wildest dreams of the planners of the late 1950's.

By 1976, under the stimulus of the Washington Square East project, rehabilitation has spread deep into South Philadelphia, extending west of the Delaware Expressway continuously to the historic conclave around Old Swede's Church. The Rittenhouse Square influence has extended to Washington Avenue. Park Towne Place has sparked rehabilitation and new construction north of Spring Garden Street which has become a fine residential center.

Temple University has become the center of a college town where many of its faculty live. The University of Pennsylvania and Drexel Institute of Technology are helping to create a university atmosphere in residential sections of West Philadelphia. The connecting link between West Philadelphia and the Parkway and Art Museum is established by the clearance for rebuilding of the Mantua area for the 1976 Exposition.

At the same time that large sections of Old Philadelphia are demonstrating the staying power of the brick row house, and the adaptability of it for renewal for attractive urban living, the newer but less well built suburbs just over the city line are deteriorating, forming a ready market for the lower income groups. So, by the process of the natural operation of the market and free choice of the individual there is automatically occurring a breaking up of large accumulations of a single income group. A wide dispersal and variety of income and cultural status is being achieved in many parts of the region. The suburban idea as the only healthy American way of life has been challenged by a significant minority who find greater values for family living in the cultural and social advantages of the city.

The fact that this can be accomplished with a commensurate improvement in the public school system has been recognized and the community has supported the measures necessary to accomplish the improvement.

Redevelopment Program

By 1976 the Federal Government has finally grasped fully the significance and magnitude of the problem of eradication of blight, and has developed a program and administrative procedures in scale with it.

The emphasis of redevelopment has shifted from intensive activity in small areas to a dispersed program which comprehends the entire area needing treatment. More and more the problem is seen as one of people's attitude, of neighborhood morale, and activities are designed to stimulate widespread neighborhood pride. The emphasis of the social work agencies has shifted from direct service to the individual which is increasingly carried on by public agencies, to that of providing and fostering neighborhood leadership as an independent counterpart to the government renewal activities.

In every part of Philadelphia handsome neighborhood centers are being built under urban renewal, centering around old and loved landmarks as much as possible, to provide, in every community, a neighborhood symbol of which the residents can be proud. Through identification with these local centers every resident of Philadelphia will come to feel himself a citizen of "no mean city." By the year 2009 no part of Philadelphia is ugly or depressed.

Housing in the Region

On the regional level, the American people have finally come to realize that their natural heritage in beautiful country was about to be irrevocably destroyed, on the periphery of cities, and they have taken steps to prevent it.

A program for the purchase of development rights, first advocated by William H. Whyte, Jr. back in 1959, has been used to preserve for all time the open stream valleys in a network throughout the region. A new concept of zoning has caught hold which establishes bands of "Open Country District" in which the minimum lot size is kept large enough to assure continuation of open country character, passing around areas of concentrated housing in which zoning sets the maximum amount of land anyone may have for his house, and so assure fairly dense development. Utilization of these two districts together on a planned basis will avoid repetition of the familiar phenomenon of a person moving to the outer edge of development to enjoy the advantages of open country, only to find that development has moved out beyond him, and he is saddled with the costs in time and money of commuting with few compensating advantages.

Because they are surrounded with "Open Country" lands, the residents of each of the concentrated residential areas are assured of permanent access to open spaces. If the maximum lot size permitted in them is too small for one's taste, one can move into the "Open Country" zone, but must assume responsibility of maintaining a large tract of land for the privilege of doing so.

In addition to the open country reservation areas, an extensive system of regional parks has been developed by the Commonwealth for active recreation and camping. As a result of increased leisure, the regional parks have become the focus of a new way of living. Many families have given up their suburban homes for a row house in the city, and have built simple cabins adjacent to one of the parks where they "rough it" over the long weekends and on vacation. And, finally, the voters have decided to get rid of the billboards which previously lined the expressways between house and cabin, and the encrustation of "Road Rash," drive-ins, hot dog stands and advertising signs along major arteries, through vigorous legislation and follow-up.

Conclusion

Of course I actually know no more about Philadelphia in 2009 than does anyone else.

I have tried to show, however, by looking backward, that a strong idea has a life of its own, and can become a dominant factor if it is clear enough, and if the leadership is stimulated to action.

I have tried to show my belief that everything is affected by the prestige or lack of it, which the city has, both in the eyes of the world, and, perhaps more important, in its own eyes.

I have expressed my belief that Philadelphia's location is most favorable to its becoming the key prestige city of the country, and that it will become so if the assets it already has continue to be developed as they are being developed now. I have tried to show that the 1976 World's Fair can become the force that will sustain the present civic effort to the year 1976, and to give the impetus to keep it going for the full half century.

And, finally, I make my most important observation.

If we want Philadelphia to be the way we want it to be in the year 2009, the time to start is now.

Chapter Two
Salesman of Ideas: The Life Experiences That Shaped Edmund Bacon

GREGORY L. HELLER

Edmund Bacon wrote "Philadelphia in the Year 2009" just prior to what is generally considered the high point of his career. During the 1960s, the Philadelphia City Planning Commission (PCPC), which Bacon directed from 1949 to 1970, would become known as one of the most active and effective in the nation. In 1964, *Time* magazine featured Bacon's face on its cover—he was one of the very few urban planners of his generation to attain this kind of national recognition.[1]

In his "2009" essay, Bacon focuses on the problems of repopulating the city, the impacts of suburban white flight, and Philadelphia's increasing racial and socioeconomic segregation. The essay illuminates a critical juncture in Bacon's career, exemplifying a hybrid philosophy of his early passion for affordable housing and his emerging obsession with restoring the commercial heart of Philadelphia on a grand scale. This biographical sketch—an introduction to the life and work of Edmund Bacon—traces the evolution of his ideas and career while focusing on a key element of his methodology: the salesmanship of ideas.

While Bacon is associated with a number of Philadelphia's major post-World War II development projects, he lacked the power, access to funding, or influence to bring these projects to fruition through his actions alone. He always relied on other actors in government or the business community. Bacon's challenge throughout his career was developing a method for implementing plans in a complex political climate.

He learned over his career to market planning ideas effectively to powerful decision-makers, gain buy-in, and make the ideas resonate in the public consciousness. He saw his position heading the relatively independent Planning Commission as the perfect venue for influencing both the public and private sectors. Renowned Philadelphia-based architect Louis Kahn said, "If your ideas are right, they—the businessmen and the politicians—will come to you."[2] Bacon, in contrast, believed that an effective planner had to sell his ideas actively in a persuasive way. Kahn called Bacon "A planner who thinks he is a politician."[3] Kahn was largely right. Bacon spent his career taking new or existing ideas, filling them out into compelling concepts, and marketing them to key decision makers. One of Bacon's staff recalled, "He made a speech to the staff, and in that speech he compared himself to Paul Klee—a great artist. And I said, 'Ed, you missed it completely. You are a great artist, but you're an artist in convincing and maneuvering, and doing things cleverly. It's not the design issue'."[4]

While Bacon was masterful in selling ideas to the business community and political elite, he was less effective at selling them to communities. Throughout his career, Bacon wrote extensively about the need to plan with the public, developing plans through what he termed "democratic feedback."[5] However, by the end of his twenty-one-year tenure, segments of the public and the media viewed Bacon as a stubborn and forceful "top-down" type of city planner.[6]

"Philadelphia in the Year 2009" shows Bacon's priorities in 1959 and his methods of persuasion as he looked ahead. Through precise argumentation and images, he communicates his ideas as tangible elements of the urban landscape. He shows how these ideas connect as a cohesive, long-term vision for the city. Then, through the notion of hosting a World's Fair (and an anticipated Bicentennial), he expresses a practical strategy for attracting money, visitors, and national attention to showcase Philadelphia's fresh image on a national stage.

Bacon wrote in "Philadelphia in the Year 2009" that "a strong idea has a life of its own, and can become a dominant factor if it is clear enough, and if the leadership is stimulated to action." This combination of a strong design idea and the right marketing was the key to Bacon's success and indeed remains just as important in 2009 as fifty years ago.

From Philadelphia to Flint and Back Again

Edmund Norwood Bacon was born in Philadelphia on 2 May 1910, the third of four children of Ellis and Helen Comly Bacon. His parents were descendants of prominent Philadelphia Quaker families.[7] In 1924 his parents moved the family to the suburb of Wallingford. The Bacons lived down the road from the Rose Valley arts and crafts community, and here Bacon befriended architect Bill Price, Jr., who invited him to his architecture studio and taught him to draw.[8]

In the fall of 1927, Edmund Bacon enrolled in Cornell University's five-year architecture program. The most relevant of his college projects to later work was his senior thesis. While his peers designed individual buildings, Bacon took on the complicated problem of designing "A Civic Center for Philadelphia." He proposed a sunken pedestrian court, abutted by courthouses, bus platforms, and a tree-lined park promenade. This latter element was the earliest of Bacon's plans eventually to be built, as the plaza now known as LOVE Park. A key element of Bacon's plan was the demolition of Philadelphia's City Hall, with the intent of reclaiming the city's central square, an idea earlier proposed by architect Paul Philippe Cret in the 1920s.[9]

A contemporary project that particularly fascinated Bacon was Radburn, New Jersey, designed by Clarence Stein and Henry Wright in 1928. As a "Town for the Automobile Age," Radburn was one of several early American suburbs adapted from the British Garden City model. The core design principles of Radburn involved separating pedestrians from automobile traffic with footways and motorways, utilizing cul-de-sacs to separate through and neighborhood vehicular traffic, and a pedestrian pathway system connecting homes to community institutions.[10] Radburn offered Bacon a vision for communities that allowed automobile use, while keeping the pedestrian realm separate and dominant. Bacon entered the workforce at a time when the popularity of the automobile was surging. Throughout his career, he would constantly turn to the Radburn principles for insight in designing downtown and neighborhood solutions that balanced the needs of those in cars and those on foot.

Graduating from Cornell in 1932, Bacon decided to see the world while waiting out the bleak Depression-era employment situation. He spent the next ten months on his own, traveling through England, France, Italy, Greece, Turkey, and Egypt, sketching the architecture he saw along the way. In Egypt, during the spring of 1933 and with money running short, he realized that he needed to return home or, somehow, find a job abroad. During his Egyptian travels, Bacon befriended a former ambassador to China who told him there was a building boom in Shanghai. With letters from his friends at home bemoaning the lack of jobs, Bacon made the decision to buy a ticket on a Japanese boat, sail to China, and seek his fortune.

Bacon was overwhelmed by Shanghai, a cosmopolitan center of banking and business, as well as gambling and prostitution, focused on the bustling central street of the Bund. Shanghai was home to many wealthy foreigners, thus feeding the demand for western-style buildings and private homes. He contacted American architect Henry Killam Murphy, who had made a career innovating architecture that melded traditional Chinese and western elements.[11] Murphy secured Bacon a job in which he designed private residences, public works projects, and an airport.

Bacon was fascinated by China, especially Beijing.[12] His time living in China and learning from Murphy exposed him to an entirely non-western aesthetic and understanding of movement through space that would influence his later work back in the United States.

In 1934 Edmund Bacon returned to Philadelphia and started working for architect William Pope Barney, a friend of the Bacon family from Rose Valley.[13] At this point, he also met Oskar Stonorov, a twenty-nine-year-old architect from Germany who was fascinated by socialist ideology and the labor union movement in the United States. Stonorov had emigrated to the U.S. in 1929, working in New York City before establishing a firm in Philadelphia. Seeking to build modern architecture that could improve living conditions for American laborers, Stonorov and his architectural partner Alfred Kastner received a commission from the Full-Fashioned Hosiery Workers Union to design low-cost housing in Philadelphia. Since neither was a registered architect in the U.S., Barney agreed to be the architect of record for a project known as the Carl Mackley Houses.[14] Through Barney's office, Bacon also worked with Stonorov on the Westfield Acres housing project in Camden, New Jersey. Stonorov introduced Bacon to his friends and colleagues, including Catherine Bauer—a rising star in the American housing movement, whose groundbreaking book *Modern Housing* came out in 1934—and Lewis Mumford—an already renowned architecture critic and author. Stonorov, Bauer, and Mumford would become influential in the U.S. public housing movement and greatly shaped Bacon's awareness and involvement in housing issues.[15] Bauer and Mumford were also members of the Regional Planning Association of America, whose ideas led to the development of Radburn, New Jersey, and the application of the Garden City principles in an American context. To this point, Bacon had been solely interested in architecture. Henceforth, however, Bacon would have a lasting belief in the need for affordable housing, as well as a deep interest in the connection between housing for the poor and modern neighborhood design.

In the spring of 1935, George Young, Jr., dean of Cornell's College of Architecture, suggested that Bacon apply to the Cranbrook Academy of Art in Bloomfield Hills, Michigan, an institution founded by Detroit newspaper baron George Booth in 1932 on a portion of his massive estate. Bacon wrote to its president, prominent Finnish architect-planner Eliel Saarinen. Evident in this letter was the influence of Bacon's public housing work in his newfound perception of the role of the architect in society. Bacon wrote:

The relation of the architect to society certainly has, and is, undergoing changes, and I should like to follow rethinking along this line. I have seen the Juniata

Housing Workers Housing Development program [Carl Mackley Houses], of which Mr. Barney was the architect, and through this I have learned that the architect has social responsibility.[16]

At Cranbrook, Bacon was one of 96 students studying architecture, sculpture, painting, weaving, interior design, and ceramics. He loved learning from Saarinen and later repeatedly cited him as one of his leading influences. He remembered Saarinen as an eccentric character, instilling insight in his students less through traditional teaching and more by walking the studio floor making critiques or through conversations with students in his on-campus home. Saarinen wrote that "it is clear . . . the city's improvement and further development must be started with the problems of homes and their environments, and not—as is usually the case—with plazas, boulevards, monumental layouts, and other showy things."[17] Additionally, Saarinen felt that "the city's 'form order' and 'social order' cannot be separated: they must be developed hand-in-hand, reciprocally inspiring one another."[18] This philosophy of urban growth developed by Saarinen, dubbed "organic decentralization," reflected the ideas of the Garden City movement and their American applications in projects like Radburn.[19] The notion that architecture and planning can have an impact on social conditions established Bacon's focus for much of his career.

Bacon had studied at Cranbrook for only about five months before Saarinen sent him to work in the industrial city of Flint, Michigan. Flint was at that time a city of 160,000 residents, dominated by four General Motors plants. Flint's municipal government, General Motors, and the Rackham and Mott Foundations supported a program for replanning Flint that Saarinen agreed to oversee, assigning students to undertake the actual work.[20] Bacon worked for the Flint Institute of Planning and Research, producing policy reports for the city's government leaders.[21] He also supervised a Works Progress Administration-funded traffic study. As the study progressed, he met with philanthropists, business leaders, and political figures, learning along the way that he would need the support of these powerful individuals and gaining an awareness of the relationship between planning and politics. The Flint Institute sponsored a public exhibition of the traffic study findings, with a large-scale wall map and a model showing a vision for Flint's business district of the future. These were Bacon's first efforts to sell planning ideas to members of the government and business establishment (which in Flint were often the same thing). He wrote to his parents, "It really seems as though politics may be combated by public education. This is a swell test."[22]

Bacon, naively confident in his power at this stage, decided to take on the Flint establishment over placement of a downtown bridge. Over

Figure 5. Worker housing in Flint, Michigan, 1938. Photo by Ruth H. Bacon. Courtesy of the Architectural Archives of the University of Pennsylvania.

time, some in Flint's political elite had gotten fed up with what they viewed as the uppity Flint Institute. Harlow Curtice, president of Buick and head of the Flint Community Association, seeing the efforts of Bacon and others at the Flint Institute as a threat to business interests, disbanded the Community Association that supported the Institute and fired its president, Seward C. Simons.[23] This turn of events shocked Bacon. However, he was allowed to finish working on the report for the traffic study.

In early 1938, the traffic study came out—Edmund Bacon's first major planning document—proposing new automobile and train routes and parking solutions. The study stressed how these improvements would be good long-term investments. It also proposed a new neighborhood planning method to curb the city's suburban sprawl, along with an idea for reclaiming the downtown with new urban neighborhoods, ideas all inspired by the Radburn principles. The report was featured prominently in the *Flint Journal* and covered in the *New York Times*. Lewis Mumford praised Bacon's attention to the new housing plans. Paul Opperman, assistant director of the American Society of Planning Officials, observed, "It seems to me that Flint is in the throes of a city-wide 'planning movement'."[24]

With passage of the Wagner-Steagall Act in 1937, hundreds of millions of dollars of interest-free loans were allocated to local housing authorities to subsidize affordable housing. Despite his previous political rap on the knuckles, Bacon had been appointed to Flint's Planning Board as its secretary. Bacon and others on the Planning Board established a Citizens' Housing Committee to lobby the city and state to utilize available federal funds. Bacon also created a grassroots group called the Flint Housing Council, comprised of forty-five different groups from a wide array of organizations, including the Genesee County League of Women Voters, the Negro Recreation Council, the Association of Flint Churches, the Flint and Genesee County Building Trades Council, and the County Real Estate Board. These organizations found success in the fall of 1938, with the state and city each adopting enabling legislation and creating a local housing commission to apply for funds. Bacon would continue to utilize this concept of promoting ideas through the formation of grassroots organizations.

Also in 1938, at the National Planning Conference, Bacon first met Walter Blucher, the director of the American Society of Planning Officials. Blucher argued for the benefits to cities of establishing a planning commission with paid staff and resources. Probably as a result of Blucher's influence, Bacon lobbied the Flint City Commission (the city council) to create such a planning body. A measure was put on the ballot and approved by the voters.

Late in 1938, Bacon and other public officials secured $3.5 million in committed federal housing funds. Many Americans were still highly skeptical of planning and public housing, viewing them as bordering on socialism.[25] With the potential of millions in federal housing dollars coming to Flint, Bacon explained, "the real estate people began to realize that I . . . was a threat to their profits they derived from building terrible shacks and selling them to the workers on contract."[26] The Flint City Commission—whose members were well connected to the local real-estate industry—voted to strip the Housing Commission of its funding, and at the same time Bacon also was informed that the Planning Division of the Flint Institute was being dissolved.[27]

An article in the *Flint Journal* reported that the dissolution of the Planning Division was due to the fact that, with a new planning commission, the Institute was no longer needed.[28] The article included a photograph of Bacon and blandly explained that "Edmund N. Bacon . . . leaves the staff of the Institute with this change, [and] will assist in the transfer of activities."[29] Correspondence from the time indicates that the editor of the *Flint Journal* had been an informant for Eliel Saarinen and others at Cranbrook.[30] Concerned that Bacon's foray into politics would reflect badly on the school, the Cranbrook contingent viewed the dissolution of Bacon's division of the Flint Institute as a way of getting rid of Bacon while saving him the embarrassment of getting fired. While Bacon thought that he had been gaining support for his endeavors, he was actually digging himself a political hole.

In a last-ditch effort, Bacon and his group convinced the Flint City Commission to put a referendum on the ballot, asking voters if they wanted the city to accept the federal money.[31] The referendum was voted down by a margin of almost two to one.[32] The events in Flint provided a learning experience for Bacon, and its lessons would shape his later career and philosophy. As he later recalled, "I was thrown out of Flint in disgrace. But I had learned that city planning is a combination of social input as well as design."[33] He learned that it took both insider politics and grassroots efforts to produce changes in a city. It would take years before Bacon again found himself in a similar role in Philadelphia.

Philadelphia's City Planning Movement

In 1939 Edmund Bacon published some of his Flint work in the *Journal of Land and Public Utility Economics*.[34] In this and a subsequent article in *American City*, Bacon argued for a proactive approach to rehabilitating blighted areas. "Under existing legislation," he noted, "the only way to restore value to the individual lot is to reassemble ownership in large areas, clear away the neighborhood factors causing blight, replan and rehabilitate the area, and again offer it to private builders on condition that it be developed according to sound neighborhood planning principles."[35] Bacon would later act on similar ideas in Philadelphia's redevelopment program, favoring rehabilitation and selective demolition, rather than the wholesale slum clearance approach embraced by some other U.S. cities.

Bacon had recently befriended Walter M. Phillips—a young, civic-minded Philadelphia native from an affluent family. Phillips and Bacon had met a few years earlier, and Phillips joined Bacon briefly in 1937 in Flint.[36] Phillips convinced Bacon to stay in Philadelphia by giving Bacon and Stonorov a commission to design him a new house. He then found Bacon a job as director of the nonprofit Philadelphia Housing Association, where Bacon lobbied the city government for affordable housing and focused on the idea that better planned neighborhoods can help revitalize declining areas.[37]

During the first half of the twentieth century, with little planning, Philadelphia's government funneled patronage contracts to party bosses who made a fortune building civic projects like the Benjamin Franklin Parkway.[38] With the city going bankrupt, Mayor John Reyburn created a Committee on Comprehensive Plans in 1909. In 1912 City Council created the Philadelphia Planning Board, whose 1915 report recommended key downtown projects and the creation of a zoning code.[39] In 1919 the Commonwealth of Pennsylvania approved a new charter for Philadelphia, creating its first City Planning Commission. The Commission was initially ignored by city leaders, with patronage projects steadily moving through the pipeline.[40] In 1924 the Regional Plan Federation was formed. This body produced the Tri-State Philadelphia District Plan in 1932, with little impact. In 1939 Mayor Harry Mackey finally appointed members to the Planning Commission. The Commission, however, was largely ineffective, suffering from a lack of funding and technical staff. With all of this background, Walter Blucher lamented in 1941, "Philadelphia is the only big city in the country that is not doing an effective job of planning."[41]

Meanwhile, Bacon's friend Walter Phillips started a progressive young people's group called the City Policy Committee. Bacon convinced Phillips to focus the City Policy Committee on lobbying the mayor and City Council to create a modern planning commission.[42] The City Policy Committee teamed up with the Lawyers' Council on Civic Affairs and the Junior Board of Commerce, creating the Joint Committee on City Planning. The group decided that the best way to convince the city leaders would be to bring the National Planning Conference to Philadelphia. Bacon contacted Walter Blucher, and Blucher, anxious to spread the gospel of planning, agreed to bring the three professional planning organizations to Philadelphia in 1941.

The members of the City Policy Committee contacted Judge Nochem Winnet, of Bacon's Housing Association board, who agreed to ask City Councilman Frederick D. Garman to introduce the city planning bill drafted by the Joint Committee. The bill was introduced but sat in committee indefinitely without visible public support. As a result, Bacon and his colleagues went on a citywide blitz, enlisting the support of civic, community, and business groups. Bacon and Phillips approached

Edward Hopkinson, Jr., a partner at Drexel and Company and one of the most powerful men in Philadelphia.[43] Hopkinson favored the idea that strong planning would equal better investment opportunities for the city, by allowing the city to match its capital expenditures with a pre-determined set of needs and long-term projects. In December 1942, when the bill got a hearing, Bacon's group brought out more than a hundred members of the public, plus Hopkinson, to testify on the bill's behalf. Surprised and impressed, City Council passed the bill, and the Philadelphia City Planning Commission (PCPC) was born.[44] Bacon had again recruited a major grassroots effort to lobby city government, as he had done in Flint. However, with Hopkinson on board, this combination of insider and outsider support was successful in a way that Bacon's efforts in Flint never were. Bacon was learning the subtleties of getting things done amid the complicated political realities of a big city. At the suggestion of Bacon's group, the mayor named Hopkinson to serve as PCPC's first chairman. There were no guarantees that the public and private sectors would allow this new commission to thrive; however, with Hopkinson at the helm, PCPC had a strong nexus with the business sec-tor. Other business leaders had been involved in Philadelphia's plan-ning in the past; real-estate mogul Albert M. Greenfield had sat on the earlier planning commission, for example. However, the commission that Hopkinson chaired had the money and staff to succeed where its predecessor had not.

Bacon and Phillips spearheaded a new group called the Citizens' Council on City Planning (CCCP)—which involved a number of the most active members of the City Policy Committee. The CCCP role was to work with PCPC and serve as intermediary between the Commission and community groups.[45] Hopkinson hired Robert B. Mitchell, pre-viously chief of the Urban Section of the National Resources Planning Board, as the first director, to the applause of Bacon and the CCCP.[46] Bacon, however, would not play a part in the Planning Commission's early years. In December 1943 he resigned his position at the Philadel-phia Housing Association and enlisted in the U.S. navy. Like so many other Americans of his time, Edmund Bacon's profound opposition to fascism spurred him to leave his family and go to war. For Bacon, who came from a long line of pacifist Quakers, however, his enlisting was a major break from family tradition. Stationed in the Pacific, he served in the battles of Iwo Jima and Okinawa.[47] By Christmas 1945 Bacon was reunited with his family, then living in New York City.

A Better Philadelphia

While Edmund Bacon was serving in the Navy, Oskar Stonorov wrote him about an idea that he had developed in conjunction with Walter

Phillips and Robert Mitchell. They saw an emerging mood of postwar optimism in America, ripe for advancing a city planning agenda, which they decided could be publicized and promoted through a major exhibition. The idea resonated with business leaders, like Hopkinson who helped established a committee to develop the concept of a "Philadelphia Exhibition," eventually known as the "Better Philadelphia Exhibition." The group raised $200,000 from business leaders and the city, and Stonorov was selected as the exhibition's designer.[48] He, in turn, recruited Bacon to work on the exhibition, and Bacon joined the staff of the Philadelphia City Planning Commission as a senior land planner in October 1946. He focused on designing the exhibition, along with Stonorov, Mitchell, and Stonorov's business partner, the increasingly prominent Philadelphia architect Louis I. Kahn. The goal of the exhibition was to show off the work of the Philadelphia City Planning Commission, promote planning to the general public, and test the waters on potentially controversial ideas, like a new Center City office district and major highway projects.[49]

Running from 8 September to 15 October 1947, the Better Philadelphia Exhibition attracted an impressive 385,000 visitors.[50] It took up two floors of the Gimbels department store, at Eighth and Market Streets in the Center City section of Philadelphia. There was no precedent for a city planning exhibition on this scale. Unlike the General Motors-funded "Futurama" exhibit at the 1939 New York World's Fair, which had envisioned an autocentric city of the future, the Better Philadelphia Exhibition focused on rebuilding neighborhoods and on tangible downtown projects that could be melded into contemporary Philadelphia. The exhibition's theme was "What City Planning Means to You and Your Children." Building on that theme, the planners introduced a city planning curriculum in a handful of Philadelphia public schools, where Bacon, Stonorov, and others at the Citizens' Council on City Planning guided exercises that allowed students to redesign their neighborhoods and schoolyards. The student plans were then shown at the exhibition.

Many of the Better Philadelphia exhibits focused on what Philadelphia could look like by its 300th anniversary in 1982. Others were light-hearted, like a series of cartoons by famous illustrator Robert Osborne, showing everyday scenarios where planning is important, like planning a football play or budgeting for shopping. Others were technologically advanced like the "Time-Space Machine," which used side-lit glass panels to demonstrate Philadelphia's physical development over time. Some displays were less dynamic but equally important, explaining what the PCPC and the city's Redevelopment Authority (RDA) did and how they worked together. The exhibition stressed the cost of capital improvements, with actual price tags attached to model buildings and parks.

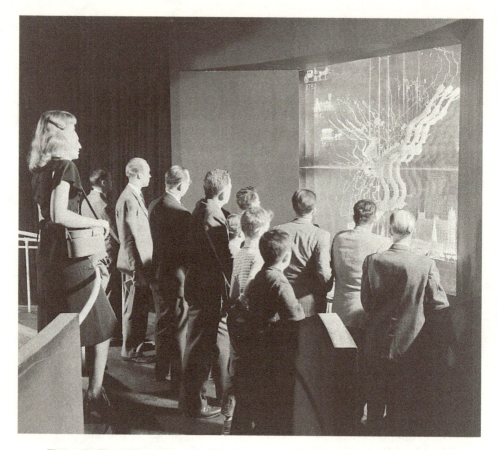

Figure 6. The "Time-Space Machine" display at the Better Philadelphia Exhibition, held at Gimbels Department Store, Philadelphia, 1947. Photo by Ezra Stoller. Courtesy of Esto.

Another room featured a massive, horizontal map of the city that marked the projects slated for development in the city's six-year, adopted capital program.

Perhaps the most spectacular exhibit was an amphitheater featuring a 30-by-14-foot model of Center City with 45,000 buildings, 25,000 cars and buses, and 12,000 trees. A recorded narrator discussed various parts of the city as a spotlight highlighted them. The model segment then lifted up and flipped over to show a future vision for each site. The model contained concepts that had been in the works for years. It showed the so-called Chinese Wall—the Pennsylvania Railroad's massive viaduct across from City Hall—gone, with new office buildings in its place. It showed a three-block mall north of Independence Hall, a concept for which powerful leaders had been lobbying for over a decade, and that was already promised millions in state funding.[51] There was a yacht basin and pedestrian promenade along the city's Delaware River waterfront. Also on display was a model for a new highway system encircling Center City, a concept that Robert Mitchell had promoted as director of the Planning Commission.[52] The model also showed a series of pathways in a historic residential section of the city. This concept, designed by Bacon, would later become the Society Hill greenway system. Another model showed 15,000 acres of undeveloped land in northeast Philadelphia, with plans for new communities on this land that were distinctly urban, utilizing the Radburn principles incorporated into the natural topography. These plans for the Far Northeast section of the city would later become a signature effort of Bacon's at the PCPC.

Better Philadelphia promoted the notion that competent planning can revive blighted neighborhoods, preventing slums from emerging in the future. One model showed an existing struggling neighborhood in south Philadelphia. Rather than proposing wholesale bulldozing and rebuilding, the exhibition promoted a more sympathetic approach of rehabilitating older homes, altering the street network to remove through traffic from local streets, and creating new open space. The models also demonstrated a predilection for historic rehabilitation, planning for pedestrians, and designing to retain natural landscapes. These ideas were progressive for a period when other cities were looking at wholesale demolition and rebuilding of slums. Certainly, the exhibition's designers believed in selective demolition. A key element of the Better Philadelphia Exhibition, however, was the idea that cities do not need to demolish and rebuild huge tracts of land—they can revive their depressed areas through small-scale demolition, weaving parks, shopping, schools, and amenities into existing areas, with new housing integrated alongside restored, older housing.

Ultimately, the Better Philadelphia Exhibition achieved what Bacon and the other designers set out to do, generating local and national publicity about Philadelphia's ambitious planning program. An article in *American City* called the exhibition "the most significant thing that has happened to planning in nearly a score of years."[53] Better Philadelphia was a major factor in building the community support necessary to advance Philadelphia's planning agenda in the coming years.

Toward a Modern City

After the Better Philadelphia Exhibition, Edmund Bacon continued to work for the PCPC as a land use planner. Much of the Commission's early work was spent planning infrastructure improvements, postwar housing, and highways.[54] The 1944 Federal-Aid Highway Act established the interstate highway system, and the Public Roads Administration designated the first system of interstate highways in 1947. By that time, a number of Philadelphia's highways were already planned, including the Schuylkill, Delaware, and Vine Street Expressways, while Robert Mitchell was pushing the fourth segment of a Center City highway loop along Lombard Street, on the south side of Center City. Mitchell soon resigned to teach at Columbia University, and the next PCPC director, Raymond Leonard, died of leukemia after just a few months. Hopkinson then appointed Bacon to the directorship; he started in January 1949.

Bacon inherited a weak government agency with little access to funding. There was no guarantee that the young agency would even survive. The PCPC was advisory to the mayor, subservient to the State Highway Department on highway planning, and took a secondary role to the RDA on neighborhood redevelopment. With limited power, Bacon knew he had to gain alliances and market the Commission's agenda. Support from Hopkinson, his chairman, was key. Bacon's assistant director, Paul Croley, was an experienced bureaucrat, invaluable in negotiating with City Council. Bacon also made connections with a newly formed business organization, the Greater Philadelphia Movement—made up of a diverse group of civic leaders formed by advertising executive Harry Batten and lawyer Robert T. McCracken in 1948 to foster "a better climate in order to attract new industry."[55]

In his first three years as PCPC director, Bacon worked under Republican Mayor Bernard Samuel. In 1949, an ongoing effort seeking home rule for Philadelphia finally succeeded, giving the city sovereignty to draft its own charter without needing state approval.[56] The mayor formed a commission to write a new city charter, adopted by voters in the spring of 1951. Bacon knew several of the charter's key authors, having served with them on the City Policy Committee, and lobbied to keep the Planning Commission independent and advisory. This independent structure worked well with Bacon's preferred approach: developing concepts on his own, then selling them to the establishment and the public. It is likely that, had Bacon been directly accountable to the mayor or managing director, he might not have had the freedom to develop ambitious design concepts. Over time, Bacon would come to rely on his own form of "planning salesmanship," based on what he called "a complete image" of the future city.[57] In his plans and presentations, Bacon showed the integration of projects into a single vision for replanning the city—thus associating himself with a wide array of historical and contemporary ideas. For example, Bacon took his Society Hill greenway system and, with a graphic of the system tied into the historical parks and buildings around Independence Hall, made these projects, separated by centuries, appear as a seamless physical composition.

In 1951 former City Policy Committee member Joseph S. Clark was elected the city's first Democratic mayor in generations. Walter Phillips and Edmund Bacon had stressed the importance of the City Policy Committee as a venue for developing civic engagement among young Philadelphians, orienting them toward political reform. Indeed, every member of Mayor Clark's cabinet was a member of the City Policy Committee.

Bacon's primary interest was still on housing and neighborhood planning. The newly created RDA and the PCPC certified the first batch of redevelopment areas in 1948. Bacon saw the Federal Housing Act of 1949 as an opportunity to realize his ideas for community planning. However, he was skeptical of the intent of the federal funding for slum clearance. In a 1949 speech, he explained his view:

The very nature of urban blight itself is complex, elusive, difficult to define. The mere spending of money, clearance of areas or building of projects doesn't necessarily constitute a valid attack on urban blight. . . . [W]e should involve the people of the neighborhood in the planning process itself. . . . Rehabilitation should be used wherever appropriate, closely tied in with clearance and new building.[58]

In the same speech, Bacon described the Planning Commission's search for the proper method of planning with communities, explaining methods that had worked and others that had failed in various redevelopment areas.[59] If community participation in planning is to succeed, Bacon explained, "The plan evolves slowly as a joint effort, and the representatives justly consider themselves as its co-creator."[60]

Bacon worked on the planning and implementation of several of Philadelphia's early federally funded redevelopment areas, with the RDA as the lead agency. These early sites, including East Poplar, Southwest Temple, and Mill Creek, were innovative in their plan and execution. Bacon was instrumental in the planning of these sites, incorporating elements of the Radburn principles and working with Oskar Stonorov and Louis Kahn.[61] East Poplar utilized a lease-to-own structure and a "self-help" approach that cut costs through use of labor donated by the future homeowners.[62] Louis Kahn worked heavily on the plans for Southwest Temple and Mill Creek. Both of these redevelopment areas called for the preservation of historic buildings and the retention of a significant amount of the urban fabric, while incorporating new, human-scale developments, connected with winding, pedestrian walkways.[63] These projects were also progressive in that they used selective clearance and historic preservation, rather than wholesale bulldozing and rebuilding.

Still, they did involve significant clearance, they did displace residents—mostly African Americans—and they did spend a lot of money on small sections of the city's worst areas. Critics cited a lack of coordination and comprehensiveness in the city's redevelopment efforts. Bacon's PCPC and the RDA were accused of displaying "projectitis."[64]

EASTWICK

In the summer of 1949, Bacon received a letter from the RDA directing him to create a plan for "Eastwick," in a sparsely developed part of southwest Philadelphia. This new community would be designed to house individuals, mostly African Americans, displaced by slum clearance in other parts of the city.[65] Since his days at the Philadelphia Housing Association, Bacon had been a critic of projects that bundled the poor together in isolated areas. It is unclear whether Bacon exerted pressure against the RDA over Eastwick; however, when the project began to take shape in the early 1950s, the "displaced persons" idea was dropped.[66] Eastwick moved ahead as the nation's largest redevelopment project, with major federal funding. Bacon viewed it as a key opportunity for selling the idea of new community design on a massive scale, and he oversaw the area's physical planning. However, despite the federal support and the city's goal of racial integration at Eastwick, its development moved slowly. There would be significant protests to the RDA's proposed condemnation from the small but surprisingly racially diverse community that occupied the existing homes in the area.[67]

Overall, by the early 1950s, Bacon believed the city's redevelopment program was on the right track, with Radburn-inspired neighborhood plans in place for reviving some of the city's most distressed areas. The goal was to build good housing for existing residents in poor, largely minority areas, fostering a fresh sense of community pride. Based on progressive planning principles, it was felt that these redeveloped neighborhoods could attract the middle class, resulting in mixed-income neighborhoods. The program, however, soon underwent a shift in focus. In 1951 the RDA changed leadership, taking on Francis J. Lammer as its new director and a new director of planning, David A. Wallace. In 1953 Mayor Clark created a new position of Housing Coordinator and appointed his former special assistant William Rafsky. David Wallace dubbed Rafsky, "almost as omnipresent, although by no means as omnipotent, as Robert Moses in New York."[68]

Bacon would continually butt heads with Lammer, Wallace, and Rafsky over the direction of the redevelopment program. For example, in 1954 the board of the RDA commissioned the Central Urban Renewal Area (CURA) study, recommending the city stop investing in the scattered neediest areas, heavily occupied by "Negroes," and focus instead on the transitional "gray areas" and on key sites around Center City.[69] Bacon strongly disagreed with this new approach, but the RDA was much more powerful than the PCPC, and Rafsky had the ear of the mayor. As the scene shifted, Bacon refocused and withdrew a bit from the redevelopment program. According to city economist Kirk Petshek, "Other approaches were tried in this period which, had they been given sufficient funds and allowed to work out their problems, might have proved that they were worth adoption by other cities; but the circumstances changed or the period under discussion ended before their worth could be firmly established."[70]

PENN CENTER

Bacon's approach was two-pronged, focusing on neighborhood planning, while also re-planning Center City to revive the city's commercial heart. Even in the pre-CURA days, when the Planning Commission was focused on the city's neediest neighborhoods, Bacon simultaneously was working on concepts for redeveloping the site of the Pennsylvania Railroad's "Chinese Wall," in the heart of downtown. The railroad had planned to remove the wall since signing an agreement with the city in 1925. There was general consensus within the architectural community that it would be a tragedy for the railroad to sell off this key site piecemeal; it was felt that it should be planned as a coordinated, iconic project in the heart of Philadelphia. There were several concepts for replacing the Chinese Wall that surely influenced Bacon. Notably, in the 1930s, William Pope Barney had been part of a design team (including Louis Kahn) that created a concept for replacing the Chinese Wall with a three-block project, containing shops, offices, cultural institutions, and a motel, including an elevated pedestrian promenade.[71]

Prior to the Better Philadelphia Exhibition, Kahn and Stonorov led a design team, called Associated Planners, under contract with the PCPC to design the "Triangle Area," including the Chinese Wall site.[72] They inserted their ideas for this area into the exhibition model, including a series of commercial buildings and a sunken plaza, resembling Rockefeller Center and replacing the Chinese Wall. Bacon later asserted that he had tried to sell Stonorov and Kahn on his own idea of including a multiblock, sunken esplanade in the model, but the idea failed to gain traction.[73] After Bacon became planning director, he helped form the American Institute of Architects' Triangle Committee, including William Pope Barney, with Kahn as Chairman to develop further concepts for the Chinese Wall site. In 1950, Kahn produced a model for the committee that replaced the Chinese Wall with eleven identical slab buildings, stretching west to the Schuylkill River, including a sunken, open-air, pedestrian esplanade running beneath the buildings.[74]

At first Bacon was enthusiastic about working with Kahn, since the two of them had similar notions about the below-ground concourse idea.[75] However, their personalities and working styles did not mesh. Bacon much later recalled,

I would say, "Let's make a model so we really show the earth transparent and show the concept," he [Kahn] would say, "Oh that's lovely but I would like to put a tower over here and a curving staircase over here and a little grove of trees over here." And I saw that Lou's creative genius, which is entirely appropriate and necessary at another phase of a total organic process, was simply obscuring the purity of . . . the concept.[76]

Bacon greatly admired Kahn as an architect and praised his work on some planning projects, like Mill Creek.[77] However, he felt that Kahn was not the right partner to convince the businessmen on the board of the Pennsylvania Railroad. Kahn left the committee to study at the American Academy in Rome in December 1950, and Bacon looked for a new partner.

After parting ways with Kahn, Bacon began working with a young architect named Vincent G. Kling. Kling was already experienced with corporate clients and had designed stations under contract with the railroad. He was also close to several of the railroad's board members and lived in the same apartment building as the railroad's executive vice president, James Symes. Bacon and Kling designed models and lobbied the executives.[78] This was planning and architecture melded with strategy, salesmanship, and marketing. They called their design "Penn Center," and produced a series of plans and models showing a system of movement. The plan had several key components: separating pedestrian and vehicular traffic; combining offices, retail, and transit connections; and incorporating a three-block, open-air, sunken pedestrian promenade flowing under the office towers that straddled the site.[79]

Bacon's challenge was to sell the conservative railroad board on this ambitious concept. Bacon and Kling secured an audience with Symes and the railroad's development consultant, Robert Dowling, the New York-based promoter of Pittsburgh's Golden Triangle development and New York City's Stuyvesant Town and Peter Cooper Village.[80] Bacon and Kling knew that Symes was more civic-minded than the railroad's board, and they were able to sell him on their vision of an iconic Penn Center establishing a positive image for the railroad as a good partner with the city. They were also able to convince Dowling to adopt a few of their design principles, like the pedestrian esplanade.[81] Dowling secured Uris

Brothers of New York as the developer and New Yorker Emory Roth as the architect.

When Symes was ready to announce that the Chinese Wall was coming down, Bacon followed with a presentation of the Penn Center plan. Bacon got the Citizens' Council on City Planning to sponsor a luncheon in February 1952 and mailed out 5,000 invitations.[82] The luncheon was held in the Grand Ballroom of the Bellevue-Stratford Hotel, and for the first time publicly, Bacon displayed images and a model of his plan. Here he sought to convince the business community, to get his vision into the collective consciousness by showing a model that people could understand in three dimensions. "Let me say, as forcefully as I can," he explained to the audience, "that these plans . . . are not orders issued by some superbody." With his PCPC position giving him no real control over the site, Bacon realized that he had to sell the plan on its design merits. In closing, he hammered home what he viewed as the most important element, telling the audience, "I hope it [the presentation] has served its purpose . . . of showing the magnificent results that can be achieved by a coordinated development of the tract as a whole and unified scheme."[83]

After the luncheon, Bacon put the model of the Bacon-Kling plan in the grand court of Wanamaker's department store, and PCPC issued a public copy of the plan—to keep Philadelphians interested and to stoke media interest. PCPC also released the results of a market analysis showing that there was a demand for downtown office space.[84] These elements were all part of Bacon's salesmanship, necessary to launch the Penn Center idea. However, there was little interest in the site among Philadelphia's real estate industry. In fact, Philadelphia real estate mogul Frank Binswanger, after seeing Bacon's plans and believing them unrealistic, advised the Equitable Life Assurance Company in New York (Equitable had shown interest in Penn Center) not to invest, and Equitable soon announced that it was passing up the opportunity.[85] Albert M. Greenfield was the only local player to make an offer, but the railroad eventually turned Greenfield down, believing he was planning to overcrowd the site.[86]

Over the coming years Penn Center would continue to be a struggle, and it would evolve significantly, in ways that differed dramatically from the Bacon-Kling plan. Dowling developed his own scheme for the site, which he felt would yield sufficient financial returns to make the project viable, and figured out an innovative leasing structure so that he would not need to identify a single buyer for the entire site.[87]

Dowling's plan covered the pedestrian concourse with a roof, like an enclosed shopping mall, and reoriented the office buildings to maximize leasable space. In the summer of 1953, the railroad appointed

Figure 7. Edmund Bacon and Vincent Kling with Penn Center model, c. 1952. Courtesy of the Architectural Archives of the University of Pennsylvania.

Bacon to a three-member Advisory Board of Design for Penn Center. Mayor Clark also appointed a Citizens' Advisory Committee, including local business leaders, planners, and Louis Kahn.[88] In addition, the local chapter of the American Institute of Architects had a committee that Bacon and Kahn sat on, to keep an eye on Penn Center. There was much attention and concern about the design of Penn Center, and rightfully so. In October of that same year, Uris Brothers unveiled a design for the first building with architecture that appalled everyone on the various committees. Douglas Haskell wrote in *Architectural Forum,* "Much of the poetry of the fine ideas Mr. Dowling accepted in Philadelphia's Penn Center is already being frittered out by third-rate architecture commissioned by well-meaning but unobserving tenants of the project."[89]

Penn Center moved ahead in fits and starts, and the railroad and its developers had continuous tension with the Art Commission, the various advisory committees, and even Mayor Clark, who hinted that he would use eminent domain if the railroad did not cooperate and insist on high-quality design.[90] Penn Center did incorporate several key elements of Bacon's initial vision, such as the pedestrian concourse, though it was below-ground, not open-air as Bacon envisioned it. Importantly, Penn Center ended up as a coordinated project, and it would act as the seed for Philadelphia's future business district along Market Street. In the end, though, Penn Center turned out vastly different from Bacon's vision and was widely considered a disappointment. The story of Penn Center clearly shows the nuances of Bacon's role amid the community of Philadelphia's postwar planners and developers. His power was expressed through advice and persuasion. Bacon's success depended on his ability to convince key actors—both in the private and public sectors—that his concepts were valuable.

THE FAR NORTHEAST

Turning to another critical project from this era, Bacon focused the Planning Commission on an undeveloped expanse of rural land in northeast Philadelphia. As previously mentioned, the Better Philadelphia Exhibition had featured drawings of a new Radburn-inspired development for this area, with homes positioned around loop streets to fit into the topography of its stream valleys, thereby preserving the streams. This land preservation idea stood in stark contrast to the typical construction method, in which street grids were laid down regardless of the natural topography, a method that usually enclosed streams in sewers. In the early 1950s, Bacon filled out this concept, positioning retail at the center of these planned communities and connecting them to downtown with transit. These were not to be suburbs; these were to be dense, urban communities with row houses. The idea required that a new zoning district be adopted, called C-1, allowing for more spacious row houses to be constructed.

The residents in the Far Northeast section of the city opposed Bacon's concept, favoring suburban-style single-family homes. A struggle ensued between Bacon, supported by the development community, and the residents in the Far Northeast. John S. Schultz, head of the Rhawnhurst Civic Association, vehemently opposed Bacon's proposed row house zoning, stating in one letter to Mayor Clark, "Mr. Bacon and the City Planning Commission have done an outstanding job in developing a street plan for the application of the C-1 residential designation, but it seems a pity that the benefits of city planning on site and street arrangement must be accompanied by the construction of down-graded housing."[91] Bacon disagreed, arguing for the benefits of the row house over suburban housing types: "The Philadelphia row house is still one of the best economical building types for the normal American family that has ever been invented. The main thing wrong with it here is the way it has been placed on the land. The endless, monotonous rows, constructed on the gridiron street plan, with no decent play space for children, penetrated by straight through-type raceways, are the things that have given the row house its bad name."[92]

At first Bacon's attempts to change the zoning were adopted by City Council but vetoed by Mayor Clark due to neighborhood opposition. Eventually, Bacon was successful in getting the new zoning classification adopted. Accompanying the zoning, Bacon's staff worked up a physical development plan for the Far Northeast that developers had to follow.[93] However, the process of working with developers to fit their projects to PCPC's master plan was seriously flawed. As time went on, developers deleted important elements like the retail centers, favoring suburban-style strip-malls. The new, mass-transit-connected community hubs were scrapped, necessitating automobile travel. Bacon and his design staff compromised with developers, shifting the loop-street system to one that favored cul-de-sacs. When finished, the Far Northeast held a large stock of affordable, urban row houses. It also preserved the stream valleys. However, several key concepts, such as the uniform design and retail centers were lost along the way. Despite its failings, the planning of the Far Northeast was applauded in William H. Whyte's 1968 book, *The Last Landscape*. "For so advanced a plan," Whyte explained, "what one sees on the ground is disappointingly ordinary. . . . But the plan works, and one has only to look to the conventional row-house developments a few miles back toward the city to see what a difference it has made . . . [the new houses] are complemented by a magnificent stream-valley network that cost the city nothing and will one day be priceless."[94]

The Far Northeast is another useful case study of Bacon's methodol-

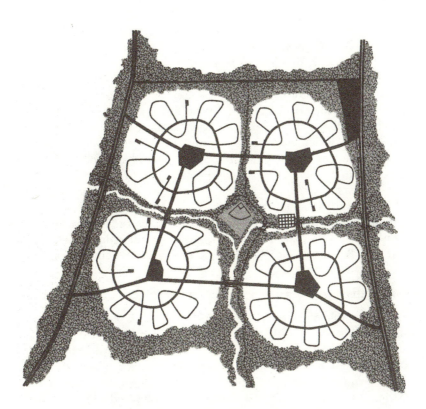

THROUGH STREETS
MAJOR LOCAL STREETS
MINOR LOCAL STREETS
RESIDENTIAL STREETS
TRAILS
COMMERCIAL
SCHOOLS
PARKS
WATER COURSE

Figure 8. Diagram from the Preliminary Physical Development Plan for the Far Northeast, published by the Philadelphia City Planning Commission in January 1955. The diagram shows the conceptual urban design framework for land use and transportation, to serve as the foundation for the development of Philadelphia's Far Northeast section. Courtesy of the Architectural Archives of the University of Pennsylvania.

ogy, but also perhaps of its drawbacks. He began with a single vision comprised of an integrated set of urban planning ideas, what he referred to as a "design idea" or later still as an "organizing concept."[95] He used the tools at his disposal to sell the concept to key decision makers, until at a certain point the implementation of the concept was largely out of his hands. Whether parts of the organizing concept stayed together or fell apart depended on Bacon's success as a salesman and the degree to which those carrying out the project understood and accepted their interdependency. In one interview, Bacon pondered, "Is there a point at where an organizing concept can be changed so that the basic idea is lost?"[96] The answer is clearly yes, and the Far Northeast is a key example. Despite the preservation of the stream valleys and the continuation of urban-style rowhouse communities, the Far Northeast in 2009 is a quasi-suburban, auto-centric section of Philadelphia—far different than Bacon's vision of a new type of urbanized community.

SOCIETY HILL

Another example of Bacon's focus on neighborhood planning is Society Hill.[97] The historic Society Hill neighborhood in the early 1950s was sometimes called the "Bloody Fifth Ward." The neighborhood was poor, full of tenement houses, and populated predominantly by ethnically Eastern European working-class families and a smaller population of African Americans.[98] The CURA report emphasized redevelopment on the fringes of Center City. Along with the development of Independence Mall nearby and the planned removal of the crowded and unsanitary Dock Street market, Bacon saw the potential in Society Hill to implement a redevelopment program that could meet CURA's goals, while realizing the pedestrian walkway system he had designed for the Better Philadelphia Exhibition. In Society Hill he could focus on historic preservation as a means to attract middle-class families back into the city.[99] Bacon explained, "The whole area cannot and should not become one large museum. It must be . . . a live city, as it originally was."[100]

In 1955 Mayor Clark did not seek reelection, and District Attorney Richardson Dilworth was elected mayor. Dilworth put political muscle behind advancing the revitalization of Society Hill, giving Bacon a key ally in selling Society Hill to the business community. Years earlier, Bacon had commissioned planning consultant Eugene Klaber to make recommendations on the potential of redeveloping Society Hill.[101] In 1950 Klaber issued a report stating that he did see great potential, and suggested that it be financed through "the creation of a limited dividend corporation" that would serve as the developer.[102] Dilworth fol-

Figure 9. Edmund N. Bacon, about 1960, with his staff, examining a model of Society Hill, with I. M. Pei's Society Hill Towers prominent. Left to right: Irving Wasserman, R. Damon Childs, Bacon. Courtesy of the Architectural Archives of the University of Pennsylvania.

lowed this recommendation and instigated the creation of the Old Philadelphia Development Corporation (OPDC) to serve as the developer for Society Hill. Few other cities at the time were restoring slum areas through historic preservation and rehabilitation, and the federal renewal program was not designed for it.[103] But, in 1957 OPDC finally found success lobbying the federal Urban Renewal Administration for $11 million in funding.[104] The city's RDA advertised a development competition in 1958 for two parcels in Society Hill.[105] Bacon was involved in assessing these entries and, though he was not on the jury, he was influential with RDA Chairman Michael von Moschzisker.[106] The RDA selected Bacon's favored plan, by New York developer Webb and Knapp with architect I. M. Pei, for the eastern section, and Thomas Jefferson Square Corporation as the developer for a section adjoining Washington Square to the west. Bacon favored Pei's design because it included low-rise modern townhouses as a transition from the historic homes to the new apartment towers.[107]

By the fall of 1959, when Bacon published "Philadelphia in the Year 2009," prospects for Society Hill seemed strong, and Mayor Dilworth had recently commissioned a faux colonial house for his family on Washington Square. Bacon's influence in planning Society Hill was less tangible than in the Far Northeast or in the redevelopment areas where he spearheaded the physical planning. In this case, Bacon used the momentum of CURA and Dilworth's early desire to create a legacy for his administration to propel the Society Hill vision. His salesmanship could not rely on the shiny image of a new project alone. Instead, he had succeeded in promoting a much more subtle and complex notion: the transformation of a living part of the city.

Society Hill's redevelopment was not without controversy. The project involved some displacement of existing residents—especially renters— though the numbers were considerably fewer than in other cities, where redevelopment sometimes cleared entire areas.[108] Also, the RDA did demolish some eighteenth-century and many more nineteenth-century structures. Society Hill's redevelopment received strong criticism from Charles Peterson, a National Park Service architect and passionate preservationist.[109] However, Society Hill ultimately received much more praise than criticism, viewed as one of the nation's most successful efforts at attracting middle-class families back from the suburbs.[110]

MARKET EAST

In the mid-1950s, Bacon shifted his view east of City Hall to Philadelphia's historic center of commerce. By that time, Market Street contained five department stores, though threats to downtown shopping from suburban shopping malls were evident.[111] One department store, Frank and Seder, had recently closed and another, Snellenberg's, in financial trouble, was sold. Bacon had an idea for a major shopping development that had the amenities of the suburbs, but in an urban context. This was similar to his thinking for the Far Northeast, borrowing elements that made the suburbs appealing but transferring them to a distinctly urban model.

Bacon and his design staff worked out a scheme that they believed could be sold to the business community, and in 1958 the PCPC released "Market East Plaza: A New Center for Transportation and Commerce."[112] The plan presented a structural diagram of how people would arrive and move around Center City, with a subway station lined by gardens, special ramps for buses to a new terminal, a six-level parking garage wrapped by an open-air retail complex, open-air walkways separating pedestrians and cars, and a direct connection to Penn Center. PCPC also proposed the idea of connecting the Pennsylvania Railroad and Reading Railroad track systems with an underground tunnel.

By 1959, there was both support and opposition to "Market East" from the Commissioners of PCPC and the business community. After the initial release of the Market East concept in March 1958, the *Philadelphia Inquirer* printed an editorial stating, "It may be found desirable even to discard the Market Street section of the plan and concentrate wholly on the bus terminal and parking garage along Filbert Street."[113] Some members of Bacon's Planning Commission felt that the parking garage and bus terminal were, perhaps, the only tenable parts of the plan.[114] In the face of a challenging climate, Bacon worked through both public and private venues to sell the concept of Market East. He continued to promote his design concepts to the media, while working with Jack Robin from OPDC, members of City Council, the Pennsylvania Railroad, and Mayor Dilworth to convince them of its worth and devise possible financing mechanisms. However, in 1959 Bacon still had a long way to go to sell the vision and get wide support from the business community for Market East.

By the time Bacon wrote the "2009" essay Philadelphia's first comprehensive plan was finished and ready for release. This 375-page charter-mandated plan laid out a program that was estimated to cost $3.5 billion. It analyzed the city's historical development, population demographics, and existing land use conditions, then set out planning strategies for industry, housing, commerce, and recreation.[115] Bacon oversaw the effort, though he was never much interested in comprehensive planning, viewing it as either too abstract and statistical or too broad-brush to make an impact. In a 2002 interview, Bacon remembered, "I regarded this [comprehensive planning] more as busy work than anything else, and kept cheerfully doing projects which together developed the whole city, without necessarily any reference to the Comprehensive Plan at all."[116]

While Bacon delegated the 1960 Comprehensive Plan to a deputy, he had a heavy hand in designing a related Center City plan, fitting together a series of downtown projects: Penn Center, Market East, Society Hill, Independence Mall, the expressways, parking, and transit.[117] To

Bacon, Center City represented a scale where he could plan for a large number of physical projects, tie them together, and communicate their interconnectivity. Other ideas in the plan included transforming Chestnut Street to a pedestrian-only street with a trolley in its center, building a park and marina on the Delaware Waterfront, and extending Fairmount Park along the eastern bank of the Schuylkill River—ideas described in the "2009" essay. Bacon also included a comprehensive transportation plan showing a system of transit and highways. These ideas were not new, but this was the first time they were combined. [118] With this overall plan for Center City, Bacon faced his greatest public relations challenge of all. Each time he gave an interview or wrote an article, he pushed the idea of this complete image of the downtown. He graphically demonstrated this image in the Comprehensive Plan, and presented it to the architectural community in 1961 at the American Institute of Architects' national conference. However, as he argues in the "2009" essay, the greatest marketing tool for putting the eyes of the nation on Philadelphia's redevelopment program was to be the World's Fair.

Hence, we arrive at 1959 and the motive for "Philadelphia in the Year 2009." The article reflects the result of over a decade of evolving concepts, pieced together like a jigsaw puzzle into a complete picture. The World's Fair was to be the venue for propelling the Center City plan into the public consciousness and then to carry the plan into reality over the next fifty years. Bacon clearly recognized how long it would take to implement the plan.

The "2009" essay shows a visionary promoter of big ideas for Center City attempting to position Philadelphia to compete with the great cities of the world through physical design. However, the essay also demonstrates a concern with affordable housing and community planning. "So, I think the second half of this period," Bacon notes, "will be a great, concentrated social and human effort. Finally, after all these years of trial and effort, of discussion, thought and shouting, we will finally turn our full energies to the job of housing our people."[119] Bacon maintained a two-pronged approach throughout his career and returned more heavily to issues of housing and community planning in the 1960s.

Beyond 1959

In the early 1960s, about 30 percent of Philadelphia's residents were African American—with one in five unemployed. The neighborhoods of North Philadelphia harbored crime, poverty, and unrest.[120] Bacon's international fame after appearing on the cover of *Time* in 1964 likely gave him greater political capital at home, and federal programs under presidents John F. Kennedy and Lyndon Johnson made new monies available to cities. Through the Community Renewal, Neighborhood Development, and Model Cities Programs, Bacon again focused on planning for underprivileged communities. In 1967 Bacon explained, "It's very important constantly to stress the point that planning must engage the problems of racial discrimination and the most underprivileged and deprived."[121] One of Bacon's major efforts in this regard was in creating a program in 1968 "for involving black planners in the planning process." Bacon presented this program to officials in Washington and reported to Mayor James Tate, "The HUD officials were impressed with the plan, and indicated there is a possibility that HUD will make funds available for this purpose."[122]

During the 1960s, Bacon took a stand against the dominant model of public housing in high-rise buildings, citing their "very serious social and moral hazard."[123] He was instrumental in developing a new approach to public housing in Philadelphia that eventually became known as the "Used House Program," in which the city would rehabilitate abandoned homes for scattered-site public housing. Initially, Bacon pitched the idea to Mayor Dilworth without success, then revived it in the early 1960s with the support of Murray Isard, a developer and member of the City Planning Commission.[124] Though the RDA was skeptical at first, "Used House" came into being in 1965, bolstered by the Federal Housing Act's Turnkey Program, allowing a straightforward means for developers to transfer properties to housing authorities.[125] The city created the nonprofit Philadelphia Housing Development Corporation (PHDC) to serve as the development intermediary. PHDC received a two million dollar revolving fund, with additional support from the Smith, Kline, and French Foundation. The Used House Program was the first scattered-site housing program in the country.[126] However, lack of funding, legal challenges, and an investigation into corruption in the Philadelphia Housing Authority would doom it to failure by 1970.[127]

TRANSPORTATION ISSUES

In 1968, Mayor Tate appointed Bacon to the dual role of planning director and development coordinator, making him a much more public figure. It was during this period that he came under significant heat from community groups, primarily in association with major expressway projects like the Delaware and Crosstown Expressways.[128] Throughout his career, the funding and planning agency for expressways was the State Department of Highways. Stanhope Browne, who led the opposition to the Delaware Expressway through Society Hill, said in a later interview, "I knew we were fighting the highway department. I knew they were our principal enemy. At that point it was really out of Ed Bacon's hands."[129]

Despite this, the question still stands as to whether Bacon could have done more to pressure the state to stop Philadelphia's highways. The answer must be yes. There is evidence that Bacon was generally supportive of the highway network.[130] He was in favor of a comprehensive transportation system for the region and shared a vision with Louis Kahn of expressways circling the downtown connected with parking garages, so that visitors could drive into town, get out of their cars, and walk into Center City.[131]

Still, by the mid- to late 1960s, it seems that Bacon had developed a true dislike of automobile travel. In 1966, Bacon said in an interview, "there is a 'revulsion' against the automobile and the destruction it does to cities and the countryside. The car is losing its luster as something worth sacrificing for."[132] Bacon recalled that he had a policy of not speaking out publicly against the mayor's administration.[133] This fact could explain why Bacon represented the city in support of the Crosstown Expressway, until Mayor Tate decided to oppose it. Another important fact is that just a few years later, after he retired, Bacon immediately became highly critical of the automobile, speaking and writing prolifically about the "Post Petroleum City," where the car was no longer viable and people got around on mass transit and by bicycle.[134]

Bacon never seemed to speak or write about highways in the way that he promoted his physical design concepts like Penn Center or Market East. However, he was passionate about a comprehensive vision for transportation, a strategy that valued public transit equally with highways.[135] This kind of vision comes through clearly in documents like the 1963 Center City Plan that show an intermeshing of rail and highway systems to bring people downtown.[136] The same idea would strongly inform Bacon's thinking about how to bring visitors to the World's Fair in 1976.

An article in *Railway Age* in 1968 noted that "Bacon doesn't preach 'balanced solutions'—he practices them, making room in his schemes for everything from high-speed mainline trains to rapid transit to private automobiles."[137] Bacon was also wildly enthusiastic about the prospect of the Metroliner for connecting East Coast cities and transforming Philadelphia's 30th Street Station into "the economic center of the northeastern United States."[138] Here, perhaps, is an example of Bacon's salesmanship failing to hit the mark. He favored a comprehensive transportation system, connected to the downtown renewal program. In the end, however, his legacy became attached to two controversial expressway projects.

Last Years

Edmund Bacon resigned after twenty-one years as director of the Phila-delphia City Planning Commission in May 1970, amid a grand jury inves-tigation of the Tate administration into political graft regarding a downtown development project (Bacon was never found to have any wrongdoing).[139] As he left the PCPC, he was distressed by negative assess-ments of his legacy. He wanted to be remembered for his affordable housing and neighborhood development work, not just his major down-town projects, like Penn Center and the still unfinished Market East. In one interview he said, "Center City has really been a sideline. . . . It is not the significant part of my work. . . . My principal preoccupation has been with housing."[140] An article in the *Evening Bulletin* titled "Bacon's Battle Against the Bulldozer" reported, "[Bacon's] voice is occasionally edged with anger as he talks of the Liberal Establishment and its 'his-toric, stubborn commitment to the bulldozer approach in neighbor-hood renewal.' It's just this approach that Bacon's more fervid critics ascribe to Bacon himself. 'How do you convince people otherwise?' asked Bacon. 'Do you keep saying, "But I'm for the poor, too'?" [141] In this sense, Bacon's salesmanship may have backfired. He was never a major player in the most destructive projects during his tenure, like the University City Science Center and the expressways. Still, with the unde-niable intensity of his personality and his efforts to make himself the face of the city's redevelopment program, he necessarily inherited the legacy of all of the city's planning and rebuilding projects of the 1950s and 1960s—not just those in which he pounded a heavy hand.

After retirement, Bacon became a vice president at the Canadian development company, Mondev. In the 1960s, Bacon had gotten involved in national policy, serving on President Lyndon Johnson's Citi-zens' Advisory Committee on Recreation and Natural Beauty, and later on President Richard Nixon's Citizens Advisory Committee on Environ-mental Quality. In his retirement letter, Bacon predicted he would "devote the major part of my energies to the problems of pollution and environmental quality."[142] In the 1970s he did so, focusing his intellec-tual energies on a new concept, the "Post Petroleum City." He wrote articles and gave speeches about the need to move past the age of oil, received a contract from Viking Press to write a book on the subject (he never finished it), and organized a conference around the idea that never finally materialized. In the 1980s Bacon developed five films dis-cussing the oil crisis and explaining designs of world cities. Bacon also famously clashed with developer Willard Rouse in the late 1980s over what became the first building to break Philadelphia's "Gentleman's

Agreement" height limit that Bacon promoted as planning director. Throughout his tenure, Bacon argued that City Hall should be the tallest building in the skyline, but despite several attempts to push a bill through City Council, the height limit was never codified into law. It was a rule waiting to be broken, and was with the construction of One Liberty Place in 1987. In the 1990s, Bacon moved into the spotlight from time to time, fighting new development projects that he disagreed with, such as the proposed redesign of the Benjamin Franklin Parkway and of Independence Mall. In one of his last public acts, he made headlines by skateboarding at age ninety-two in LOVE Park, in protest of the mayor's ban on the sport. Edmund Bacon died on 14 October 2005.

Although Edmund Bacon held a limited role in postwar Philadelphia's development policy system, he found significant success. Unlike Robert Moses in New York City, who had the power and funding to push projects from beginning to end, Bacon relied on his skills in salesmanship and networking to make ideas resonate with Philadelphia's citizens and its leadership. Bacon's strength, and the key to understanding his successful initiatives, was his ability to comprehend the power structure and work through the right channels to advance his concepts. Bacon promoted his ideas to decision makers and then (if he was successful) stepped away as others carried out his visions. Through this tenuous process, it is apparent how easily development projects evolved differently than Bacon planned. In his career he deferred to developers, the Pennsylvania Railroad, the RDA, and powerful actors like the board of OPDC, mayors, and the development coordinator. Both the successes and limitations of Bacon's methodology had to do with the fact that he marketed his ideas to others in the urban development network of postwar Philadelphia, a varied group who took the Planning Commission's ideas and became their primary force toward implementation. Of course, Bacon continued to play a role in these projects, maintaining the ear of the business and political elite as best he could through a very dynamic and often tumultuous period in the city's history. However, with most of his projects he ceased, at a certain point, to be the key decision maker. This fact sets Bacon apart from his famous contemporaries, powerful twentieth-century urban planners like Robert Moses in New York and Ed Logue in New Haven and Boston, men who were in much more central positions to control those cities' redevelopment programs.

In 1964 Bacon was highlighted as the key player of Philadelphia's renaissance, with his face on the cover of *Time* magazine. It is surprising that Bacon received such national publicity. Other American cities had ambitious renewal programs, and in Philadelphia, arguably, others like Bill Rafsky were equally if not more influential than Bacon.[143] These facts highlight Bacon's skill as a planner who understood the intricacies and politics of selling a vision to key decision makers, to the media, and to the public. Bacon was not in a more powerful position than planners in other big cities. He simply was able to do things that other planners could not or did not realize were necessary for advancing their plans. One element of Bacon's approach was figuring out how to gain access and work with key decision makers. Another element was communicating ideas through clear, coherent, and compelling models and drawings. A third was Bacon's skill at gaining media coverage and obtaining large-scale venues to present his plans to the public. Bacon expanded both new and existing ideas into complete physical concepts and presented them in a way that others could readily understand, ideas that would resonate.

Certainly a number of Philadelphia's projects built in the 1950s and 1960s leave much to be desired. Still, planners in 2009 have much to learn from Edmund Bacon—if not from his ideas, then from his methodology. Edmund Bacon's fame and his lasting influence largely stem from his ability to forge the link between planning and implementation, creating a new role for the city planner as both an active civic participant and salesman of ideas. This was just as rare a feature for planners in 1959 as it is today. The challenge for planners in 2009 is to understand and excel at this subtle art of selling ideas, inspiring decision makers to adopt ideas and transform them into a vivid reality.

Chapter Three

A Utopian, a Utopianist, or Whatever the Heck It Is: Edmund Bacon and the Complexity of the City

GUIAN McKEE

In February 1965, University of Pennsylvania professor Paul Davidoff launched a withering attack on Philadelphia's highly acclaimed city planning and urban renewal programs. Speaking before the Citizens' Council on City Planning (CCCP), a local planning advocacy and "watchdog" group, Davidoff charged that while Philadelphia "has men of international fame for its planning, it has become increasingly plain that they have provided a renaissance façade covering the host of problems. [The planners have] failed to examine [the] relationship between economic and social and physical objectives." The CCCP members in the audience would have immediately recognized the target of Davidoff's reference to "men of international fame," as Philadelphia City Planning Commission (PCPC) Executive Director Edmund N. Bacon had appeared just months before on the cover of *Time* magazine. Continuing, Davidoff noted that the city's planners had based their work on "physical values such as land use," while failing to see that "land is used to serve members and classes of society having different ideas and resources . . . for whom is it assembled and why?" Even the recently completed Comprehensive Plan had completely failed to consider "what groups or classes are aided or harmed by the public act?" Finally, Davidoff noted that "planning, renewal and policy are clearly political matters. They should be debated. It should not be quieted; it should be encouraged." Bacon, the Planning Commission, and the city's Redevelopment Authority (RDA), he charged, had done the opposite.[1]

Davidoff's attack might have been dismissed as the ranting of a disgruntled academic if it had not followed a period of growing controversy about planning in Philadelphia. Instead, in the same month that *Time* presented its laudatory account of a Bacon-directed quest to rebuild

Center City, *Architectural Forum* observed that "the blight has been removed from one [Philadelphia] neighborhood only to appear in another" and concluded that the city should direct "renewal at the fundamental human and economic problems by which physical blight is produced."[2] Locally, *Greater Philadelphia Magazine* noted that "a strange and apologetic silence has overtaken formerly voluble politicians and planners" who "know that the grand design has failed . . . because the planners isolated themselves from realities that conflicted with their preconceived notions" and pursued their aims "solely by manipulation of the physical environment."[3] Meanwhile, North Philadelphia had suffered through days of violent, racially charged upheaval during August of 1964. Few events spoke to the failure of planning and urban renewal more immediately than this rebellion in the city's largest low-income, African American neighborhood.

Edmund Bacon did not constitute the sole target of such rage or of these journalistic critiques. The *Greater Philadelphia* article, for example, placed greater emphasis on city development coordinator William L. Rafsky. Bacon's image and reputation, however, have since become so intertwined with the memory of city planning in Philadelphia that the upheavals of the mid-1960s serve as pointed reminders of the significant limitations and failures of the great Philadelphia planner himself. Paradoxically, though, critical reassessment of Bacon's work may lead to a more realistic understanding of what he actually accomplished. Edmund Bacon cared greatly about his city, about the people who lived there, and about the problems with which the city and its people struggled. His only avenue to act on these commitments, though, lay in physical design and in efforts to promote his ideas about urban form. Although Bacon believed very strongly in the power of both design and ideas, his career would ultimately demonstrate the inability of such an approach to address the massive social and economic changes of the mid-twentieth-century American city. The key challenge in assessing Bacon, however, consists of determining whether these characteristics of his work primarily reflected the constraints of the political and policy environment in which he worked or whether they reflected deeper and ultimately more limiting intellectual boundaries of his own approach to planning and the city.

Constraints: The Reality of Bacon's Position in Politics and Policy

In recent years, Edmund Bacon's role in Philadelphia's postwar planning and renewal efforts has been exaggerated. Beloved at the end of his life for his cantankerous personality, his self-styled image as a visionary, his spirited fight against the renovation of his design for Independence Mall, and such noble acts as riding a skateboard, at age ninety-two, across LOVE Park in protest of Mayor John Street's ban on skateboarding in the park, Bacon has been granted an outsized role in the city's memory of its planning, development, and housing policy during the era of his life's major work.[4] This exaggeration arises from a failure to apprehend either the constraints of the position that Bacon held or the limitations of his own approach to city planning—the very shortfalls that Paul Davidoff pointed out in 1965.

Bacon's importance in Philadelphia has frequently been compared to that of Robert Moses in New York and Edward Logue in New Haven, Boston, and New York state.[5] Such comparisons, though, are poorly drawn, as Bacon lacked the concentrated authority over planning and renewal that these men held in their respective cities. Bacon understood this well, observing in 1975 that

Robert Moses directly manipulated and controlled vast amounts of money. And Ed Logue, by the designation or assignment of political power . . . from the Mayor of Boston and later from Governor Rockefeller of New York, exercised direct political power. I never had this privilege. I never exercised either control of large amounts of money nor direct political power, and I was indeed not given that by the mayors whom I served. I invariably had to work by motivating other people to do something which seemed appropriate.[6]

Considering that Moses and Logue implemented massive and often destructive urban clearance programs which produced at best mixed results, Philadelphians may well be grateful that Bacon was *not* in fact comparable to either of these iconic master builders.

The constraints on Bacon's power originated from four structural features of Philadelphia's politics and its city government. First, in terms of direct influence over policy development in the areas of urban renewal and housing, Bacon occupied a distinctly secondary position behind that of William L. Rafsky. Rafsky was a Polish-born graduate of the City College of New York who had worked for the War Production Board during World War II and later as research director for the left-wing Hosiery Workers Union. During Philadelphia's political reform movement of the late 1940s and early 1950s, he emerged as an activist with the local Americans for Democratic Action chapter. This brought him to the attention of reform mayoral candidate Joseph S. Clark. Following Clark's 1951 victory, he asked Rafsky to serve as his executive secretary. Rafsky impressed the new mayor with his "computerlike mind" and his grasp of "the problems the city faced" and soon became Clark's most important advisor. By 1954 Clark had become frustrated with the lack of policy coordination between the PCPC, the Redevelopment Authority, and the Philadelphia Housing Authority and appointed Rafsky to the new position of Housing Coordinator. Two years later, Clark's reform partner and mayoral successor, Richardson H. Dilworth, broadened Rafsky's portfolio with the title of Development Coordinator. This position gave him authority over all aspects of the city's housing, urban renewal, and economic development programs. With this backing, Rafsky was assumed to speak with the authority of the mayor. Later in his career, Rafsky retained much of this influence when he served as director of the powerful quasi-public Old Philadelphia Development Corporation during the 1960s and of the city's Bicentennial Corporation during the late 1960s and early 1970s.[7]

Rafsky's broad authority and his access to the mayor relegated other policymakers such as Bacon to a distinctly secondary position. It was Rafsky who determined overall policy, Rafsky who sat on the mayors' cabinets, and Rafsky who coordinated the many public and quasi-public agencies involved in Philadelphia's urban renewal and economic development programs. Bacon lacked such control and access, except as he could attain them through Rafsky or others influential in city government or through the PCPC's central (but not exclusive) role in setting the city's annual and six-year capital programs. Under the reform mayors Clark and Dilworth, Bacon and Rafsky frequently clashed over differing priorities and about the latter's growing influence. Rafsky, it should be noted, was not a Moses-Logue figure either. He preferred to operate quietly, exerting his influence privately rather than seeking publicity, whereas Moses and Logue often transcended the mayors for whom they nominally worked. Rafsky also held what remained a more limited position than Moses or Logue, as he had control over broad policy formulation but not over the actual operation of the different agencies in his purview. Nonetheless, his powerful presence and the authority with which he spoke greatly limited Bacon's capacity to act autonomously.[8]

Second, Bacon's surprisingly weak connections to the reform mayors Clark and Dilworth exacerbated his structural disadvantage relative to Rafsky and other key figures in the mayoral administrations. Mayor Clark viewed Bacon as a potentially untrustworthy holdover from the Republican administration of his predecessor. The result was that Bacon stood at significant remove from the reform leadership with whom he is now too easily associated. As Bacon himself recounted, "I had really very little access to [Clark] personally and as far as I can recall, I may be wrong about this, I never met with him in cabinet."[9] Bacon's situation did not improve under Mayor Dilworth, who informed Bacon that his position was "subordinate" to Rafsky and threatened to fire Bacon after the planning director engaged in "politicking in City Planning Commission and in City Council" over a disagreement regarding the design for the new plaza west of City Hall.[10] Only late in his career, under Mayor

Figure 10. William Rafsky, who at various times served as housing coordinator, development coordinator, executive director of the old Philadelphia Development Corporation, and director of the Bicentennial Commission, 1963. Courtesy of Temple University Libraries, Urban Archives.

James H. J. Tate (the more traditional successor to the reform mayors), did Bacon's direct authority increase.[11]

Third, although Bacon and the Commission could certify areas of the city for renewal and could engage in broad conceptual planning for such sections, the city's Redevelopment Authority had final responsibility for detailed project planning. The RDA had been established in 1946 to allow Philadelphia to take advantage of Pennsylvania's 1945 urban redevelopment law, which allowed cities to establish public authorities that would implement redevelopment plans.[12] This did not exclude the PCPC from a role in urban renewal, but as with Rafsky's role in policy coordination, it limited Bacon's field of influence and activity. To a lesser degree, similar points could be made about agencies such as the Philadelphia Housing Authority and the Philadelphia Industrial Development Corporation (PIDC). In a similar vein, the development of basic plans for the highway and mass transit systems took place outside of Bacon's purview, initially in the Urban Traffic and Transportation Board study of the mid-1950s and later in the Passenger Service Improvement Corporation and Southeastern Pennsylvania Transportation Authority (SEPTA) in the 1960s. Transportation planning represented a crucial component of the city's overall planning process, yet it took place outside of the PCPC. Bacon did not set the basic parameters for this defining urban system. Had Bacon, rather than Rafsky, held the development coordinator position, he might have been able to use the PCPC as an operational base for controlling Philadelphia's renewal, housing, and economic development policies. The PCPC executive director's position alone, however, did not offer such power.[13]

Fourth, and finally, the private sector played a critical role in guiding much of the city's development process. From Penn Center to Market East to Society Hill, Bacon's plans had to find support first from such powerful local business organizations as the politically active Greater Philadelphia Movement and, ultimately, from private investors and developers who often came from outside the city. Influential figures such as real estate mogul and Democratic Party power-broker (and for a time, PCPC Chairman) Albert M. Greenfield operated as competing and sometimes overwhelming sources of direction—although occasionally, as allies as well. Proudly proclaiming the "power of the idea" in his theorizing about the planning process, Bacon claimed a unique ability to influence such private sector decision making through his own design vision. Often, though, the implementation of those ideas would be badly crimped by the reality of what the private sector would invest in. Penn Center and Market East represented the clearest cases of such constraint. In projects aimed more directly at human and neighborhood needs, lack of private sector support ultimately undercut even Bacon's most socially sensitive designs. The slow progress of the East Poplar Redevelopment Area in North Philadelphia stood as a glaring example. Ultimately, these barriers contributed to Bacon's overemphasis on design and his inattention to social and especially economic issues, as they meant that for much of his career he simply lacked the authority and the policy tools to address such matters. Whether, and how, he might have done so had he occupied a position that granted him such power is the remaining question of this essay.

Planning: Edmund Bacon's Vision of the City

While significant, the political and policy constraints that impinged on Bacon's autonomy do not fully explain his approach to planning. A more complete assessment of Bacon's vision requires attention to the historical context in which "Philadelphia in the Year 2009" was written and to that which followed its publication. When Bacon drafted the essay, Philadelphia's urban renewal programs had recently undergone a critical shift in strategy. This change would shape the nature of the programs themselves, the legacy of the individuals who worked on them, and the contours and character of the city for decades to come. Although this policy transformation would have a tremendous, even defining, influence on Bacon's career, his role in and reaction to that change have been poorly understood.

In a speech at Temple University five years after he left the PCPC, Bacon declared himself "a utopian, a utopianist, or whatever the heck it is."[14] This strand of idealism appeared early in his career, when Bacon and his staff helped to pioneer an innovative approach to urban redevelopment. This process began even before the 1951 triumph of Philadelphia's political reform movement. Although Bacon's reputation would eventually be based primarily on his work in Center City and northeast Philadelphia, much of his early tenure at the Planning Commission focused on housing issues in older neighborhoods. Following the passage of the Housing Act of 1949, Philadelphia established a redevelopment program that avoided the massive clearance projects of such cities as New York and Chicago.[15] Instead, Bacon and counterparts such as David Wallace of the Redevelopment Authority sought to employ a mixture of clearance and rehabilitation in relatively small project areas. Low-cost housing would be woven into the projects, ideally with little stigmatizing demarcation. Further, community institutions such as churches, clubs, and schools would be maintained. As Bacon explained in early 1952, "there is a structure of institutions (in all neighborhoods) which has vitality . . . which tie the people together. Redevelopment, whenever possible, should give these institutions new strength and vitality."[16] This was a notable insight during an era in which planners typically disregarded such relationships within the existing urban fabric.

More broadly, though, Bacon and the Philadelphia planners operated on an assumption that the immediate removal and replacement of the worst spots of "blight" could create "spores of good" that would inexorably exert wholesome and improving influences on the surrounding neighborhood. *Architectural Forum* characterized this approach as relying on "penicillin" rather than "surgery," and as a "repatterning rather than replacing of neighborhoods." The plan for the East Poplar area embodied this idea, as it featured a mix of new public housing, green spaces, pedestrian corridors, and existing housing rehabilitated by the Quaker Friends Service Committee. In the Morton area of Germantown, the planners pushed this strategy even farther, placing public housing "in scattered, beautifully designed small sections of row houses that manage to be both contemporary and neoclassic." As in East Poplar, older houses were renovated when possible.[17] One commentator even enthused that the "color of each house is separately considered."[18] In these early projects, Bacon encouraged a method of continuous interaction between planners and neighborhood groups that was not entirely dissimilar from the methods later advocated by Paul Davidoff.[19]

This subtle, mixed approach to redevelopment had much to commend it. In actual practice, though, these early projects generated problems unanticipated by the planners. Most critically, while the projects avoided the total clearance of other cities, they still displaced large numbers of low-income residents, many of them minorities (albeit still fewer than in other cities). In the late 1940s, Bacon and the RDA planners certified the semi-rural Eastwick area of Southwest Philadelphia as a redevelopment area with the assumption that it could become a relocation area for low-income African Americans displaced from homes miles away in North Philadelphia. Critics called it a dumping ground. "Conceived in sin," as one planner later put it, this conception of Eastwick was abandoned in the early years of Clark's mayoralty. Eastwick, though, remained a renewal site. With Bacon's support, Rafsky and the reform mayors pushed through an ambitious and costly plan to transform the area, against the wishes of residents in its existing, partially integrated working-class neighborhoods, into a model "city-within-a-city" intended to demonstrate what planning and urban renewal could achieve.[20] Meanwhile, plans for mixed-race public housing projects on sites scattered around the city stalled because of white opposition to racial integration. As a result, the Housing Authority placed most new public housing units on clearance sites in redevelopment areas. Increasingly, the Authority built stark, isolated high-rise towers instead of low-rise row house units. Little integration took place, and almost all Philadelphia

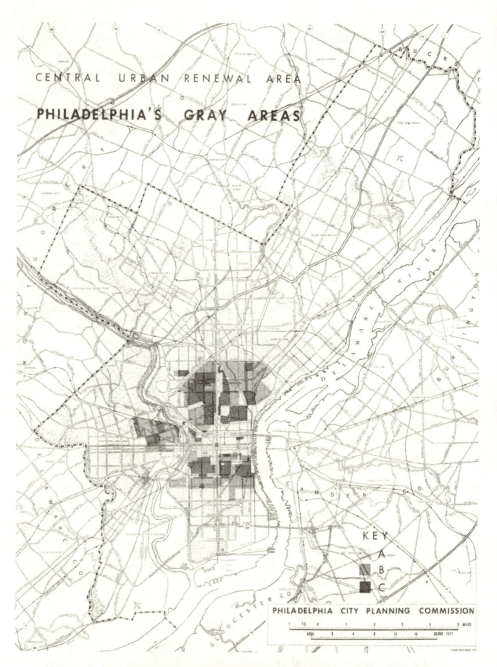

Figure 11. RDA Neighborhood Map-RDA/City Redevelopment Authority plan of the East Poplar, Northwest Temple, and Southwest Temple Urban renewal areas, 1960. East Poplar shows the mixture of rehabilitation and clearance in Philadelphia's early urban renewal projects; the other areas, planned later, show a heavier reliance on clearance. Courtesy of University of Pennsylvania Libraries.

public housing became single-race.[21] The quality of planning in the urban renewal areas declined as well, and some North Philadelphia projects sat empty for years after clearance because of lack of interest from private developers. Failure to complete, or even begin, such projects led to disillusionment among residents who had participated in the community planning sessions.[22]

Regardless of quality or character or speed of completion, the number of public housing units in Philadelphia simply proved inadequate relative to the demand. William Rafsky later explained that, as a result, most displaced residents simply crowded into nearby neighborhoods, further hastening decline: "while we were working on this blight, adjacent blocks were adversely affected when those who were dispersed from the clearance . . . began overcrowding the existing structures nearby. While we were working on this, other neighborhoods somewhat removed were deteriorating, and because of obsolescence and population movements were creating new problems for us."[23] Finally, the strategy of targeting the first areas proved to be tremendously expensive, costing as much as a billion dollars.[24]

Not all these problems, of course, could be blamed on Edmund Bacon. Others in city government and the private sector also supported the "worst-first" approach. Nonetheless, Bacon remained a determined advocate of this "sore spot" strategy, even as displacement, delays, and cost became apparent. Bacon's emphasis on the city's most troubled neighborhoods, though, offers evidence that he did take an interest in the city's social issues. Bacon himself argued this in 1975: "the thing that interested me the most was the problem of the deterioration of neighborhoods and of the quality of life in the communities, including the poorest."[25] Bacon no doubt believed this. The difficulty, though, is that his favored solutions to such problems, and his understanding of the city itself, relied on a model of physical determinism: the idea that manipulation and improvement of the built environment of homes, streets, commercial areas, and open spaces could strongly influence, or even control, social and economic outcomes. The argument that Edmund Bacon's focus on physical design reflected a disinterest in the social dimensions of urban life must thus be qualified. The problem was not that Edmund Bacon cared only about design: it was that he believed far too deeply in its power.

Change: The CURA Policy and the Transformation of Urban Renewal

Regardless of such subtleties, both Bacon's leadership of the PCPC and his preferred "worst-first" redevelopment strategy came into serious question during the first years of the Clark administration. In 1954, Rafsky hired the Chicago-based planning consultant Walter Blucher to evaluate the Commission's operations. Blucher concluded that because of Bacon's emphasis on project planning, the PCPC had made little progress toward fulfilling its charter-mandated responsibility to prepare a comprehensive plan.[26] Blucher also noted the Commission's neglect of social and economic issues, and argued that "the development of a comprehensive plan requires a high degree of economic and social planning at its base."[27] With Mayor Clark's endorsement, the Blucher report soon led to the appointment of deputy directors for administration and for comprehensive planning, with the latter charged with beginning a major push toward completion of a comprehensive plan. This meant a significant shift in the Commission's work, pushing it away from the scattered-site redevelopment plans that Bacon had been pursuing.[28]

This had been part of Rafsky's intent in arranging the Blucher report, as completion of the Comprehensive Plan represented his priority and that of the RDA, rather than that of Bacon. Lennox Moak, who served as Clark's first finance director, later recalled that "Bacon fought [the Comprehensive Plan] all along the way."[29] The Blucher report, though, reflected a deeper conflict between Bacon and Rafsky. David Wallace recalled an episode in which "Bill Rafsky turned to [him] in the elevator and said 'Bacon has to go. He is totally unreconciled to the concept of coordination'." Continuing, Wallace indicated that "in fact Rafsky at that point convinced Joe Clark that Bacon had to go, and then the Blucher report was asked for and finally brought a compromise approach. The first draft of the Blucher reports really asked for Bacon's resignation but only a very few people saw that and the later report was a compromise by recasting the Planning Commission." Such accounts suggest that Bacon's acceptance of the Comprehensive Plan—and the accompanying reorganization of the PCPC—represented not an expression of a broad planning vision but instead a defeat in an internal bureaucratic struggle.[30]

These staff changes proved to be but the beginning. In March 1956, the RDA completed an initial draft of the Central Urban Renewal Area (CURA) study. Based on a three-year evaluation of the city's urban renewal program, the CURA study reviewed Philadelphia's existing program and outlined future alternatives. The results were both striking and disturbing. Not only had the worst-first approach failed to reverse deterioration, but it had actually made the problem worse through displacement and overcrowding.[31] As Rafsky later explained, "as a result of inadequate funding what we were able to do in the early 1950s was to create an island of good surrounded by a sea of bad, which in effect continually played havoc with the good things we did, and produced negative influences on decent housing."[32] Rafsky's point about inadequate funding raised another key concern: the study found that clearance of all "blighted" areas in the city would cost approximately $1 billion. In contrast, Philadelphia's existing program funding from federal and local sources stood at just $45 million. Further, the slow pace of Philadelphia's program meant that costs might rise even more because additional areas would deteriorate as existing projects moved toward completion.[33]

During the year that followed, the new Dilworth administration assessed the study's implications, particularly those related to the high costs and limited benefits of intensive "sore spot" clearance." In March 1957, Rafsky presented the city's new policy. The CURA study had classified neighborhoods in the central city as A, B, or C, ranging from blighted to conservable, with the C areas consisting largely of white neighborhoods that lay in a ring around the central core. The "intermediate" B and "most blighted" A areas, in turn, formed successive, roughly concentric rings nearer the Center City business district; most of the "A" areas were occupied by low-income African Americans or were in the process of racial transition. Reflecting the inadequacy of federal and local funds to "accomplish the job on a large enough scale," as well as the concern that outlying areas might be "hopelessly lost" during an extended "worst-first" program, Rafsky indicated that the new CURA policy would no longer focus redevelopment efforts on the "A" areas.[34] Instead, it would concentrate on "conservation" of the outlying "C" areas: this approach involved a mixture of conservation, rehabilitation, highly targeted clearance, and intensive code enforcement. Projects already underway in the "A" and "B" areas would be completed, and code enforcement would be enhanced, but at least initially no new redevelopment work would be undertaken. Meanwhile, the city would also undertake a three-track economic development program that would include extensive Center City redevelopment, expansion assistance for universities, and industrial renewal to stem the loss of manufacturing jobs.[35] The goal of the new policy was to establish a strong central business district core while "protecting" outlying areas from decline caused by "overspill of people from the center having an adverse effect in accelerating decay."[36]

The CURA policy shift had distinct racial, economic, and political implications. For the residents of the primarily African American "sore spots" in North Philadelphia, this change had mixed implications: major physical improvements to their neighborhoods would be delayed indefinitely—outside of the East Poplar and Southwest Temple project areas, where work had already begun—but future residential displacement would be significantly limited compared to continuing the full-

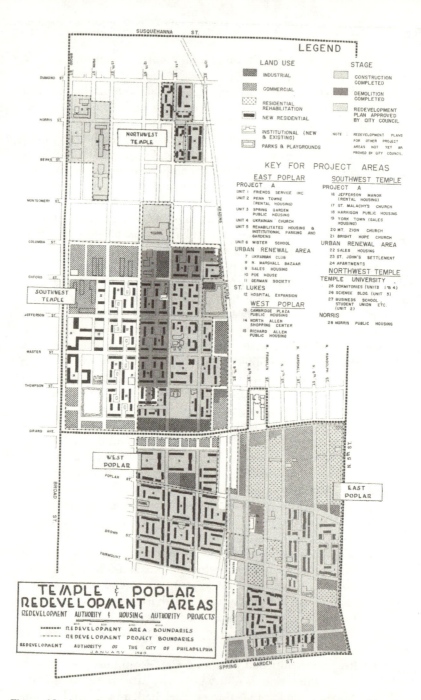

Figure 12. A version of the neighborhood classification map developed by the Central Urban Renewal Area (CURA) study, showing areas marked for eventual reconstruction, rehabilitation, and conservation, c. 1957 ("A" and "C" designations have been reversed from the original study). Courtesy of University of Pennsylvania Libraries.

scale, "worst-first" clearance strategy. West Philadelphia, where the University of Pennsylvania and Drexel Institute of Technology soon undertook major expansions, constituted an exception to this point, as did the Society Hill area.[37] Nonetheless, CURA's shift away from a clearance focused strategy in North Philadelphia limited at least *some* of the worst consequences of urban renewal. By the 1960s, other policy efforts would again target the poorest sections of the city, but they would do so through means other than urban renewal's almost exclusive focus on physical reconstruction.

For Edmund Bacon, the new policy had yet another implication. With the most blighted areas removed from urban renewal's reach, and with housing policy constrained to public housing projects and conservation, Bacon would simply have far fewer opportunities to engage the city's social problems through planning. As a result, the CURA policy constituted a shaping force in Bacon's career, as it directed his work away from Philadelphia's slums and concentrated it in the Center City area for the final fifteen years of his public career. Existing assessments have not appreciated the significance of this change. It is not that Bacon was uninterested in Center City to begin with, but that the policy contours that CURA established helped to shift Bacon's gaze toward the center rather than the neighborhoods.

At the time, Bacon opposed this policy turn. His resistance, and the eventual adoption of the policy, delineated the internal politics of planning and renewal in the late-1950s. Although initially Bill Rafsky also had doubts about the CURA study, he quickly adopted it as his own when he recognized that the new policy direction represented an opportunity to consolidate his authority and enhance his role as "the real coordinator."[38] Managing disparate conservation, rehabilitation, and economic development strategies called for some measure of centralized direction. Eventually, Rafsky even became "wedded to the conservation approach."[39] Bacon, in contrast, argued in favor of continuing with a scattered site strategy focused on the most blighted neighborhoods— even if not all such areas could be rebuilt at once. At least in part, his resistance to CURA rested in his opposition to the expanded coordination role that Mayor Dilworth had already granted to Rafsky, a role that would be enhanced by CURA.[40]

Bacon's stance, though, could not be attributed entirely to such concerns. Instead, Bacon apparently believed that it was a mistake to abandon the poorest and "most blighted" sections of the city. In January 1957, shortly before Rafsky announced the new policy, a statement by the Commission staff explained this point:

while we recognize that mistakes were made in some of the redevelopment work so far undertaken, we also recognize that the elimination of blight is a very difficult problem at best, and we do not think the difficulties attendant upon the efforts in the more blighted sections should lead us to a policy that abandons these areas altogether for any sustained period, but rather to a policy in which a portion of our energy is directed toward developing new solutions to these older areas which overcome the major problems revealed by our old approach.[41]

If the "worst-first" approach really had to be abandoned, Bacon and his staff suggested an alternative of focusing all program resources on a "pilot project" that would undertake the complete redevelopment of a single large area in West or South Philadelphia. Such an experiment would provide experience in comprehensive renewal. More importantly, it would "demonstrate in concrete terms to the community at large that the city has not lost sight of the problems in the poorer areas, and that it is following an orderly program to meet them."[42] While subject to the critiques that such an approach would have perpetuated problems of displacement and that it still relied on a physical determinist model of urban life, this position seems to have reflected in concrete policy terms Bacon's real interest in urban social problems. The planning director, it seemed, did not want to abandon the slums in the way proposed by the development coordinator, and he clearly cared about issues far broader than grand planning designs in Center City alone.

Factories: Bacon's Inattention to Economic Change

Bacon remained concerned about low-income sections of the city, and not just about the relatively elite Center City areas for which he is best known. During the 1960s, for example, he pushed Mayor Tate to adopt a "used-house" renovation initiative as part of the city's low-income housing program (an idea he had long championed).[43] Such concern, though, did not mean that he fully understood the problems of these areas, especially the economic challenges that they increasingly faced. Bacon's approach remained focused exclusively on the removal or improvement of decayed structures and "improper" land uses, as he viewed "the problems in the poorer areas" as rooted primarily in the built environment. He had little grasp of how other variables—low-wage work, employment discrimination, failing schools, rapid economic change—interacted with that environment. In particular, Bacon had little understanding of the implications of deindustrialization, which by the 1950s had already begun to affect inner city areas of Philadelphia and other older U.S. cities.

As such, Bacon's opposition to CURA may have reflected his lack of sensitivity to Philadelphia's growing economic plight as much as his concern for housing and the interests of the poor. For it was in its economic strategy that the CURA plan did something unprecedented: it focused local public policy on addressing deindustrialization. Most existing accounts of urban policy in postwar Philadelphia have emphasized that CURA responded to the interests of the business community and large institutions by shifting urban renewal resources toward Center City and the universities. This offers only a partial picture of a far more subtle policy history. CURA also gave new impetus to calls for an active, local-level policy response to the loss of manufacturing jobs. During the Clark administration, city economist Kirk Petshek had conducted detailed economic studies that traced Philadelphia's loss of industrial firms and jobs during the post-World War II period. His analysis warned that these losses represented something more dire than a simple cyclical downturn. "Philadelphia," he argued in November 1955, "is obviously suffering from a chronic illness which goes deeper than merely lagging behind the national recovery."[44] Earlier, Petshek had pointed out that the effects of such long-term economic decline would fall hardest on the unskilled, African Americans, older workers, and women in "particular industries."[45] In response to Petshek's warnings, city commerce director and reform leader Walter Phillips wrote a series of detailed policy memos that argued that a lack of suitable land for new factory construction lay at the root of Philadelphia's loss of manufacturing. Phillips proposed that the city establish a reserve of industrial land and that it create a nonprofit, quasi-public authority to manage the construction of new, modern industrial parks where Philadelphia-based firms could build the spread-out, single-story factories that industry increasingly favored during the postwar decades. This could be done, Phillips suggested, on publicly owned land near the city's airports in southwest and, especially, northeast Philadelphia. Overburdened with other priorities, Mayor Clark made little move to act on Petshek's prescient warnings or Phillips's persistent proposals.[46]

Edmund Bacon remained mostly unsympathetic to Phillips's ideas, at least in their details. Initially, he objected to Phillips's suggestion that the industrial project be managed through a public-private partnership, arguing instead for either a full-fledged public authority or the sale of the land through a process of open competitive bidding.[47] Phillips countered that the "proposals for a non-profit corporation seek to avoid involving a public authority in speculative land ventures. It is our thought that competitive bidding works against public policy in regard to the objectives of our program. Real estate transactions for industrial land are conducted in highly confidential negotiations."[48] More broadly, the rationale for the public-private structure was to bring the business community into the project as a partner and thus overcome business distrust of the Clark administration. Still, these were differences of opinion, and while Bacon's position reflected an unrealistic assess-

ment of the local political climate and the attitude of many manufactur-
ers toward city government, a defensible claim could be made for clear
public control of the future program.[49]

Bacon's differences with Phillips, though, actually extended much farther, to a conflicting understanding of both the purpose of city planning
and the nature of Philadelphia's problems. These deeper disagreements
remained unresolved, and in early 1955, they revealed themselves in a
conflict over the Planning Commission's newly completed Preliminary
Plan for the Far Northeast (the first component of what would eventually become the city's Comprehensive Plan). In the mid-1950s, the "Far
Northeast" section of Philadelphia still contained large tracts of undeveloped land, much of it still forested or used for agriculture. Phillips
had identified a number of tracts around the city's Northeast Airport
and along Roosevelt Boulevard as key components of the proposed land
reserve for the industrial program. The Commission's proposed plan,
however, failed to set this land aside for industrial use.

At a 20 January 1955 meeting of the Planning Commission, Bacon
presented the Far Northeast plan for approval by the Commission.
Unfortunately, he had neither provided Commission members with
prior notice that the meeting would include such a formal review nor
circulated copies of the completed draft before the meeting. As a result,
Commission members had not had a chance to examine the plan in its
final form. Walter Phillips, whose position as director of commerce enti-
tled him to a position on the Planning Commission, angrily objected to
problems of both process and substance in the plan. The following day,
he composed a lengthy letter to Bacon and, at the suggestion of Rafsky,
sent copies to all members of the Commission. In the letter, Phillips outlined his specific complaints concerning the allocation of land uses proposed in the preliminary plan. Particularly problematic was the devotion
of a large amount of airport land to park space, despite both Phillips's
specific requests and the Planning Commission's approval of industrial
zoning for the airport tracts.[50]

Phillips saw the plan's overall inattention to Philadelphia's pressing
need for more industrial land as indicative of Bacon's lack of awareness
of the city's deteriorating economic situation. Although a recent reces-
sion had highlighted the problems of Philadelphia's industrial sector
and demonstrated the weakness of the city in relation to the surrounding area, Phillips worried that problems of manufacturing employment
seemed of little concern to Bacon or his staff. Bacon and his staff had
offered a plan that would drastically increase the population of the Far
Northeast while making no provision for employment needs, either in
that section or in Philadelphia as a whole. Although the Far Northeast
constituted some of the last open land in the city that could accommo-

date modern industrial parks, the planners had allocated most of it for residential or recreational use. In Phillips's view, the failure to address industrial needs represented a deliberate choice on the part of the planners. Such an omission, Phillips argued, suggested fundamental questions about planning priorities:

The big point is that the open land that can still be rezoned for industry is needed more by the whole City for that purpose than for housing. . . . Either I am mistaken in believing that land for industry is a very important planning consideration, or it actually is important, and either you were not aware of the problem, or you deliberately chose to ignore it and to withhold from the Commission one of the most basic of the policy considerations it should have had before it.[51]

This disagreement indicated that two views had emerged within city government about Philadelphia's future. Bacon and his planners anticipated that the city would retain at least a stable level of population and employment over the next quarter-century. For them, the key to successful planning lay in a reduction of housing density and an overall emphasis on design excellence that, they believed, would secure the city's future by providing a functional, pleasant, and socially healthy environment. In contrast, Walter Phillips and his staff of economists and industrial development experts saw a bleaker future in which obsolete, crowded factories would interact with a changing economy and a racially segregated population to create an environment inhospitable for economic survival, much less growth.[52] Although both sides emphasized variations on a primarily physical theme, Walter Phillips's Department of Commerce had presented a glimpse of what actually lay ahead for much of Philadelphia. Without an adequate supply of jobs, even the best planned, best designed, and most socially sensitive housing would inevitably slip into deterioration.[53]

Phillips's objections, though, had an effect on the planning process for the Far Northeast. Immediately, he delayed both the PCPC's final review of the plan and a series of public hearings. In February, Phillips and Bacon reached a procedural compromise, under which the PCPC moved ahead with its hearings but presented the Far Northeast Plan merely "as the tentative thinking of the Commission."[54] In the aftermath of the hearings, the PCPC determined that, just as Walter Phillips had suggested, the relationship between the Far Northeast and the city as a whole needed additional study. As a result, it delayed adoption of any final plan for the area until the Comprehensive Plan had been completed. Bacon agreed to reconsider the use of land at Northeast Philadelphia Airport, and ultimately, the Planning Commission devoted all excess land there to industrial uses.[55]

In 1958, Philadelphia finally created an industrial renewal program. Managed by the Philadelphia Industrial Development Corporation, the program experienced significant success in renovating inner city factories and establishing new urban industrial parks on open land, even as it ultimately remained inadequate to the scale of the deindustrialization problem and insufficient in addressing the more complex challenges of racial isolation, employment discrimination, and inner city poverty.[56]

This was the context in which Edmund Bacon composed "Philadelphia in the Year 2009" (published as "A Fair Can Pace It"). William Rafsky had gained the upper hand in the struggle to determine the direction of the city's urban renewal policy, shifting it away from Bacon's favored approach. Meanwhile, Philadelphia's manufacturing base had gone into notable decline and its population had become increasingly divided, both spatially and socially, on lines of race and class. In the "2009" essay, Bacon offered only passing reference to the transformative changes underway in the city's racial makeup, its economy, and its politics. Instead, he offered a fanciful vision of Kabuki dancers in the City Hall courtyard and "open-sided electric cars" traversing Chestnut Street. In the essay, Bacon briefly noted that the city's failure to appeal to the "out-of-town visitor" had negatively shaped "the decisions of . . . businessmen and industrialists considering locating their enterprises here" and suggested the need to develop industrial parks "in many parts of the city." He offered little sense, though, of how urban design, form, and image would actually address the city's most pressing problems, especially economic ones. This was a defining characteristic of Bacon's approach to planning, and one that he would never successfully resolve.

Adjusting: Edmund Bacon and Center City

Edmund Bacon lost the debate over the CURA program but would soon adjust to the altered policy environment. This capacity to adapt, to learn, and to change in accordance with shifting circumstances was an important factor in his longevity as planning director. One PIDC planner observed that "Ed Bacon has the definite capacity for growth. He fights this growth himself but eventually he gets there and once he gets there he really thoroughly believes in it." Although another participant in the Philadelphia policy community remarked that Bacon "pounds on the table and yells," Walter Phillips observed that the planning director had managed to survive despite the personal dislike of numerous powerful figures in Philadelphia politics: "Bacon is very smooth and bends with the wind."[57] So it was with CURA. Bacon not only accepted PIDC but found career-defining opportunities in the CURA policy, which he used to pursue his own interests in the redevelopment of Center City. Bacon's "2009" essay represented part of this process, as it marked an effort by the planning director to assert his centrality in a transformed policy environment. In many ways, Bacon would succeed at this task, but in doing so, he would come up against the limitations of his own approach to planning.

The details of Bacon's Center City projects are treated elsewhere in this volume, and only key interpretive points need be mentioned here. Bacon's senior thesis at Cornell, his work on the Better Philadelphia Exhibition, and his partially successful effort to steer the Penn Center project away from mediocrity show evidence of his long-standing interest in Center City. CURA, though, provided the policy framework for developing his ideas about urban function and for testing the true "power of the idea" in city planning. With the Market East project, Bacon explored his concept of planning for the "simultaneous movement systems" generated by thousands of people encountering and traveling about the city.[58] Yet as the design for Market East evolved through a series of designs, often under great pressure from Center City retail interests, much of the original planning concept was torn away. Market East's four-block sweep shrunk to just two blocks, its innovative commercial concourses morphed into a commonplace suburban shopping center, its office towers were never built, and its final, quasi-brutalist style made Penn Center seem iconic and innovative in comparison. Its presence may even have sucked the economic life out of another Bacon project, the Chestnut Street pedestrian mall, which had been outlined in the "Philadelphia in the Year 2009" essay.[59] Flaws aside, though, Market East found significant functionalist redemption, as it maintained a significant retail presence in Center City and became the shopping destination of choice for many inner city residents.

Bacon's grandest triumph, Society Hill, retains more regard today than his other Center City projects. Relying on the architecture of I. M. Pei, the project skillfully blended new construction with eighteenth-century structures, even integrating Pei's high-rise towers with the two- and three-story townhomes that surround them. Although aspects of the project struggled financially in its early years, Society Hill emerged as a popular core of the city's historic district and arguably as a critical base for Center City itself. Society Hill came with a social cost, however, as it caused significant displacement among the area's existing population, much of which was low income and minority.[60]

Still, for all the human-scale success of Society Hill, Bacon supported another nearby project that threatened to impose exactly the opposite values on Center City Philadelphia.

Conceived in the early 1950s, the city's transportation plan envisioned

Figure 13. Society Hill prior to clearance of riverfront area for the Delaware Expressway (I-95), showing the historic connection of the area to the river. Courtesy of Temple University Libraries, Urban Archives.

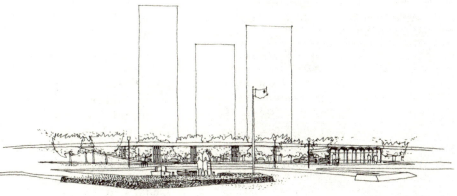

view from river

Figure 14. Model of Society Hill Washington Square East urban renewal area by Webb & Knapp and I. M. Pei, clearly showing an elevated Delaware Expressway, 1960. Courtesy of Pei Cobb Freed & Partners Architects LLP and University of Pennsylvania Libraries.

a web of circumferential and radial highways beginning in Center City and extending into the wider metropolitan region. The plan placed the Delaware Expressway (I-95) along the Delaware River.[61] Throughout much of the planning period, both engineers and planners conceived of the expressway as an elevated highway. Such a structure would have created a massive barrier that severed Society Hill's historic connection to the waterfront. It also would have caused intense traffic noise and pollution. The human experience of Society Hill would have been greatly diminished. Edmund Bacon, though, initially accepted this conception of the expressway, arguing in December 1964 that it represented "the wisest course under the circumstances."[62]

This position illuminates Bacon's most serious failing as a planner and, even more, as an urbanist. The elevated road reflected an understanding of the relationship between the automobile and the city that by the mid-1960s had already become an anachronism. The model assumed the existence of a technological remedy for the effects of traffic, a physical solution composed of garages and express highways that would painlessly whisk cars in and out of the city. It failed to recognize the great incompatibility of the highway with the city: the irretrievable destruction of the existing urban fabric, the pollution and noise that automobiles imposed, and the urban "dead zones" that highways created for other types of movement and for social and economic interactions.

Bacon, as was so often the case, did not bear sole responsibility for the elevated design, which was largely dictated by state and city highway engineers. Nor, to be fair, was he an unequivocal advocate of urban highways, and shortly after defending the highway in 1964, he suggested to Mayor Tate that the city might push for a redesign of the elevated structure. Nonetheless, he did endorse the original Delaware Expressway design, and every Bacon-approved model of Society Hill from the 1947 Better Philadelphia Exhibition to the mid-1960s included an elevated highway along the river. Furthermore, his priority throughout the controversy that erupted in 1964 consisted of avoiding delays in the overall highway project.[63] As one local activist exclaimed in 1965, "I never thought Mr. Bacon would do a thing like this to us!"[64] After significant community protest, the federal government agreed to build the expressway below grade through Center City, a plan that Bacon eventually supported.[65]

The struggle over the expressway demonstrated the underlying difficulty with Bacon's approach to planning. The city and its infrastructure would never be the orderly world of the planner's scale models and sketches of "simultaneous movement systems." It was a place where people interacted with one another, with the built environment, and with technology, and where one element, such as an expressway or a poorly conceived commercial development, could easily overwhelm and even destroy the other. What Edmund Bacon never fully grasped was that in the complexity of urban reality, design itself could be an instrument of destruction as well as salvation.

Assessing: Edmund Bacon's Shifting Self-Conception

Even as Edmund Bacon achieved his greatest success with the Society Hill project, he faced growing public criticism.[66] Like Paul Davidoff, critics increasingly charged that his work had neglected the true nature of urban problems in favor of grand, physically based construction projects that offered more disruption than solution. William Rafsky faced similar criticism. CURA's conservation efforts had proved limited and underfunded, and code enforcement in the "worst areas" had been largely ineffective. Meanwhile, Center City was rebuilt. This disparity generated a tense conflict that increasingly posed neighborhoods against Center City.

By the early 1960s, a new planning effort, known as the Community Renewal Program (CRP), sought to establish procedures for a more integrated form of city planning that encompassed the social and economic as well as the physical needs of urban communities. Ironically, given their past records, Bacon and Rafsky served as co-chairs of the

CRP. Most of the extensive work on the project, conducted through nineteen technical reports and studies, took place at the staff level. Much of it was done by young economists and planners who worked far more in the economically oriented tradition than in the grand design style of their immediate superiors. Elizabeth Deuterman, who wrote the CRP report on economic development, noted that, despite the staff's broadened focus, "Bill Rafsky and Ed Bacon keep coming back to physical planning and [the staff] sometimes feels that nothing is happening." She observed, though, that Bacon had exhibited increased sympathy for her position.[67] Ultimately, the CRP reports suggested a failure not just of CURA but of Philadelphia's entire approach. Whether working from the periphery to the core or the core to the periphery, physical planning could not ignore the social and economic dimensions of the city's problems. Completed within the context of the federal War on Poverty, CRP contributed to a partial shift of resources back to the city's lowest income, most deteriorated neighborhoods. Neither Bacon nor Rafsky felt comfortable with the results, although Bacon gradually integrated some of the new thinking into his public statements.[68]

Bacon's appreciation for the social side of planning would increase further in the years after he left the City Planning Commission in 1970. Four years later, speaking as part of a Temple University series on the city's future, Bacon drew a connection between modern warfare and modern city planning, based on the Vietnam documentary *Hearts and Minds*, which he had just seen. Recounting a bomber pilot's description in the film of the impersonal, mathematical precision of an air raid, Bacon identified a similar process in urban renewal: "the bomb would be released and it would go right to its target. [The pilot] said: 'We didn't see the people. We didn't hear the screams. We didn't smell burning flesh.' There it is! You don't see the people, you don't hear the screams, you don't smell the burning flesh! . . . Unless we can get back to seeing it exclusively in terms of individuals, and individuals as members of a family, and families as members of a family of families and a community, we are absolutely sunk."[69] Bacon, of course, had not necessarily dropped the urban renewal "bomb" in Philadelphia, but he had helped to plot the course. Even more, his 1959 vision of the future city had invoked the promise of fairs and festivals without considering how such entertainments would—or would not—address the consequences of the flight of factories and jobs from the city's neighborhoods.

Two years earlier, in his speech at Cornell, Bacon had argued that his primary concern had always been for low-income neighborhoods. He then evaluated whether the trade-offs involved in shifting his focus toward Center City had been too great:

I did not allow my concern for this, or the very vocal concern of other people, to deter me from also working to keep center city alive. Had I let center city go down the drain, as many people urged me to do, I would have done a disservice to all people, including the urban poor.[70]

   This was Bacon's dilemma, forced on him by CURA and the failures of early redevelopment policy, and his answer to it had provoked much controversy and opposition by the 1970s. Yet as he also pointed out at Cornell, "I am not interested in an apology for myself in this regard. Everybody knows that society has not provided me or anyone else with the tools necessary for a fundamental attack on poverty, and to blame the planners for this deficiency is foolish."[71] These two observations captured the essence of his career. Edmund Bacon believed too deeply in the power and utility of design and had an underdeveloped comprehension of how the social and economic dimensions of urban life such as poverty, racial segregation, and deindustrialization would undermine and compromise even the best design. In the end, however, he lacked the power within his own city to do even all that a strong planner might have done in these areas, and cities in the United States as a whole lacked the policy instruments and financial resources to combat these wider problems. The difficulty, of course, is the question of whether Bacon might have done better with the tools he did have. Saving Center City, or at least providing a strong base for its powerful revival at the turn of the twenty-first century, did matter, and it constitutes part of Bacon's legacy. The other part of his legacy, though, is the question just posed. It raises the painful possibility that even more ambition from this man of sweeping design, more vision from the visionary, might have accomplished something far more important by closely linking planning to the needs of the people who lived and worked in the city—to their need for jobs as well as carefully planned neighborhoods, to their need for education and training as well as a strong downtown core, and to their need for economic planning as well as for functioning "simultaneous movement systems." These were needs that transcended anything that physical design alone could ever accomplish.
   This review of Edmund Bacon's career suggests a final, broader point about how historians should assess planners and city planning. Scholars have long rejected the "great man" model of history in which a single, significant individual shapes events through personal power, force of will, or superior judgment, in favor of a model of the past that places individuals within the context of the wider events and social forces of their times. Although historians of planning have by no means ignored this wider shift, the subfield often inevitably involves the study of key individuals. This is not entirely a mistake—individuals did affect the tra-

jectory of planning in individual cities and, to a lesser extent, in national and international contexts as well. Certainly, city planning in Philadelphia cannot be understood without reference to Edmund Bacon. Yet this tendency brings with it dangers. Bacon, and other planners, cannot be understood or adequately evaluated by treating their legacies on a project-by-project, biographical basis. The emphasis cannot be on planning in isolation. This assessment of Bacon has shown that planners—and planning history generally—must be studied amid the rich historical context within which they operated—amid the public and private institutions with which they interacted, the political cultures that they inhabited, and the social movements that challenged or supported them. Planning history cannot be a field unto itself. It must be cognizant of the wider dimensions of urban history, of social history, of political and cultural history that shaped the actions of planners. For all the limitations outlined in this essay, Edmund Bacon did struggle throughout his career to contextualize his work within the human framework of the city, as he understood it. Historians should do no less.

Chapter Four
Staying Too Long at the Fair: Philadelphia Planning and the Debacle of 1976

Scott Gabriel Knowles

In 1682, 1776, or 1876, the optimism of Edmund Bacon's remarkable 1959 vision for Philadelphia's future—"Philadelphia in the Year 2009"—would have surprised no one. From its founding, Philadelphia's unfolding futures were consistently dynamic, focusing the energies of colonial expansion, democratic governance, and industrialization in one urban crucible. No other city in America exhibited each trend so dramatically. It was the Centennial Exhibition in Philadelphia in 1876—with the glass and steel dome of its Memorial Hall, its displays of telegraphy and the telephone, its prototype steam automobiles—that first demonstrated to Americans what an industrialized nation might really look like. Ed Bacon was an enthusiast of world's fairs and public exhibitions, writing and speaking of them throughout his career to illustrate and promote trends in urban development, and working in the genre himself to advance a far-reaching planning agenda for Philadelphia in the postwar decades.

Philadelphia emerged from World War II burdened by creaking infrastructure and a housing shortage, its Center City business district underperforming against rival cities. Deindustrialization was already noticeable by the mid-1950s, an emerging economic reality that foretold difficulty in achieving the social goals of a new and aggressive generation of reform-minded political leadership.[1] Residents were embarking for the suburbs at a steady clip, with the city falling by 1960 from third to fourth in population behind Los Angeles.[2] Bacon's 50-year vision projected against this backdrop might have struck the reader as cheerful but unrealistic, even naïve. But what good is a prophecy if it does not reveal a hidden future, a future obstructed? Bacon's future was a city revitalized, beautified, and modernized in time to host the nation's Bicentennial celebration and a simultaneous 1976 Philadelphia World's

Fair. Imaginative planning was his method, enabling the political gate-keepers along with the citizens of the city to see with him decades ahead and to grasp the occasion of a fair to accomplish lasting change for the city's built environment and its people. "Philadelphia in the Year 2009" builds its case on this one powerful idea: a world's fair could transform it into a model of humane urbanism.[3]

Considering his vantage point in 1959, it is possible to imagine why Ed Bacon might predict the future of Philadelphia with such mesmerizing flourishes. The Philadelphia City Planning Commission (PCPC), under his directorship, was in the midst of one of the longest winning streaks any urban planning body had or has ever achieved. With Penn Center, Society Hill, Independence Mall, the neighborhoods of Eastwick and the Far Northeast each underway or finished, Bacon and his team of young planners were totally in their stride in 1959, working to think, dig, and build the city out of its rut. The Market East transportation center, a pedestrian-friendly Chestnut Street, and a tourist-friendly Delaware waterfront were all on Bacon's drawing board, too. These were the varied pieces, described in turn by each of the authors in this volume, of a full urban-renewal portfolio advanced consistently over more than two decades by the PCPC. Postwar federal legislation enabled city officials for the first time to broadly exercise eminent domain powers, moving masses of residents and bulldozing whole sections of the city, planning and building anew.[4] Ed Bacon's PCPC was certainly of its time in this respect and forceful in its place, stirring up both wonder and backlash. The old industrial city, the city that had lain fallow through the Depression and World War II, was awakening slowly to the possibility of high-rises and integrated transportation hubs, and at the same time redis-covering its walkable character and the vernacular beauties of its historic neighborhoods. Bacon's idea was to liberate William Penn's grid from over a century of industrial-age clutter and to make the city simultane-ously auto-, pedestrian-, and investment-friendly. Bacon understood the power of display and salesmanship as keys to making his idea of the next Philadelphia into something tangible. In this spirit, his "2009" essay arrived on newsstands in 1959.

Could new high-rises and a suburban-style shopping center downtown reverse massive job losses and a suburban exodus? Whether the PCPC's projects were comprehensive enough remained an open question in 1959. In this context, the Philadelphia World's Fair could provide a shared goal, a focused way for Bacon to complete the projects he wanted. Market East, the Chestnut Street pedestrian mall, and even the heliports and Kabuki dancers really pale in comparison, though, to his essay's boldest claims. In 2009 Philadelphia will not have any bad neigh-borhoods, suburbanites will have moved back bringing their vitality and tax dollars with them, greenways will ring the city, transportation options will be rational and varied; the entire metropolis will reflect the best and brightest ideas that modern urban planning can deliver. Bacon's predictions still astound with their self-confidence, and throughout the 1960s and into the 1970s, from City Hall to the halls of academia and elite architecture firms and bankers' offices, from newsrooms to neighborhoods across the city, Philadelphians would grapple with the idea that a world's fair could help deliver the future city they desired.

This chapter examines the fair-as-urban renewal formula that Ed Bacon worked with to promote his long-range planning objectives in Philadelphia. The "2009" essay was just one of the many publications and speeches he used to stimulate and sustain interest in the manifold projects of the PCPC. But here was a truly seductive model of development. If a world's fair could leave useful permanent structures behind while simultaneously rejuvenating public faith in the city, then what was the downside? Ed Bacon and scores of Philadelphians would take up this challenge, shaping it over a 15-year period to fit their own visions for the future of their city. From London's 1851 Crystal Palace Exhibition to New York's 1939 World's Fair, such events periodically announced new eras in technology and science, in business, and in culture. As Bacon and other key players in Philadelphia intuited, they also offered host cities opportunities to innovate in urban design. Starting with Brussels in 1958 a new generation of postwar world's fairs began, and the planning for the Philadelphia Fair took place as fairs were held in Seattle (1962), New York (1964), Montreal (1967), San Antonio (1968), and Osaka (1970). The difficulties of the New York Fair and the success of the Montreal one especially played defining roles as the Philadelphia planning process went forward. Learning and applying lessons from fairs in other cities and other eras proved difficult for Philadelphia's planners.

The chapter develops two main analytical points. First, world's fairs have historically proven as different and mercurial as the cities and time periods of their creation, and have rarely inspired large-scale urban renewal in host cities in predictable, linear ways. The historical lessons and legacies of world's fairs for urban planners were (and remain) decidedly ambiguous. But by studying the period of gestation for a fair, and perhaps by extension any large-scale civic undertaking, we gain critical insight into the dominant conflicts shaping the modern city. As the planning process moved into the 1960s and early 1970s, it became more and more evident that the Philadelphia World's Fair of 1976—if it was to happen—would not recreate the 1876 Centennial Exhibition or launch an urban renaissance so much as reflect the clashing ambitions of citizens caught in a declining American industrial metropolis. The final plan, to the extent there ever was one plan, deviated starkly in both intention and design from Bacon's 1959 vision. This leads to the second point. The deviation from Bacon's "2009" vision shows two quite specific urban historical processes working in conjunction: the decline of the "master planner" and by extension New Deal/Great Society urban liberalism, and the rise of a consensus-seeking planning model driven by the maturation of urban community-based protest movements. The evolving plans for the World's Fair vividly show these trends defining one another, with plans for (and protest against) the Fair emerging from all quarters of the city, diluting the strength of Bacon's 1959 vision, while at the same time adding elements more desirable, more democratic, to the multiple communities affected. Between 1970 and 1972 planning for the Fair broke apart amid a prolonged season of racial strife, intergenerational resentment, federal disinvestment, and a creeping urban pessimism. Combined with hesitant municipal leadership this climate of urban uncertainty clouded the vision of a fair-as-catalyst to a utopian "Philadelphia in the Year 2009."

The Ghost of Fairs Past

American cultural history overflows with tales of world's fairs, expositions, exhibitions, centennials, and good, old-fashioned trade shows. Fairs have been closely scrutinized, proving their utility as historical lenses, moments through which to view the values and aspirations of a city, even a nation, at a given time and place. As Robert Rydell argues, such events are rich in meaning and have never been simply about recreation, but always "reflected profound concerns about the future and deflected criticism of the established political and social order."[5] Rydell, John Findling, and Kimberly Pelle outline the various schools of thought that have emerged among the many historians who have analyzed world's fairs. From reviewing arguments for fairs operating as tools of elite cultural hegemony to seeing fairs as techno-utopian emporia, the authors conclude "no consensus exists among scholars, but they do seem to be moving toward a view that stresses the complex and often contradictory nature of fairs . . . expositions [seen] as arenas of debate."[6]

One critical perspective deserves more attention—namely, that the planning and construction processes of a fair are *in themselves* critical moments in urban evolution, be they pathways to renewal or bellwethers of decline. Cultural critique is important, but why limit it to the fairgrounds? If we want to understand the modern American city, we might also pay close attention to world's fairs as economic gambits and large-scale projects that illuminate struggles within city government, between citizens and their government, and among planners and architects. Historian Neil Harris argues provocatively along these lines for the use of a "life cycle" metaphor in thinking about the built urban environment. For Harris, "examining buildings through their life stages and modes of representation encourages us to conceive of them not simply as places but as sets of events, affixing a temporal dimension to their existence that is not simply an add-on but fundamental to their nature."[7] This is a productive way to think about the 1976 Bicentennial and World's Fair planning in Philadelphia, a case where the period from idea to action was relatively long, contained many dramatic turning points, and in the case of the Fair ultimately never came to life. To overlook the planning and construction of Bacon's "Philadelphia in the Year 2009" projects that were built, despite the glaring fact that there ultimately was no Fair, would likewise be to miss a critical period in Philadelphia's postwar history. In this case we should consider both the built and the unbuilt environments simultaneously as keys to understanding the dynamics of a city undergoing a rapid set of changes. As suggested in *Unbuilt America*, a remarkable 1976 compendium of architectural and urban planning projects that never came into existence, there "are almost an infinite number of explanations—many of which are so complex to determine and interpret that they can only be hinted at by terms such as 'unbuilt.'"[8] Herein lies the challenge: piecing the false starts, lost plans, and distant voices back together into a whole that reveals the Philadelphia that was, and how that urban reality constrained what might have been. The Fair that never happened is perhaps just as instructive—if not more so for understanding the Philadelphia of the 1960s and 1970s—than it would be to us now had it actually taken place.

A brief review of the lessons drawn from the history of world's fairs creates a context in which to see how Philadelphia's Fair planners developed their ideas. Ed Bacon pointed to world's fairs as both indicators of urban health and catalysts for growth. He believed that late nineteenth-century America expressed a striking dichotomy in its cities. On the one side were the "romantic" forms, "expressed in curved flowerbeds and winding paths attempting to emulate the forms of nature," as seen in New York's Central Park. On the other side stood the behemoth, the industrializing metropolis. To Bacon, the dichotomy was "dramatically embodied in the 1876 Centennial Exposition in Philadelphia." Here we saw "the huge Corliss engine which drove 23 miles of shafts and 40 miles of belts in machinery hall. The new energy spawned new technology which spilled out into the cities and choked the streets with poles, wires, advertising signs and confusion."[9] The Centennial was certainly a turning point in American life, the first time that a complete picture of industrialized life was displayed, in a city that was itself rapidly moderniz-ing.[10] Funding for the Centennial was generated mostly privately and was a concern throughout the planning. Though a United States Cen-tennial Commission was created to assist in planning and fundraising, the federal government insisted that a congressional appropriation of $1.5 million be returned as a loan when the fair closed.[11] The legacy of the Centennial was a mixed one. The psychological effect on Philadel-phians seems to have been positive, a point not difficult to fathom when learning that 9 million people of a national population of 46 million came to the city for the event, held in Fairmount Park, the nation's largest urban park.[12] Fairmount Park's landscape design was trans-formed by the Centennial, but aside from Memorial Hall and Ohio House little remains—most of the exhibits were temporary. The imprints of the fair on Fairmount Park and on collective memory were lasting, but the physical effect on the rest of the city was minor.

Bacon saw in Chicago's World's Columbian Exposition of 1893 a posi-tive lesson for renewal and planning. He waxed enthusiastic over plan-ner and architect Daniel Burnham's design for the fair: "Here Americans came and marveled at the White City . . . a new understand-ing of the possibility of an urban environment devoid of the confusion and squalor which had sprung up in the Victorian American city."[13] He was similarly taken with the innovations of landscape architect Frederick Law Olmsted, Burnham's colleague in planning the Columbian Exposi-tion. Bacon observed that "Olmsted's idea of simultaneous movement systems . . . gave America a completely new idea of what the city could be. The landscape design carefully integrated white buildings, statues, canals and reflecting pools in a coherence and clarity beyond anything America had known."[14]

Still, the planning process for the World's Columbian Exposition in Chicago was not without difficulties. The fair was scheduled to open in 1892, rather than 1893, and had been planned to memorialize Colum-bus's discovery of America. As would happen decades later in Philadel-phia, site selection was a problem, with the railroads, as they also would later, strongly shaping the site decisions.[15] However, architect and direc-tor of the Exposition Daniel Burnham had some advantages that Ed Bacon would have envied. Funding was mostly raised privately among Chicago's elites, removing the need to lobby Congress or the president for money once Chicago had been officially named as the site. Also, organization of the Exposition was designed to put Burnham fully in charge, giving him wide-ranging powers to hire and fire architects and builders and to design the fair as a single, coherent project.[16] Burnham imagined and presented an ideal "white city," an urban space where the technologies of the industrial age, particularly electricity, would serve the aims of civilized living. Judging by accounts at the time and ever since, he achieved his goal.

Burnham's skills as a raconteur rivaled his talents as a designer. According to historian Carl Smith, Burnham "understood how much the actual enactment of proposals depended not only on its inherent merits but also on attracting and shaping public opinion. He alternately cajoled reporters into keeping quiet about work in progress and made certain that they would attend and tell their readers about important presentations. . . . He used lantern slides and artists' renderings," and even executed a watercolor of the Chicago waterfront on his own, when he decided he needed a striking visual.[17] After the widely heralded success of the Columbian Exposition—27 million people attended in six months—Burnham was sought after to turn his "City Beautiful" concepts loose on the increasingly chaotic streets of real American cities. Even though he did not accept fees in many cases, the planning work that followed in Washington, D.C., Cleveland, and San Francisco added to his fame and to his income, and launched an aesthetic revival in the American city. And it enabled him to be the central figure when the progressive Commercial Club of Chicago commissioned a plan to direct the growth of the Chicago region.

In his influential 1909 *Plan of Chicago*, Burnham invoked the World's Columbian Exposition as the genesis for his ideas. The Exposition was "the beginning, in our day and in this country, of the orderly arrangement of extensive public grounds and buildings." Bacon would have nodded with agreement toward Burnham's assertion that the Columbian Exposition succeeded because commercial men "had learned the lesson that great success cannot be attained unless the special work in hand shall be entrusted to those best fitted to undertake it. It had become the habit of our business men to select some one to take the responsibility in every important enterprise; and to give to that person earnest, loyal, and steadfast support."[18] As Burnham argued, the design and expenditure were possible because of public-spiritedness and "entrusting great works" to "trained" men.[19] The primary outgrowth of the fair, he noted, was the gaze of the city shifting to the waterfront, around the Jackson Park area; this resulted in the South Park commissioners' proposing lakefront development as early as 1894, with the Columbian Exposition still fresh in collective memory. The process of planning carried forward from there. Burnham called for material changes very similar in effect to those Bacon would ask for fifty years later: "improvement of the Lake front . . . a system of highways outside the city . . . improvement of railway terminals . . . an outer park system . . . a systematic arrangement of the streets and avenues within the city, in order to facilitate the movement to and from the business district . . .

development of centers of intellectual life and of civic administration, so related as to give coherence and unity to the city." Writing in a mode that Ed Bacon echoed in his "2009" essay, Burnham laid the success of the project at the feet of the people of Chicago: "Every one knows that the civic conditions . . . of to-day will not be tolerated by the men who shall follow us. This must be so, unless progress has ceased."[20]

Bacon was highly impressed with Burnham's ability to take the model city of Chicago in 1893 and transform it into the *Plan of Chicago* in 1909. It was magnificent and "resulted in a fine lakefront development." Nonetheless, he judged in the final analysis that Burnham's plan had not achieved its larger aims, that it had "little effect on Chicago in depth."[21] Daniel Burnham worked out the formula of a world's-fair-as-catalyst to substantive urban renewal, but he could not apply it vigorously enough to enact his full 1909 plan—he died in 1912. Burnham's work in Chicago would prove more influential as the expression of an American City Beautiful planning ethos taking shape in numerous cities than in transforming Chicago into the utopian white city of the Columbian Exposition. In this way one might argue that the Columbian Exposition was illustrative of the ways that visionary landscape architecture was leaving a mark on the American city. But as urban planning historian Peter Hall concludes, American cities did not adopt wholesale changes along the lines promoted by Burnham in 1893 or in 1909, and the big ideas of the City Beautiful movement ended up in the realm of piecemeal "City Functional" changes.[22]

One of New York City Parks Commissioner Robert Moses's ambitions had long been to transform the wastelands of Flushing, Queens, into a park.[23] As early as 1936 Moses was actively detailing the fantastic transformation to come to the future "Versailles of America in Flushing Meadow Park."[24] This area, immortalized by F. Scott Fitzgerald in *The Great Gatsby* as "a valley of ashes—a fantastic farm where ashes grow like wheat into ridges and hills and grotesque gardens," was selected as the site for a world's fair in 1939. A world's fair in a garbage heap as Europe readied for war and the Depression economy lingered? Robert Moses has never been characterized as an urban planner without moxie, and his plan worked as an urban renewal gambit.[25] The physical site of the fairgrounds was more than three miles long, stretching out over 1200 acres, and was served by the New Deal-funded Grand Central Parkway, as well as the Long Island Railroad and local subway lines.[26]

The content of the 1939 New York World's Fair was a triumph of corporate-sponsored showmanship—science and engineering capturing the imagination (26 million imaginations) in pavilions like the General Motors "Futurama," where the public could witness a stunning autocentric city of 1960 designed by Norman Bel Geddes.[27] In this new America, an America arising from the Depression, private wheels rolled gracefully along publicly subsidized highways. Corporate enthusiasm and dollars coupled with scaled-up New Deal federal support allowed planners and designers to let their imaginations run wild. However, Moses's plan to turn the valley of ashes into a grand urban park met its demise in World War II. And, in fact, it would take a second fair on the same site in 1964 before Moses could complete his planned vision for Flushing Meadows.[28] Still, there was a lesson in 1939, and it died hard—that a city could host a world's fair and use it to rehabilitate an area, that designers and planners could enhance their portfolios, and that the bill could be pushed over to eager corporate patrons, with government at all levels making up the difference.

At the time of the 1939 Fair Ed Bacon was living in Philadelphia, getting by at an architecture firm, having recently left his position with the housing authority in Flint, Michigan. It is not clear from the record whether he visited the World's Fair in New York, but he was certainly affected by it. One of the young designers involved closely with Futurama was Austrian-born émigré designer Oskar Stonorov. Bacon and Stonorov would work closely in the ensuing years—and Stonorov's experience with Futurama would prove critical in Bacon's introduction to the power of visionary futuristic displays, the 1947 Better Philadelphia Exhibition.

The 1947 Better Philadelphia Exposition opened the way for Bacon's eventual ascendance as executive director of the Philadelphia City Planning Commission, and it provided a deep well of ideas to draw from when he later began thinking about the 1976 World's Fair. Stonorov and Philadelphia architect Louis I. Kahn, along with Bacon, worked on developing not only the content but also the methods of display. Gregory Heller and Harris Steinberg each discuss the ambitions and legacies of Better Philadelphia in this volume, and some elements of it are worth stressing here as well. First of all, the stakes of any sort of large-scale exhibition were high in the city following the bad memories of the 1926–27 Philadelphia Sesquicentennial. Poorly planned and late in construction, politically divisive and ultimately bankrupt, the lightly attended Sesquicentennial showed what might happen if a city blustered into a world's fair without an adequate plan for its funding or its design.[29]

More modest than the spectacle or cost of a major world's fair, Better Philadelphia did use new technologies to impress the visitor and to advance the argument for a specific development agenda. Better Philadelphia's design stressed four elements: simple ideas clearly expressed to the public; the use of sound, color, and motion in presentation; accessibility of concepts to the layman, stressing participation rather than watching; and movement from the general (the city) to the specific (the home). As pioneered in Futurama, multimedia techniques showed visitors the future of their city. The diorama at Better Philadelphia showed the city as it might look in 1982, "if you support city planning."[30] Philadelphia public school students were also involved in Better Philadelphia:

pupils arranged for conferences with members of city planning groups. They discussed their proposals and studied the viewpoints of experts. They joined neighborhood planning committees and visited their councilmen to talk over the need for ordinances that would provide playgrounds, good lighting, and safe streets. They said *"Now we'll have to get all the people interested. That's the only way we'll get the kind of city we want!"*[31]

Architectural Forum ran a special issue describing Better Philadelphia. The "exhibition boasted three-dimensional models, a huge aerial photo map, movies, a diorama, murals, wall panels, cartoons, a reproduction of an actual street corner and mechanical gadgets—every device known to the display artist—to sock home what is wrong with Philadelphia and what, specifically, can be done about it."[32] The exhibition opened with an eight-foot copper hand and the words "A Better Philadelphia Within Your Grasp." *Architectural Forum* noted that the entrance "with ramps leading to a dimly illuminated area, is strikingly reminiscent of the Futurama at the World's Fair."[33] Visitors walked down a ramp into a diorama of the region and then into the "Time and Space Machine." A full-size row house was shown, and a "photo-mosaic" that "features only projects already approved by the City Council." This was important, *Architectural Forum* noted, "in gaining the confidence of a public made cynical by utopian futuramas and the inertia of local politicians." The central display was the 30-by-14-foot scale model of downtown from the Delaware River to West Philadelphia:

As the visitors approach down a ramp, they first see the city as it now is. Then, synchronized with an explanatory dialogue and section-by-section spot lighting, portions of the model flip over to show the proposed improvements. Eventually, the entire model is reversed, showing the center of Philadelphia as it could be in 30 years if all improvements were carried through."

Major improvements included "a widened Vine Street . . . an express highway along the Delaware River . . . new bridges and apartment house projects, a stately mall to set off Independence Hall . . . and the replacement of the 'Chinese Wall' with a new midtown boulevard." The model took nine months and $50,000 to build, "and contained 45,000 buildings, 25,000 autos and buses and 12,000 individually made trees, fashioned of buckram."[34] Before Better Philadelphia opened, a survey showed that 10 percent of Philadelphians knew something about city planning, but 64 percent of 365,000 questionnaires turned in afterward said "yes," that citizens would be willing to pay higher taxes, slightly, to get the planning so dramatically displayed in Better Philadelphia done.[35]

Ed Bacon was ecstatic, writing in a post-Better Philadelphia think-piece titled "Are Exhibitions Useful?" that when "390,000 people take time off to bother with city planning, that is news."[36] In the piece, Bacon becomes a student of the Exhibition, noting which elements were successful and which were not. Not everything worked as expected. "A 30-year plan with realizable possibilities, reduced to that scale," he noted, "does not make for very spectacular changes." He liked the Time and Space Machine, but he really liked the aerial mosaic, gushing that it "was an unforgettable experience to see people of every sort leaning over the maps, translating their interest in their own homes into city planning as it affected these surroundings."[37] Here was a way for city planners to inspire in citizens deep and durable emotional bonds to a new vision for their city. Better Philadelphia used the tools of modern advertising, window display, and audio-visual persuasion gleefully and to great effect. With a model Center City flipping over and over, students planning in their schoolrooms, and visitors reading secret messages from the mayor written in invisible ink and encouraging them to embrace this fresh look at the future city, it was a new day in the art of the exhibition.

On New Year's Eve 1947, in the aftermath of Better Philadelphia's success, an exultant Stonorov fired off a memo to a handful of key city planning officials, imagining out loud the potential Better Philadelphia demonstrated to reach an even larger public in the future. And what kind of forum was Stonorov imagining? "A world fair in the midst of Philadelphia!"—the Philadelphia Fair of 1953, an event that would be soon made possible by tearing down the "Chinese Wall" and Broad Street Station and creating a vast expanse of land in Center City for redevelopment:

Independent and without interfering with the city's life—a single air-conditioned glass structure 50 feet high and 20 feet above the street level—so as not to interrupt street traffic—might extend from the Schuylkill across from 30th Street Station to City Hall, branching out laterally . . . to Logan Square. . . . This structure internally would be served by an overhead mono-rail electrical road traveling at low speed through the various subdivisions of the show.[38]

This vision for a 1953 World's Fair contained within it two broad concepts. First, it would showcase the "peaceful intentions" of the United States, highlighting "the power of democratic ideas" and the "physical skill of American technique." Second, "the Philadelphia Fair would transform the city into a whirlpool of life and activities for a year or more" and enable the construction of not only the glass structure but also an airport, Independence Mall, and the revitalization of Market Street in West Philadelphia, among other projects.[39]

Could these concepts—democracy, technique, and urban renewal—be bound together successfully at the core of a Philadelphia World's Fair? Could the planning for such an event propel the Philadelphia City Planning Commission forward as it unveiled its aggressive plans for a revitalized Center City, new housing, and integrated transportation networks? The past provided mixed messages, depending on how one read them. A World's Fair in 1893 nourished the City Beautiful movement and a bold plan for Chicago that spurred lakefront redevelopment, but ultimately fell short of achieving Daniel Burnham's comprehensive changes for his city. In 1939 the New York World's Fair began the transformation of an abandoned area into a park rivaling Central Park—a site that would rest for 25 years before hosting a second World's Fair in 1964. In these cases the planner with a long view and an ability to maintain power and sway could find rewards in the world's fair idea. It was with these lessons and those of Better Philadelphia at hand—the power of a coherent fair-to-renewal plan, interlocking public/private funding mechanisms, public fascination stoked by skillful display—that a World's Fair plan was taking shape in Ed Bacon's mind when the first discussions of a Bicentennial celebration for Philadelphia began in the late 1950s. To succeed—to leave behind permanent structures, not lose money in doing so, and deliver an experience that would galvanize the city around an urban planning vision—Ed Bacon would have to top the success of his own city in 1876, its failure in 1926, and do at least as well if not better than Daniel Burnham in Chicago and Robert Moses in New York.

Philadelphia in the Year 2009

The 1950s were an extraordinarily productive time for Bacon and for urban planning and renewal projects in the city of Philadelphia. It is little surprise, then, that when the idea for a Bicentennial in Philadelphia was first mentioned, Bacon was soon in on the discussion. The first serious inkling of the Bicentennial occurred in 1957, when Mayor Richardson Dilworth picked up the idea and handed it off to the Junior Chamber of Commerce for development. More than a year went by and little was done, but Bacon obviously saw this as a rare moment of opportunity to hitch his Better Philadelphia urban renewal agenda to a new star. He added on a World's Fair to the planning concept for a Bicentennial and wrote it up in 1959, providing the first serious description of

what a combined event of this magnitude might look like. It was published in a special 50th anniversary issue of *Greater Philadelphia Magazine*
that included essays covering a broad swath of Philadelphia's recent history and future prospects.

The critical tension in Bacon's essay resides in a struggle between the
need for a Bicentennial and World's Fair as central to a celebration of
patriotism and democracy on one side, and the same events as vehicles
for Philadelphia's urban renewal on the other. Philadelphia will host a
"reconsideration of the ideas of 1776," with all the pageantry, pomp
and circumstance one would expect. However, Bacon also believes "the
Fair should inspire the Federal Government to lend special support to
see to it that the main features of the downtown plan are actually completed by 1976, and completed at a high level of engineering and
design, as a part of its world strategy." After waving at the temporal
aspects of a fair, Bacon elaborates his vision, rooted in a physical planning agenda certainly familiar by 1959 to anyone following his career
and the work of the PCPC. Throughout the essay he shifts back and
forth from a strictly descriptive mode of speaking to a more dogmatic,
more ideological style. For example, he submits that in 1976 the
"Washington Square East redevelopment project . . . will still be
regarded as the finest achievement of American redevelopment." Here
he is boosting projects already underway, projects under the control of
the Planning Commission. Contrast that with this: "By 1976 the Federal Government has finally grasped fully the significance and magnitude of the problem of eradication of blight." This is sweeping,
imploring the reader to consider an active set of federal policies that
creates a new context for American cities more generally. Like Stonorov's 1947 memo, Bacon is asserting that localized urban renewal would
emerge as part and parcel of broader trends in progressive governance,
anticipating policies like President Lyndon B. Johnson's "Model
Cities" program. Even this early, Bacon is focused on an event far more
grandiose than a patriotic Bicentennial celebration.

Some critical elements are left wanting explanation in Bacon's 1959
plan, elements that in retrospect predict the rough waters ahead for the
Philadelphia World's Fair. First, the money—with the federal government on the verge of a hard-fought contest between Nixon and Kennedy
this was a vexing concern, and it would remain so as the federal patron
careened left and right in its financial relationship with American cities
into the 1960s and 1970s. Also, how exactly would the plan take shape;
what would be the mode of citizen engagement and neighborhood
input; would there be another Better Philadelphia or some other
method of keeping the public charged up for the idea? Bacon summons
Chestnut Street to come alive as a commercial corridor, a "backbone"

connecting revitalized Delaware and Schuylkill River waterfronts. However, this would require closing a major east-west arterial route through
Center City. He assumes a planned Crosstown Expressway will succeed
as a high-speed route cutting across the south side of Center City. Each
of these elements would prove contentious, as would the necessity of the
grand East Market transportation center, with its "air conditioned moving sidewalk" hovering above the streetscape. Last, one encounters his
enthusiasm for neighborhood renewal, and the idea, for example, that
the neighborhood of Mantua, standing between West Philadelphia and
the Franklin Parkway and Art Museum areas, would undergo "clearance
for rebuilding." Perhaps no single phrase in "Philadelphia in the Year
2009" would seem so reasonable when it was written and look so trouble-
some in retrospect.

In July 1960 Bacon moved to have the Planning Commission take over
the Bicentennial and World's Fair planning. In confidential reports to
Mayor Dilworth, he recounted the history of Fair planning to that point.
The Junior Chamber of Commerce planning committee had decided to
push City Council for a resolution asking the Bureau of International
Expositions (BIE) in Paris—the body that determined when and where
official world's fairs could occur—to reserve 1976 for Philadelphia. That
was a good first step, but not much else was happening except for a suggestion by one of the Junior Chamber members that someone be sent
to New York to work with Robert Moses on the plans for the upcoming
1964 New York World's Fair.[40] "I question whether the committee, as
presently constituted," Bacon wondered, "is sufficiently vigorous and
astute to carry through these actions." He suggested that the mayor find
someone highly enough placed to be helpful to the effort and suggested
Senator Joseph Clark, the former mayor. He spelled out his strategy
plainly: "I do believe that the idea of interesting the Federal Government in helping to complete the Downtown Plan as a proper setting for
the Fair has enough merit to be given a try."[41]

In 1961 Bacon put together a richly photographed and illustrated
issue of the *Philadelphia Inquirer Magazine*, titled "The New Face of Philadelphia." In it, he asserted that Better Philadelphia, the "vision of Postwar Philadelphia . . . has kindled the imagination of the City and,
through the medium of international exhibitions, has stirred the interests of a much wider sphere. Now, fifteen years later, we are perhaps half
done in the realization of much of that vision. But the hardest half lies
ahead." He called for a full effort—wrapping it in the gung-ho language
of the cold war—"So we will have properly done the work of our generation, and will have contributed our part to the World War of Ideas."[42]
"One of the things that would impress world opinion today," Bacon
summed up, "would be the full realization of a totally efficient, totally

human and totally beautiful center city, an expression of the highest that American technology and culture can achieve. And we are well on our way to accomplishing just that." In this he again marries the notion of urban renewal in Philadelphia to the broader ambitions for the age, enunciated so forcefully earlier that year in President John F. Kennedy's inaugural address, reprising that balance of local success in urban planning with broader national goals. Then he set forward, just as he had for the mayor the previous year, the case in all honesty: "we must seek from the Federal Government the extra assistance needed to bring some of the more daring projects to completion." Bacon looked back at Better Philadelphia and felt hard-earned pride. Penn Center, the Schuylkill Expressway, Independence Mall, Independence Historical Park, "if a serious person had prophesied that all this would be done in fifteen years, the citizens would have considered him to be visionary indeed."[43] The Market East transportation center was the major piece of Bacon's vision unrealized at this point. Market East to Bacon would be critical in helping achieve the goal of drawing suburbanites back into the city, at least to visit downtown and shop. He also revisited the idea of closing Chestnut Street to traffic. At the end of the article, Bacon laid out the plan for the Bicentennial and World's Fair for 1976, polishing up again the major elements of his "2009" essay.

Mentions of the Bicentennial and Fair appear over the next two years in Bacon's updates to the mayor, but little concrete planning for it was done. Bacon and his staff had plenty to keep them busy aside from normal duties hosting the 1961 American Institute of Architects conference, producing the film *Form, Design, and the City* to promote the Planning Commission, contributing to the 1962 "Avenue of Architecture" exhibit in Penn Center, and working on the Center City Plan. In 1962 city Development Coordinator Bill Rafsky and Ed Bacon first met with Ewen Dingwall, general manager of the world's fair then under preparation for Seattle. Dingwall was a specialist in pushing world's fair financing through Congress and would go on to advise on San Antonio's "Hemisfair," as well as the Philadelphia Fair.[44]

The first formal plans for the fair emerged at the direction of the new mayor, James Tate in 1963. Mayor Tate wrote to the Planning Commission in late 1963, wanting a Bicentennial and a "Free World's celebration" for Philadelphia in 1976. In 1964, the Planning Commission published Tate's requested report, *United States of America Bicentennial: Philadelphia, 1976*. This book set forward the plan for the combined Bicentennial and World's Fair, and Tate submitted it to President Johnson for consideration. Five years after publication of the "2009" essay, Bacon's Bicentennial/Fair concept was now at last in front of the policymakers who could make it happen.

Unsurprisingly, *Philadelphia, 1976* contained a comprehensive outline for the Planning Commission's projects, richly illustrated with regard to those but with little or no specific attention paid to buildings, themes, or events related to the Bicentennial or World's Fair.[45] The buildings were to be sited in Fairmount Park, but it was thought that

for the most part, the City's hundreds of thousands of Bicentennial visitors will concentrate much of their interest in Center City, which embraces all of Philadelphia's historic past. Penn's Landing is being recreated as a park. Nearby, the old dwellings of Society Hill are being faithfully restored. The whole Independence Hall area—embracing as it does the very heart of Colonial America—is an authentic national shrine. . . . Historical shrines, however, are only one part of the story. Center City in Philadelphia, already a national model of breathtaking redevelopment, with its stately buildings and magnificent vistas, is being steadily revitalized in accordance with a spectacular basic plan. By 1976 everything will have been completed—and ready for the world to see.[46]

By now this was a familiar pitch for Bacon, though he did return to one of Stonorov's more fantastic 1947 ideas as well, an overhead cable car system that would connect Fairmount Park to the west bank of the Schuylkill, cross the river, and link with the electric tram system planned for Chestnut Street.[47] The focus was still 100 percent on the urban renewal plan, with unique fair elements to be determined later. "Detailed plans for the Bicentennial Celebration and its concurrent World's Fair," the report explained, "will be developed from this point forward through the actions and interaction of the many groups, private and governmental, interested in the success of these projects. We are presenting here a new concept involving total community effort and participation and thus to assist those whose efforts must come later."[48] This statement was significantly more accurate than Bacon might have imagined in 1964. He was about to lose primary control over the plans for 1976, a control he would never regain. From 1964 forward, a wide-ranging array of public officials, business leaders, architects and designers, community activists, outside consultants, media observers, and even average citizens would pick up these tasks, and in doing so modify Bacon's plans in ways he could not anticipate or rein in.

With the release of *Philadelphia 1976*, Mayor Tate and City Council President Paul D'Ortona formed a 200-member organizing committee for Bicentennial and Fair planning, placing city councilman John B. Kelly in charge and effectively moving the process into the realm of machine politics and patronage. Little of substance—other than pushing forward for permission from the BIE—took place for over a year, but bad omens were all around. Despite the strong-willed planning of Robert Moses, or rather because of it, the 1964 New York World's Fair closed to highly unfavorable reviews and low turnout, losing millions of dollars. Critics in New York were castigating Moses and crying that the old model of the fair was dead.[49] Corporations were seemingly no longer willing to underwrite fairs as they had been in the past. In the age of television, General Motors, DuPont, and Westinghouse had better tools at their fingertips to engage the imagination of the American consumer. Additionally, Philadelphia faced competitors for the Bicentennial and Fair. Bacon reported to the mayor that Boston was looking to host a World's Fair in 1975, commemorating the Battle of Bunker Hill. Chicago also wanted a World's Fair in 1976 and commissioned a feasibility study by the Real Estate Research Corporation. The report was damning. The first conclusion was that Chicago did not have a "site adequate in size, suitability and accessibility to accommodate an undertaking of the magnitude envisaged." Bacon wrote a memo to Tate drawing the conclusion that this was, in fact, good news for Philadelphia: "As you see, lack of a suitable economically feasible site is a major consideration. In this regard," Bacon judged that "Philadelphia is very fortunate." More worrisome, though, might have been the report's conclusion that "World's Fairs of the traditional type are apparently obsolete" because of high costs, public apathy, and "studies indicate that the concept of reusing land brought into being for a World's fair for private entrepreneurial development subsequent to the Fair's use likely would be uneconomic." Here was a cold, sober assessment of the possible pitfalls in planning a fair and using it to achieve long-term development goals.[50] Shortly thereafter, Chicago withdrew itself from consideration to host a world's fair.

In late 1965, Mayor Tate convened a nineteen-member Bicentennial Planning Committee, placing retired Atlantic Richfield Company president Henderson Supplee, Jr., as chairman. The Bicentennial Committee was charged with preparing specific location, facilities, and theme recommendations. At the same time, Tate was also trying to bring the Olympics to Philadelphia. Tate, John B. Kelly, and Bacon traveled to Chicago in 1966 to make the case to the United States Olympic Committee for Philadelphia as host of the 1972 Olympic games, proposing the Planning Commission's model neighborhood of Eastwick, near the airport in the southwest section of the city, as the ideal site for an Olympic village. Bacon described it enthusiastically, writing that in Eastwick, there "is being created virtually a complete new city within a city with some 12,000 new homes. . . . Through the heart of the area runs a pedestrian spine, a landscaped series of squares and walkways, completely separated from automobile traffic, bordered by garden apartments, churches, schools, recreation areas and shopping centers."[51] True to form, if a catalytic event could bring outside funding into Philadelphia to accomplish Planning Commission renewal goals, Ed Bacon was there to make the pitch. Kelly was such a staunch advocate of the idea—no doubt in part because both he and his father had been Olympic medal winners—that he came under criticism from the press for suggesting that an Olympics for Philadelphia was a better idea than a world's fair. Over the years to come, an Olympics in Philadelphia for 1976 was also discussed, though the committee appears never to have strongly considered Philadelphia for the 1972 or 1976 bids.

In early 1966 President Johnson proposed the creation of the federal-level American Revolution Bicentennial Commission (ARBC). This Commission was charged to help state, local, and private groups plan for the Bicentennial. "In planning this bicentennial celebration, we must remember that we are celebrating not only the birth of American ideals, but the birth of ideals that today encircle the globe," Johnson intoned. Johnson's announcement mentioned names like Washington and Jefferson, but also Pierre L'Enfant, the famous planner of Washington, D.C., a hopeful sign perhaps for Bacon's agenda. "These were men of vision. They were men of courage. They were men of ideas," Johnson said.[52] Few specifics were set forward, but cities were encouraged to begin preparing their proposals. In March 1967 Mayor Tate and Councilman D'Ortona folded the two existing advisory committees into one 50-member board. This was incorporated as the Philadelphia 1976 Bicentennial Corporation (BC), vested with the power to move forward on preparing a plan for consideration by the federal government. Supplee was named to chair the board, Kelly was named president, and Dingwall was hired as a consultant. Bacon chaired the committee charged with preparing physical site plans. Moving forward, success would require rallying local, state, and federal political support, getting the nod to host an international exposition from the BIE in Paris, and pushing the whole effort ahead on pace.

A Permanent Revolution

Early in 1966, a thirty-year-old Philadelphia architect named Richard Saul Wurman wrote a letter to President Johnson explaining his vision of a Bicentennial celebration not confined to specific cities, but stretching over the "full East coast contained in the boundaries of the thirteen original colonies," from Boston to Savannah.[53] The plan would include a high-speed rail line from Boston to Washington, a complete interstate highway, port development, and waterway beautification, along with innovations in "Phon-A-Vision, television and the communications satellite." Each major city would play its role: Boston, for example, would display science and history, while New York would show off business, finance, and entertainment. Philadelphia's role would be in culture, history, and city planning.[54] Wurman's ideas and his brashness in sending them to Mayor Tate and former Mayor Dilworth, Senator Clark, planning officials in Boston and Philadelphia—not to mention Lyndon Johnson—provoked a reaction from Bacon that would come to represent one of the critical fault lines developing underneath the World's Fair. Bacon was not amused. He responded to Wurman that in his view it was "uncalled for and totally out of the spirit of what we are trying to do. Everyone agreed that the celebration would have national aspects and that it would have to have a focal center and that this focal center would be Philadelphia."[55] Wurman reassured Bacon that he would "participate with all vigor to describe the image of my city and the processes, methods and aspirations that were necessary to arrive at its form in 1976."

But Wurman was also "disturbed" that Bacon saw such an effort as counter to the planning effort underway for the Bicentennial and Fair.[56] Bacon's notion that "everyone" was in agreement about the Fair's plan was starting to become a matter of great contention in Philadelphia, as would a series of related and thorny questions. Should Philadelphia and its local planning agenda comprise the core of the 1976 events, and if so, what would be the right balance between physical planning in Center City and in more dispersed neighborhood, regional, and national development? Also critical, how should new ideas be funneled into the process? As planning went forward the needs of minority communities would come more to the fore of the process, as would the energies of a rising generation of Philadelphia architects, designers, and urban activists. New voices and new visions were undeniable by 1967 and by 1970 would in fact move the planning of the World's Fair to a new, more representative, and ultimately conflict-ridden course.

In 1967 the BC commissioned the Franklin Institute Research Laboratories to prepare two studies, on ideas for the Philadelphia World's Fair, and on the Montreal International and Universal Exposition (Expo 67). This was the second major study, with the Stanford Research Institute concluding in 1965 that Philadelphia was favorably positioned to host a world's fair. The Franklin Institute report was delivered by Technical Director Joel N. Bloom and included a concept, an action plan for the city's presentation to the ARBC, and an implementation plan.[57] The report predicted that "by 1976 . . . the developments of science will make it possible for people to sit in their living rooms and watch the exploration of space by astronauts on 3-D color television. With such exciting entertainment so readily available, *there will be little appeal to the public from a spectacle-type World's Fair like those of the past.*"[58] What was needed was a "Fair Without Walls," a "city-wide and regional fair," where visitors would call into a supercomputer, state their preferred itinerary, and receive complete instructions on where to go, what to see, and how best to travel.[59] Another aspect of the Fair would be "research for humanity," where food and water, transportation, housing, and health would each be featured in a dedicated building: "It will consist of actual, operating institutions functioning to eliminate the scourges of mankind." Laboratories would be built and leading scientists would be invited to live on-site. "The physical facilities for these research centers can be built around the existing excellent research laboratories (for example, Franklin Institute Research laboratories' new building)." The idea was that this connected to President Johnson's charge that the fair emphasize "ideas associated with the Revolution which have been so important in the development of the United States, in world affairs, and in mankind's quest for freedom."

Voices from outside the formal Bicentennial Corporation also began to speak out about the World's Fair in Philadelphia. With the mayoral election heating up in the late summer of 1967, Tate's Republican challenger Arlen Specter released a report alleging political "cronyism" in the assignment of Bicentennial Corporation positions, and publishing a list of political contributions Tate had received in the primary season from various BC members. Specter went on to argue that Tate had not been aggressive enough in promoting Philadelphia's 1976 plans in Washington. He also pointed to the Stanford Research Institute Study, and its $22,500 price tag, as examples of questionable spending and lack of follow-through by Tate. Specter pledged, if elected, to remove politics from the Fair's planning (a tricky claim in the midst of a campaign), as well as moving quickly to decide on an "imaginative concept," and insisting on permanent improvements from the Fair.[60] Tate won the election, but Specter's criticism seemed to reflect a broader critique— new people and fresh ideas were on their way into the BC.

"Some people in town, mainly younger people," explains Stanhope S. Browne, "were beginning to feel very disappointed about the planning that was going on." Browne had moved in 1964 as a newlywed and young attorney into the Society Hill Towers, where he quickly became involved in the leadership of a citizen-based effort to depress and cover the Delaware Expressway (I-95), just to the east of the neighborhood that had emerged as one of Bacon's signature PCPC projects.[61] Browne and his committee went up against Bacon and the variety of establishment bureaucratic players pushing for the elevated highway project, and succeeded, a parallel to a similar effort to entirely shut down the long-planned Crosstown Expressway project.[62] In a 1967 letter to Henderson Supplee, Browne offered the services of a new "informal committee," a "highly motivated, inter-disciplinary group willing to do some intense and protracted thinking on a matter we feel very deeply about."[63] The Committee for an International Exposition in Philadelphia in 1976, or the "Young Professionals" (YPs) as they came to be known would greatly influence the direction of World's Fair planning from 1967 onward.

The YPs were a diverse group, and represented a cross-section of the city's aspiring shapers. They came together around the shared belief in the necessity of a BIE-sanctioned Philadelphia World's Fair—nothing corporate or nostalgic like the 1964 New York's World's Fair. They had in mind something much more focused on social problems like Montreal's Expo '67 then underway, with its theme of "Terres des Hommes" (Man and His World). Browne and his Society Hill neighbor Martha W. Schober were fresh from the Delaware Expressway fight; Robert J. Sugarman was deeply involved in the protest against the Crosstown Expressway. Architects and planners included Boston transplant John Andrew Gallery, who then worked at the PCPC, James Kise, Thomas A. Todd, and Richard Saul Wurman; through Wurman, Lou Kahn participated as an outside advisor. Members also included representatives of the city's development and banking communities, like Robert McLean, III, and Theodore T. Newbold, both of the Old Philadelphia Development Corporation, and John R. Bunting, head of First Pennsylvania Bank. Media figures participated, led by D. Herbert Lipson, chairman of *Philadelphia Magazine.* Government officials included congressman and future Philadelphia mayor William Green, and Yvonne S. Perry, who worked for the federal Department of Housing and Urban Development in its Model Cities program. Academics played a strong role as well, with Anthony N. B. Garvan and Murray G. Murphey from the American Civilization Department and John E. Wideman from the English Department at the University of Pennsylvania.[64]

Late in 1967 the YPs came forward with "A Proposal for an International Exposition in Philadelphia in 1976." Through this planning process, the YPs sought to address what they saw as the pressing social problems of the city. Philadelphia had been rocked by race riots in the summer of 1964, and though a tense peace had been restored, it was impossible to avoid the signs of impending crisis in the schools, in the industrial economy, and in the neighborhoods. But that was not all—the YPs looked to the World's Fair as a chance to advance a much broader agenda. The idea was that the Bicentennial and Fair as imagined thus far were backward looking and would overlook human problems. They needed to recognize "technological, social, and cultural advances" and should join "with other nations in a declaration of mankind's universal aspirations." The theme chosen was "The Permanent Revolution"— perhaps a little ominous considering the simmering events of 1968 on the horizon—but expressive of an attempt to connect thematically the political revolution of 1776 to an ongoing revolution that embraced physical, political, and social needs.

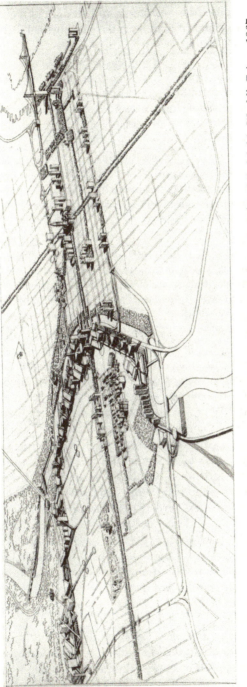

Figure 15. Megastructure plan diagram developed by the "Young Professionals" for the 1976 Philadelphia World's Fair, c. 1967. Courtesy of Temple University Libraries, Urban Archives.

Alongside the theme, the architects and designers among the YPs started working on a physical plan, with its core physical feature being a "megastructure," a 4.5-mile cover over the Pennsylvania Railroad's 30th Street Station railyard on the west side of the Schuylkill River that would serve as the site for the World's Fair. The megastructure's "central location and prototypical form . . . [could] be extended over trackage and expressways to North, South and West Philadelphia." It would disrupt no one, they argued, was close to transportation, and would "bind the inner city areas together in a new relationship to one another and to Center City." The system was made of minirails and moving platforms with other systems branching off. "More importantly, it must provide a generally applicable method for overcoming the social and physical problems of the ghetto. In addition to physical deterioration, these areas are often isolated, physically and psychologically, by railroad tracks and expressways." Thus, funds used would "demonstrate a solution to the needs of people in the urban environment, not only locally, but throughout the world."[65] It was an ambitious idea, and one that would alter the city's form dramatically if it were to succeed.

Early in 1968, Philadelphia historian Catherine Drinker Bowen, a friend of the Bacons and a member of the federal American Revolution Bicentennial Commission, wrote a letter to Ed Bacon, in effect opening a channel of communication from the ARBC to Philadelphia's planners. She was distressed by the megastructure, wondering whether it was ill-advised, with Vietnam underway, the "Negro problem, the urgent terrible problem of poverty, the schools, our cities and ghettos." Additionally, she wondered, "What part is black Philadelphia to play"? She saw this as more important than building megastructures. "Isn't there something inappropriate, even offensive, in such a gigantic plan of city advancement along lines which do not take into account the urgent and dangerous problems with which the city is now involved?" Bowen continued, "It is hard for me to believe the Federal Commission would welcome such a plan." Bowen agreed that the megastructure plans are "stimulating, and I have said so in public. But only in connection, I want to add, with a different world than the one we live in today."[66]

Even children were asking tough questions about the Fair at the time. In January 1968 Ed Bacon passed along a note from his nine-year-old son Kevin to Ewen Dingwall: "Are they going to have something worthwhile, or is it going to be corny. . . . Will it be something that the people are really interested in or just rides?"[67]

Though Henderson Supplee, Ed Bacon, and Ewen Dingwall all expressed reservations about the YPs' ideas, time was ticking and the city needed concrete proposals to show to the ARBC in Washington.[68] Mayor Tate thus directed that the Bicentennial Corporation absorb the YPs and their ideas.[69] John Bunting joined the Economic Aspects Committee, while Stanhope Browne and Theodore Newbold became "Members at Large." John Andrew Gallery joined the Bicentennial Site Committee, soon to take over physical planning and the negotiations with the Pennsylvania Railroad over the 30th Street Station air rights.[70] The BC's efforts accelerated into 1969, hiring architect and planner David A. Crane to work on technical aspects of the megastructure, with additional sites developed incorporating the area around North Philadelphia rail station and the Penn's Landing area on the Delaware River waterfront into the overall plan. Bacon, meanwhile, was pushing for a relocation of the Fair to the ancestral home of Philadelphia fairs, Fairmount Park, an idea that faced staunch public opposition.[71] Bacon had by this time moved to the periphery of the World's Fair effort.

In September 1969 an assembly of BC notables embarked from 30th Street Station amid the clamor of speechmaking and high school bands on their way to present the city's finished proposal—now called "Toward a Meaningful Bicentennial"—in Washington. The BC's leadership, and its ideas, now reflected a synthesis of YPs and establishment Philadelphia. Mayor Tate, Henderson Supplee, Bill Rafsky, and Ed Bacon all spoke, as did Anthony N. B. Garvan, Stanhope Browne, and John Bunting. The richly-illustrated accompanying book detailed the key elements creatively and in seemingly every way possible in print: in words and maps, in timelines, in schematic drawings and photographs. The emphasis was to be on people first, along with a historical evaluation of the nation's successes and failures, an "Agenda for National Action" to meet pressing social problems, and international participation. The megastructure was at the physical core of the Fair, but so now were ideas for "innovative housing demonstrations" and "experimental residential environments" where visitors might stay, but that would also be permanent additions to the city. Modern telecommunications would be employed "before and during 1976 to discuss goals and problems," and would become "a permanent communications network for the sharing of mutual concerns." A "Museum of Failure," was included, cultural displays of all types, alternative transportation demonstrations, and the list went on and on. In 10-years time the Philadelphia World's Fair had been transformed from a catalyst for completion of the items on Ed Bacon's PCPC clipboard to an "occasion for a break with previous tradition and the initiation of a new direction more relevant to our times."[72]

Along with the shimmering imagery of the "Toward a Meaningful Bicentennial" proposal there appeared a hard-nosed projection of the impact. The BC anticipated 51 million visits: 2 million from abroad, 13 million from Philadelphia, 16 million from the region, and 20 million from outside the region. The revenue projection was $1.1 billion dollars,

Figure 16. "Bicentennial Corporation board Chairman Henderson Supplee, Jr., addresses the crowd gathered at the Penn Central's 30th Street Station to bid farewell to the city's delegation leaving for Washington to make the city's bid for the 1976 celebration of American independence." *Philadelphia Evening Bulletin*, 24 September 1969. Courtesy of Temple University Libraries, Urban Archives.

with $140 million from Philadelphians and the remainder from outside. The 1972–1976 construction period would see 20,000 new jobs created, including construction, suppliers, and a total of 75,000 jobs available in the Bicentennial year. For the city itself it was projected to raise $51 million in wage taxes, $93 million in sales taxes for the state, and for the city $400 million in new taxable properties. The estimated price tag was $860 million, with 20 percent coming from private funds, 5 percent from the city, 10 percent from Pennsylvania, 10 percent from the federal government, and 40 percent from public financing (with 15 percent miscellaneous).[73]

By this time BC efforts to reach out to African American community leaders were visible. The YPs had always contended that the megastructure was desirable in part due to the positive effects it would have on the neighborhoods bordering it, particularly Powelton Village and Mantua, two of the city's poorest.[74] It had the added advantage of not necessitating any neighborhood "clearance," the bland terminology for the eminent-domain bulldozing some neighborhoods in Philadelphia had witnessed in the urban renewal era.[75] The BC now had a number of African American members, some of whom participated in the Washington presentation. These included two Mantua community leaders, Andrew Jenkins, president of Mantua Community Planners, and Herman C. Wrice, president of the Young Great Society. Harold Haskins from the Temple University Health Sciences Center was on hand, as was Augustus (Gus) Baxter, executive director of the American Architect Institute Workshop.[76] Baxter spoke about the BC "Agenda for National Action," an effort focused on "the creation of a more humane social environment" for urban communities. "Toward a Meaningful Bicentennial" stated the issue and at the same time raised the bar for success, pointing out that since the "majority of Philadelphia blacks are living in the worst sections of the city. . . . Greater participation in policy decisions by members of minority groups can be the first significant step toward establishing a meaningful Bicentennial."[77]

In 1970 the BC hired Catherine Susan Leslie to serve as the new Agenda for Action Coordinator for Community Development. Leslie had a long resume in community organizing—including two years with the Philadelphia Council for Community Advancement (PCCA), where she worked closely with West Philadelphia organizer W. Wilson Goode (later Philadelphia's first African American mayor). In this role Leslie had also worked with Bill Rafsky, a member of the PCCA board, and it was Rafsky who first approached her about joining the BC. Leslie remembers Rafsky's pitch: "You know we're going to have this 200th birthday of the United States," he explained, and "Philadelphia has been given the go-ahead to develop a program, and you could switch your community groups, leaders, neighborhoods over to that program and bring them into it and then expand from there."[78] Leslie accepted the offer, welcomed the pay raise, and set to work hiring consultants and organizing the city's different neighborhoods to participate in the World's Fair.

In this way Leslie's office became a crucial gateway for grass roots involvement in the Fair, and the effort to build strong public support among communities that by 1970 had seen a generation of postwar decline. Leslie would confront resentment against the largely white City Hall establishment that had by 1970 simultaneously fostered community apathy and cynicism on one hand and a growing Black Power movement on the other.[79] A strong argument Leslie had on her side was that the events of 1976 were seen as inevitable and coming up fast, a guarantee of sorts that the city's power structure had to take action to clean up the neighborhoods and get them ready for the world to visit, instead of just repeating empty promises.[80]

Leslie had white and African American assistants on staff, "down to earth people, they had all the technical knowledge but they were down to earth. And so that's about as much as the community wanted to see." She found spirits willing with the Nicetown-Tioga community in North Philadelphia, with the Puerto Rican community, the Irish residents of Fishtown, and with Herman Wrice and the Young Great Society group in Mantua, among others. Leslie remembers that in the Agenda for Action's interactions with the community:

[They] didn't want all this theory . . . all this architectural language, we knew that had to be done, maybe for Washington, but not for this . . . when we made presentations to community groups . . . and when we were listening to them, we didn't want the big bosses coming down to the community . . . so Ed Bacon and [and executive members of the BC] never showed up at any community organization . . . they wouldn't have gone over well . . . and they didn't want to either, but they were supportive.[81]

In Leslie's vision each neighborhood would oversee its own Fair planning initiative, focusing on the cultural expressions they were comfortable with, and that would attract international visitors. In this way every neighborhood would be connected in a seamless but diverse fabric—a culturally-expressive fabric—guiding the visitor across the city and back to see local museums, listen to music, and eat ethnic foods. Such an effort, a "clean up, fix up, paint up" out in the neighborhoods, she knew, seemed less grand than many of the ideas floating around, but would also leave the kind of lasting impact on the city's communities that her experience indicated was truly needed. This was World's Fair planning up from the streets, but would it work? Were the citizens of Philadelphia prepared for the expense, the construction, the potential crush of 38 million out-of-town visitors to their neighborhoods? In the spring of 1970 several members of the Powelton Civic Homeowners Association sent a delegation to Washington to register with President Nixon their rejection of the BC's plans for their community.[82] It would prove a sign of the times ahead.

Too Long at the Fair

In the spring of 1970 the word coming from Washington was that Philadelphia's World's Fair was in jeopardy—failure to select a site and cost concerns were raising red flags.[83] In June the ARBC finally voted, 18–14, a close outcome, in favor of allowing Philadelphia to go ahead with planning for a World's Fair. The result was endorsed by the Nixon administration. However, with the Pennsylvania Railroad filing for bankruptcy protection that same month, the drawn-out struggle to obtain the air rights was thrown into disarray. The megastructure concept was now priced out at the mind-boggling estimated cost of over a billion dollars, an extraordinary sum considering that the city's entire annual operating budget at that time was roughly half that amount.[84] At the same time, a narrative was building that the African American leaders on the BC—including Baxter, but especially Sam Evans, chairman of the Philadelphia Anti-Poverty Program and Goldie Watson, Philadelphia's Model Cities director—were "selling out" the neighborhoods and going along with whatever the white establishment on the BC wanted to build.[85] Division along generational lines, the very type of division that had produced the YPs, was now apparently affecting the African American community as well on issues related to the World's Fair.[86] *Philly Talk* magazine captured the "angry and adamant" spirit of the season, declaring it time to push the Bicentennial Corporation "up against the ghetto wall, via real social awareness and involvement." This "might provide some initial antagonism, as it has in the past. But at the risk of losing any help for our city's most needy areas in any 1976 celebration, it's worth it."[87]

Two tense meetings of the Bicentennial Corporation board took up the site issue yet again in October 1970, with the 30th Street megastructure concept winning in a racially polarized vote. In an unfortunate slip of the tongue, Henderson Supplee apparently called the board to vote, asking those in favor to raise their "white hands," drawing "both laughter and groans of disbelief from the audience," according to the *Philadelphia Inquirer.*[88] Moments later the African American members of the board stormed out of the meeting. A spontaneous sit-in and impromptu press conference followed immediately in the Bicentennial Corporation's office, with African American community members opposed to the megastructure answering the phones, telling baffled callers that the Fair was canceled, and airing their grievances to the assembled members of the press. Increasingly unsure of the future for her neighborhood initiatives, Catherine Susan Leslie had called on members of the Agenda for Action community planning groups to attend the meeting en masse. The move branded her as disloyal among BC brass, and she was fired.

The next month the ARBC itself (by now with only a handful of Johnson-era appointees left) reconsidered the cost and community opposition to the megastructure proposal and voted to reject it. The megastructure now entered the realm of the "unbuilt," and the Bicentennial Corporation was back to the drawing board.[89] From this point, World's Fair planning spiraled out of control, becoming a daily staple

Figure 17. Sit-in at Bicentennial Corporation headquarters, following the racially divided vote to approve the megastructure plan. *Philadelphia Inquirer*, 23 October 1970. Courtesy of Temple University Libraries, Urban Archives.

for news reports about the hapless and overpaid Bicentennial Corporation leadership. Henderson Supplee and many other longstanding board members resigned. Fairmount Park was briefly reconsidered as a site, then dropped. The reconfigured Bicentennial Corporation board looked over the map for open spaces and good transportation links, and the neighborhood of Byberry in the Far Northeast section of the city was suggested, the site of a closed hospital with apparently ample acreage. When local residents found out about the idea, spontaneous protests broke out. Apparently afraid, based on what they had heard, that the World's Fair was going to create a huge publicly funded housing project for low-income Philadelphians, code for African Americans, many white Byberry residents spoke out. In an era when site decisions about housing projects routinely brought Philadelphians—white and black—into the streets, this was an unfortunately predictable outcome of years of dithering over plans, negative press, and neglect on the part of the Bicentennial Corporation to engage citizens in a meaningful way in the Fair's

Figure 18. Public hearing and protest in Byberry against the World's Fair, April 1971. Courtesy of Temple University Libraries, Urban Archives.

planning. Not nearly all, but enough of Byberry resisted the fair long enough to force consideration of another site, this time a two-state idea, including the Port Richmond neighborhood, Petty's Island in the Delaware River, the Camden, New Jersey waterfront, and Penn's Landing. A remarkable plan for the site was begun by Kevin Roche John Dinkeloo and Associates; it featured a 1,250-foot-wide bridge connecting Philadelphia and Camden, and providing 40,000,000 square feet of space on 4 levels. Each level was a glass barrel-vault, with the lower two levels available for an interstate highway connector between Philadelphia and Camden. The designers argued that the bridge could become a multi-use work and living environment after the Fair.[90]

Port Richmond residents reacted much like those in Byberry before them, with suspicion and protest. This season of the Fair's planning shaped up in the midst of a mayoral race, and Democratic Party candidate and former police chief Frank Rizzo entered the fray, on the side of the predominantly white working-class Port Richmond and Byberry residents. Rizzo's racialized "tough policing" tactics in the 1960s had made him a hero to ethnic whites in the many Philadelphia neighborhoods where the color line was still strictly enforced. He now used the chaos of the site planning to score valuable political points with his base. Playing it both ways, he declared that

In my opinion the right of self-determination, whereby communities decide on matters of interest to them, is the essence of democracy. I am aware, however, that an International Exposition would generate much-needed revenue for Philadelphia. Therefore, I have no objection to such an exposition provided it has the prior approval of the residents.[91]

Rizzo certainly knew that "prior approval" would take a while to obtain in any neighborhood, if the BC could decide from whom to actually obtain such a pass. Short of a city-wide referendum (politically impossible by this point) it was impossible to truly gauge citizen opinion on the World's Fair, and so the struggles over community participation and community protest carried on in fits and starts.

Once elected, Mayor Rizzo could barely restrain his antipathy to what was becoming a World's Fair farce. At one point, Rizzo went on the Mike Douglas television program and, sitting next to Sammy Davis, Jr., berated the recently unveiled Bicentennial logo, with its "interlocking continents" design, saying he would not pay eight dollars for it (it had cost over $30,000, and did look a bit like a broken Pentagon). Rizzo's enraged populism was reflected in dozens of letters to editors in local papers.[92] The Bicentennial and the World's Fair were now a standing joke in Philadelphia, but the planning continued. Mustin Field and Fort Mifflin were both briefly discussed and dismissed as options, before a last-ditch effort with Rizzo's strong support was proposed, a return to the 1966 Olympic bid location at Eastwick. Rizzo had come out in support of Richard Nixon for reelection in 1972, a move that seemed to suggest hope for Philadelphia with the White House, but in May 1972 the ARBC voted to reject Eastwick as a suitable site, and Rizzo summarily folded the Bicentennial Corporation. The Nixon administration was decidedly uninterested in paying for a World's Fair that promised a continuation of Johnson-era Great Society urban renewal initiatives, in a state they had already locked down for the election.[93] Bicentennial planning would go ahead, but on a radically smaller scale, resulting in a lightly attended, predictable, and mostly forgettable summer full of patriotic events in 1976.[94]

As the files were boxed up on a World's Fair for Philadelphia, 1959 seemed long gone, and Ed Bacon's 2009 was even farther away.

The Built and the Unbuilt

Failure of the City to come up with a site . . . is a civic tragedy.—Ed Bacon

By the time the Bicentennial year arrived the consensus was in— Philadelphia had stayed far too long in planning a World's Fair that

Figure 19. Discussion of the World's Fair and Bicentennial plans on Philadelphia television station KYW, 21 March 1972. Left to right: Samuel Evans, John Bunting, Mayor Frank Rizzo, Vince Leonard, Governor Milton Shapp, William Rafsky, and John Gallery. Courtesy of Temple University Libraries, Urban Archives.

would never happen. In the year 2009, Ed Bacon's prophecy remains bold but unfulfilled in its broadest ambitions. Market East is finished, Chestnut Street was closed to traffic for over 25 years, and waterfront development appears finally to be underway again. However, the outflow of people and tax dollars to the suburbs has continued unabated. Housing and neighborhood deterioration are real and continue to drag down the standard of living for many, many Philadelphians. The city waits to see what comes next, at the frayed eastern edge of the American rustbelt.

There is much Bacon did not predict in 1959—the strengthening of African American resistance to white political control, federal disinvestment in East Coast cities, the emergence of a community planning ethos—each in its own way making the climate for a triumphant World's Fair less and less plausible. Each reflects a macro-trend outside the reach of a single city planner in a single city, no matter how creative or persuasive. Could he, though, have predicted that Philadelphia was going to continue its long, bitter period of economic decline, accelerating population dispersal to the suburbs, and that by 1976 the city might not be up to the challenge of hosting the world? That by 1976 the flow of dollars for "big idea" projects might dry up and leave a portfolio of unrealized dreams to remind everyone of opportunities lost? That a new generation of young planners might find the visions and methods of his generation confining? These possibilities were not outside the scope of understanding for an urbanist as sophisticated, curious, and talented as Bacon. Maybe, then, we should see his essay as less a prophecy than a gamble, a hope that big ideas could win the day, while achieving some serious and useful results along the way.

Ultimately, a planning strategy based on enthusiasm for a World's Fair in Philadelphia led to a debacle. The World's Fair proved an unreliable catalyst, especially one that deviated from previous fairs so starkly in its reliance on federal funding and insistence on permanent structures. But this was only part of the story. American cities in the 1960s and 1970s faced challenges for which the successes of the New Deal and early postwar era left planners ill-equipped; Philadelphia's failed Fair exemplifies the dizzying array of miscommunications possible between and among local and federal policymakers as they sought to enact urban renewal in the Johnson-Nixon era. The Fair attempted a grand civic gesture but instead exposed deep rifts in the city's multiple "renewal" constituencies, rifts that broke and flung the pieces of Bacon's World's Fair plan into disarray by the early 1970s.

Peter Hall pithily describes the changes in the urban planning profession taking place at just this time: "in 1955, the typical newly graduated planner was at the drawing board, producing a diagram of desired land uses; in 1965, s/he was analyzing computer output of traffic patterns; in 1975, the same person was talking late into the night with community groups, in the attempt to organize against hostile forces in the world outside."[95] Such was the case in Philadelphia, as witnessed by the rise of the YPs and the efforts of Agenda for Action community planners. In retrospect we can see these groups actually standing right on the edge of what planning theorist John Friedmann terms "radical planning," an enterprise "distinctive in drawing on organized citizen power to promote projects pointing toward social transformation." To Friedmann it is "as mediators" that "radical planners are in an excellent position to connect community groups with politically effective social movements."[96] The ideas about housing, transportation, communication, and a non-destructive urban renewal process focused on people embedded in the BC "Toward a Meaningful Bicentennial" proposal undoubtedly fit this description of "radical planning." The Agenda for Action was in a position to close the gap between low-income and minority Philadelphians and their perhaps better-educated but willing counterparts. Much more remains to be written on this topic, but it will suffice to at least start by saying that a process that could have been a tool of community-building instead pitted communities against one another. Radical planning did not take hold in the context of the World's Fair effort. More than one of the participants in this tragedy looked back with melancholy that meaningful communication along racial and generational lines proved *so* difficult. The legacies of urban segregation would not be wiped out by a single planning project, no matter how wide its appeal.

Ed Bacon probably never expected in 1959 that a mind-boggling billion-dollar fair proposal would eventually emerge for the World's Fair. He probably also never anticipated that a crippling racial divide would stall all meaningful planning by 1971. Furthermore, and much more damaging, the World's Fair planning effort made its own problems as it went ahead, sidetracking gifted young planners and policymakers from long-range planning efforts that might have helped stem the flood of violence, disinvestment, and overall malaise facing the city in the years to come.

Along the way, though, the World's Fair planning process led to a raucous and democratic debate over some vexing questions. What role should citizens and neighborhoods play in planning, especially in racially and class-diverse cities? Is the federal government a trustworthy steward of urban renewal? What is the shelf life of an urban spectacle? Most critically, can a "big event" focus political, private-sector, and citizen attention over a long enough span of time to see the vision harden into a new urban reality? Traditional answers to these questions were reexamined in the 1960s and 1970s, and new answers emerged, giving way to an era in which the world's fair was buried, big-ticket urban renewal programs were treated with suspicion, and "masterful" urban planning was forced to grapple at last with community-based solutions.

Chapter Five
Philadelphia in the Year 2059

HARRIS M. STEINBERG

Philadelphia: A New Hope, from Broad Strokes to Choke Holds

For nearly 300 years, Philadelphia had a brilliant run.

From its founding in 1682 by William Penn as a proprietary colonial capital through the heady, federally funded urban renewal days at the end of World War II, Philadelphia was often at the forefront of national and international trends in city planning, public works, technology, industry, and the applied arts. Straddled by two great rivers, the Delaware and the Schuylkill, Philadelphia's rise to prominence was fueled by the confluence of ideals, leadership, natural resources, and location. Powering America's ascendancy as the "workshop of the world" from the end of the Civil War to the dawn of the Cold War, a prosperous and expanding Philadelphia was at the epicenter of the American experiment.[1]

At the beginning of the new millennium, the city was fighting bankruptcy, its factories were shuttered, and great swaths had succumbed to blight. Disinvestment that had begun decades earlier was reaching crisis proportions.[2] Overcome by autocentric suburbanization, high taxes, white flight, failing schools, and poor city services, the middle class was gone to greener, suburban pastures, and the city was left a hollowed-out and vacant postindustrial core.

This extraordinary sweep of urban history is best embodied by two city planners standing at opposite ends of three centuries marked by invention, expansion, growth, and contraction. At the beginning stands William Penn, a questioning aristocrat, an egalitarian who converted to Quakerism and imbued his young colony, granted by King Charles II of England for a debt owed his father, with bedrock values of tolerance, patience, pragmatism, and mediation. Pennsylvania, along with her principal city of Philadelphia, was an Enlightenment-era religious experiment and a significant real-estate undertaking—paving the way for cul-

ture and commerce to coexist and flourish along the banks of the
Delaware River.[3]

At the end of this period stands Edmund Bacon, a charismatic and
willful urban planner who imparted a late twentieth-century modernist
order on Philadelphia. Dismantling the messy remnants of the city's
great industrial age with federal urban renewal funds and state-granted
condemnation privileges, Bacon aimed, as the executive director of the
Philadelphia City Planning Commission, to position Philadelphia as a
"prestige" city at the dawn of the Cold War.[4] His planning concepts were
abstract and formal, not value-based like William Penn's. Bacon's ideas
were shaped by the imperial processions of Beijing's Forbidden City, the
works of Pope Sixtus V in Rome, and the Paris of Baron George Hauss-
mann.[5] These were men who remade their cities through slum clear-
ances and the creation of grand, baroque axial lines of power and
privilege.

Between Penn and Bacon are intellectual, artistic, and entrepreneurial leaders who fostered Penn's legacy. These are the people who built
Philadelphia. They are the giants of city planning and design upon
whose shoulders we stand today as we struggle to revive her at the dawn-
ing of the twenty-first century.

Penn's vision for Philadelphia balanced the concept of protecting the
public good with private gain. His 1682 city plan, first published in 1683
to market the colony in London, was a simple Cartesian grid of streets
stretching from the Delaware to the Schuylkill River and framing five,
generous public squares. It privileged no single person; in essence, it was
the nonhierarchical design of a Quaker meeting house on a city scale.
What Penn called his "greene country town" was laid out by his surveyor
general Thomas Holme to reflect the highest safety and public-health
standards of the day. With lessons learned from the 1666 Great Fire of
London, Penn created ample-sized city lots that were originally intended
to be four acres in size for light, air, fire protection, and orchards, with
the brick London townhouse serving as the standard for fireproof construction.

Penn bordered the north and west of his city with verdant liberty
lands, a green belt around the city in which "First Purchasers" received
land both outside the city proper *and* a city lot. This established the precedent for the city's incomparable park system and started Philadelphia
on a trajectory of national and international leadership in the integration of the natural and the manmade. Most notably, his five squares,
modeled on the "Moore-fields" in London, were leading-edge public
spaces in an era of monarchy and prestige.[6]

From the outset, Penn created an influential framework of government for his colony that vested power in the governed.[7] At the same

Figure 20. Wood Street steps. Photo by Harris Steinberg. Courtesy of Harris Steinberg.

time, he created a physical plan for his city that became a prototype for *the* quintessential American city plan—the archetypal urban grid that marched westward as the city and the nation expanded. This relationship between democracy and physical planning was critical to Philadelphia's success from the beginning—a part of the city's civic DNA, embedded deep within the public psyche. Penn understood that cities and governments must be flexible and change over time without trampling core values.

Penn initially intended that the bluffs of the Delaware would be clear of development like the five public squares. Almost immediately this principle was challenged by Samuel Carpenter, who in 1684 sought to build a commercial wharf along the river. Penn's ruling allowing Carpenter to build a wharf and storage facilities along the banks of the river included provisions for public river access; over time, ten sets of municipal stairs connected the public with the waterfront. Penn's balance of public and private interests highlights the measured and pragmatic civic vision that he brought to the New World. Today, the sole remaining municipal steps that connect the original city with the river exist at Wood and Water Streets, the rest gone to the march of time and the building of I-95. The remaining Wood Street steps are testimony to the enduring, if not frayed, power of values-based planning.[8]

We have repeatedly fallen short of realizing Penn's promise for the interrelationship between democratic values and physical planning. This promise has been tested from James Logan's infamous Walking Purchase of 1737 to the Pennsylvania legislature's passage of Act 71 in 2004 stripping Philadelphia of its land use prerogative over the siting of two casinos.[9] The tension between the rights of the governed and the rule of law is continuous, yet Philadelphians retain a strong, if at times inconsistent, civic voice.

Philadelphia's ascendancy as a great port city second only to London in the English-speaking world was driven, in part, by its proximity to abundant natural resources such as a protected harbor, an ample supply of timber, arable lands and, ultimately, vast coal deposits in northeast Pennsylvania. With a foundation of personal freedoms established by Penn and its central location in the colonies, early Philadelphia was a cosmopolitan laboratory for ideas and innovation—fueled by waves of immigration that brought drive, grit and know-how to the shores of Penn's "Holy Experiment."[10] Religious tolerance and intellectual freedom made it democracy's crucible less than one hundred years after Penn founded his city. Philadelphia, in turn, helped give birth to the American idea—the coexistence of technological innovation and commerce within a democratic framework.

Benjamin Franklin's inventiveness further shaped the intellectual, technological, and institutional landscape of Philadelphia, along with leading minds such as David Rittenhouse in astronomy, Benjamin Rush in medicine, and Charles Wilson Peale in art and naturalism. With others, they forged the character and quality of Philadelphia as a place where practical, applied theory was at the forefront of innovation and discovery. Indeed, to this day, Franklin's college, the University of Pennsylvania, prides itself on his tenet to teach "Things that are likely to be most useful and *most ornamental*"—distinguishing the University of Pennsylvania from its Ivy League counterparts in its clear and conscious blending of theory and practice.[11]

The world came to early Philadelphia to witness the American experiment. The Marquis de Lafayette, Alexis de Tocqueville, Charles Dickens, and a host of European intellectuals and dignitaries learned from Philadelphia's principal civic, municipal, and public works—works of great social importance and architectural design that aspired to fuse human aspiration and social principle with grace, dignity, and elegance. Young Philadelphia was a leader in public institutions with path-breaking projects ranging from the nation's first hospital, Pennsylvania Hospital, in 1751, to the revolutionary (if not ultimately discredited) design of Eastern State Penitentiary in 1829. Frederick Graff's seminal Fairmount Water Works at the Schuylkill Dam, designed in 1812 to protect the citizens of Philadelphia from a series of yellow fever epidemics, was the first municipal waterworks in the United States. Graff's design, studied worldwide in its time, is a stunning combination of then-state-of-the-art engineering and Greek Revival design. It remains today one of Philadelphia's signature sites, as citizens visit the Water Works, as they did in Graff's day, to seek refuge from the crowded metropolis, to be cooled by river breezes, and to take pleasure in the elegant and urbane riverside setting. This demonstrates how Philadelphia's early institutions were often democratic, humanitarian, artistic, and technological triumphs.

Ideas and innovation have always mattered in Philadelphia. Its rise to greatness rested upon a culture that, within the context of its time in America, was an open society. While slavery existed in early Philadelphia and religious toleration had its limits, Philadelphia was a society that valued the creation of new knowledge supported by an abundance of natural and intellectual resources. From the first paper mill in the colonies in 1690 to the development of the world's first electronic digital computer, ENIAC, in 1946 at the University of Pennsylvania, Philadelphia often responded to society's challenges with elegant and humane solutions that were tied to commercial purpose.

Ultimately, however, events beyond the city's control caught it unaware. Tectonic shifts in transportation, economic markets, and sweeping social changes in the middle class after World War II marked the beginning of the end of Philadelphia's extraordinary nearly three-hundred-year successful run. In the postwar era, time and history conspired to drain Philadelphia's spirits and coffers, and the city was left at the brink of bankruptcy by the dawn of the twenty-first century. What had once been an expanding universe drawn from the interrelationship between culture and commerce was threatened with contraction. In retrenchment, city leaders relegated urban planning to the backseat, electing to focus on real-estate deal making over integrated planning. Thus began the era of the planner-in-exile, as civic leaders and non-profit organizations arose to provide stewardship over open space, commercial corridors, historic properties, neighborhood revitalization, and a host of design-related projects aimed at protecting Philadelphia's promethean civic legacy. Today, as a global economic crisis once again imperils Philadelphia's urban promise, the city finds itself poised to capitalize on its existing urban transportation network, its dense housing stock, and its central position in the Northeast Corridor between Washington, D.C., and Boston.

History by Design

From William Penn's time to today, the physical history of Philadelphia is a great urban fabric woven by design. Beginning with Penn's bold, formative strokes and leading to Edmund Bacon's dynamic twentieth-century interpretation of Penn's grid, many have built upon and embellished Penn's germinal plan for a healthy, safe, and prosperous city.

Generations of Philadelphians expanded upon Penn's original concepts. Fairmount Park, a 9,200-acre park stitched through 63 neighborhoods in the city, was officially founded in 1855 with the purchase of Lemon Hill, an estate northwest of the current location of the Philadelphia Museum of Art. The impetus for the park grew out of repeated epidemics of yellow fever—thought at the time to be waterborne—that began to plague the city in the 1790s. In response, the city first commissioned Benjamin Latrobe's handsome 1801 Centre Square pump house, followed by Fredrick Graff's aforementioned Fairmount Water Works. These were both groundbreaking municipal designs that heralded the city's confidence in its engineering and artistic capabilities. To ensure a continuing supply of clean water for the burgeoning industrial city, civic leaders began the acquisition of private estates and industrial sites on both sides of the Schuylkill River above the falls at Fairmount following the Act of Consolidation of 1854, creating the centerpiece of today's sprawling park—a healthy lung in the heart of the expanding city.

The Centennial Exhibition held in Fairmount Park in 1876 significantly affected the landscaping and planning of the park while serving as an international debut for America, much as the 2008 Beijing Olympic Games were for China. The Centennial drew nearly ten million people to Philadelphia from across the country and around the world. It solidified Philadelphia's, and by extension America's, reputation as a global player in the new industrial order, with the massive Corliss steam engine and Alexander Graham Bell's telephone both being introduced at the fair. Among the two hundred or so buildings on the Centennial grounds stood thirty-four designed by a young German immigrant engineer named Herman J. Schwarzmann. Designed as an art museum, his Memorial Hall, a highly influential building in its day, is one of the few remaining structures from the fair and reflects a shift away from the city's confidence in local design talent. More Ringstrasse than Broad Street, the stolid imported classicism of Schwarzmann's Memorial Hall contrasted greatly with Frank Furness's and George Hewitt's contemporaneously exuberant mixture of Thoreau-inspired naturalism and industrialism at the Pennsylvania Academy of Fine Arts on North Broad Street. To this day, we Philadelphians tend to favor outside talent over local architects for our major commissions.[12]

It could be argued that the great French architect Paul Philippe Cret did more to affect the physical face of Philadelphia than any other architect or planner besides William Penn. While Edmund Bacon, a Philadelphian, is credited with the comprehensive replanning of the city after World War II, it was in fact Cret, who taught architecture at the University of Pennsylvania from 1903 to 1937, who largely created our image of modern Philadelphia.[13] Cret was a member of the city's Art Jury, the predecessor to the current Art Commission, and oversaw the design of many municipal works. His work took him from Texas to Washington, D.C., and he designed many of the landmarks of early twentieth-century Philadelphia. His oeuvre ran the gamut from railroad bridges to power plants to parks—a seamless merging of industrial might and urbanity. His remarkable legacy includes Rittenhouse Square, arguably the finest public space in America; the Benjamin Franklin Bridge, the longest bridge span of its day; the Federal Reserve Bank on Chestnut Street; the Barnes Foundation in Merion; and the gracious Rodin Museum on the Benjamin Franklin Parkway, the finest composition of building, garden, and site design in the city.[14]

The 1927 Wissahickon Memorial Bridge at Henry Avenue demonstrates the power and poetry of Cret's contributions to place-making in Philadelphia. Soaring above Wissahickon Creek and Lincoln Drive with a transcendent arched masonry span, the bridge is both ancient and modern. The bridge commands the gorge as if a fragment of a Roman aqueduct were enlarged to contemporary scale and stretched tautly

Figure 21. Wissahickon Memorial Bridge, Paul Cret, 1927. Photo by Harris Steinberg. Courtesy of Harris Steinberg.

across the creek to facilitate car passage across the Wissahickon. At Henry Avenue, Cret combined elegance and technical brio in a timeless contribution to Philadelphia's promise, unmatched by the aesthetically challenged and traffic engineering-led Streets Department of today.[15] Cret's Philadelphia was a sophisticated mixture of fine design and daily life—of urban planning and an attention to craft and detail that gave Philadelphia an unsurpassed quality in the public realm. He combined elegance with human scale; he created places of lasting beauty and significance that are landmarks to this day.

In many ways, Edmund Bacon assumed the Cret mantle just as Philadelphia was unknowingly entering a long period of decline. The Better Philadelphia Exhibition of 1947, with its mesmerizing images of the Philadelphia of tomorrow, created a public appetite for modernization. It was a potent planning vision for the future, sweeping the city clean of industrial blight and introducing gleaming modern office towers where elevated rail tracks stood. It included a revitalized waterfront where docks and industry crammed the shores of the Delaware, and planted the seeds for what would become the iconic Society Hill greenway system. The genius of the exhibition was that it connected citizens to planning, with students' design ideas figuring prominently, and set the stage for what many believe to be Philadelphia's golden age of planning with Bacon as planning director.

Bacon rode a wave of post-World War II optimism and propelled Philadelphia planning to the center of the national dialogue at a time when a convergence of federal urban renewal and highway funds, a postwar baby and housing boom, a surging economy, and powerful, prewar, European-based planning philosophies were irrevocably reshaping the American urban and suburban landscapes.[16] He was part of what became known as the "Philadelphia School," centered on the University of Pennsylvania's Graduate School of Fine Arts and its dean, G. Holmes Perkins, who established Penn's planning department in 1951.[17] The Philadelphia School was a dazzling constellation of design and planning talent brought to Penn by Perkins—Louis Kahn, Robert Venturi, Denise Scott Brown, Romaldo Giurgola, Herbert Gans, Ian McHarg, Robert Geddes, among others—who placed Philadelphia at the heart of America's planning debate.

A View from Afar

In 1959, when Ed Bacon, as executive director of the Philadelphia City Planning Commission, peered over the horizon and wrote "Philadelphia in the Year 2009," he did not see the warning signs just beyond the bend—the end of the dominance of the industrial North, the impact of the Federal Aid Highway Act of 1956 on cities and their surrounding regions, and the gathering social and cultural upheavals of the 1960s. From the vantage point of 1959, in an era flush with federal urban renewal funds and America having emerged as a superpower, Bacon's view of the future was rosy. He saw a city in 2009 that had been transformed by federal investments in a 1976 Philadelphia World's Fair, making the city free of blight and slums, full of clean industry, and connected to its region with efficient traffic and transportation systems.

Philadelphia in 2009 is a very different city from the one that Bacon imagined in 1959.

Blight dominates the city's post-industrial core today and diminishes its soul. Burdensome wage taxes, along with significant challenges within the public education system, continue to drive the middle class from the city despite a resurgence of young graduates and empty-nesters repopulating Center City and its adjoining neighborhoods. The city's business-tax structure depresses innovation and entrepreneurialism, and it has failed significantly to capitalize on the intellectual capital generated by its great research universities. Industry packed up and left town ages ago, first going south for cheaper labor, larger building sites, and greater highway access, before heading overseas. And as the city stopped manufacturing things, its tax base shrank. We Philadelphians inherited a city planned in 1960 for 2.5 million people that today is barely holding at 1.45 million. Today, a host of nonprofits and special service organizations provide routine city services.

And yet, much of Bacon's physical vision from the postwar period has come to pass—demonstrating the power of his planning vision and salesmanship and the appetite of the times for large-scale urban renewal. A critical examination of his work is called for, as his planning legacy is a checkered one in which sweeping, grand physical plans often trumped subtlety, nuance, social values, and human scale.

In "Philadelphia in the Year 2009," Bacon presciently predicts the return to downtown living. Today, Logan Square, Old City, Society Hill, and Rittenhouse Square are just a few of the thriving compact, urbane residential sections of downtown Philadelphia. Indeed, a revived Center City has recently leaped across its historic boundaries of Vine and South Streets and is now defined by the edgier boundaries of Girard Avenue at the north and Washington Avenue at the south. Bacon also presaged the completion of the Schuylkill River trail from the Art Museum to Lombard Street that has catalyzed development along the east bank of the river. His vision for the Center City Commuter Tunnel connecting the former Reading and Pennsylvania Railroads under downtown Philadelphia is a marvel of engineering and transportation planning. Completed in 1984, the tunnel represents the last great work of municipal infrastructure in Philadelphia.

However, Bacon's idea of an enclosed suburban-style shopping center atop the rail tunnel he describes in "Philadelphia in the Year 2009" was realized as the Gallery at Market East, and it is not a success from an urban planning or civic design perspective. Rather than serve as a catalyst for the revitalization of the famed shopping street, it helped destroy the life of the street by bringing activity inside the Gallery and off the sidewalks. Today, Market Street struggles, and the story of the Gallery is a cautionary tale about mega-projects. The Gallery reminds us that building scale, sidewalk treatment, and attention to the quality of the pedestrian realm matter greatly in the civic life of cities.

Another large-scale planning project that Bacon supported was the creation of Independence Mall, the three-block expanse to the north of Independence Hall between Fifth and Sixth Streets. While he did not originate the idea, it figures prominently in "Philadelphia in the Year 2009." Many critics of the time, including Lewis Mumford, saw the creation of the mall as nothing more than baroque foolishness. Indeed, the late Anthony N. B. Garvan, former chair of the American Civilization Department at the University of Pennsylvania, decried the creation of the mall, which demolished many significant Old City historical structures, saying that "they took one of the largest buildings in the colonies and made it a paperweight on the desk of Independence National Historic Park."[18] Today, despite over $300 million in improvements to the landscaping and visitor center following a master plan from 1998, the mall remains a scale-less civic no-man's land.

Bacon imagined the Delaware waterfront as a new recreational area, only to cut it off from the city with the tourniquet of I-95. He foresaw the rise of the leisure class and predicted the importance of cultural tourism for the local economy. He saw the gleaming new office towers of Penn Center where elevated train lines once separated the northern and southern sections of west Market Street in an attempt to create Philadelphia's version of Rockefeller Center. In retrospect, however, the march to develop west Market Street with office buildings started the current trend of depopulating older office buildings when we build new ones, as we are no longer adding new jobs to the local economy. Instead, the Center City office market has become a kind of shell game for office space with many older, class-B office towers rehabilitated as residential and hotel towers. Finally, Bacon created Society Hill, one of urban America's most successful downtown revitalization efforts despite being clouded by the displacement of poor, minority Americans.

Bacon fought, unsuccessfully, for the Crosstown Expressway that would have placed South Street below grade, like the current expressway at Vine Street, and connected I-95 to the unbuilt Cobbs Creek Express-way. The project created a heated civic backlash, driven by the new residents of Society Hill, and it brought Bacon head-to-head with another Philadelphia planning legend, the young Denise Scott Brown, in Philadelphia's version of the Robert Moses–Jane Jacobs battle between top-down power and bottom-up grassroots planning and activism.[19] In the end, South Street won.

In many ways, Bacon was swimming against a tide that could not be held back with physical planning alone. He was a big thinker in an era when "big ideas" were de rigueur in planning—the International Style of Le Corbusier and Walter Gropius having a clear impact on his comprehensive design hand. At the same time, Bacon was distinctly Philadelphian. He had a complex relationship with Philadelphia's physical history, editing the grid when needed and using the great organizing axes of Broad and Market Streets as well as the Benjamin Franklin Parkway to implement his vision of a modern Center City Philadelphia. Bacon wrestled with William Penn's grid in ways that were often not successful—the scale-less caverns of Penn Center and the deadening streetscape of the Gallery shopping complex are two such examples. And while the greenways of Society Hill are among some of the more successful human-scaled walks in the city, they display an edited and calcified "colonial" Williamsburg chill in an area devoid of commercial and multilayered historic vibrancy.

Bacon's "Philadelphia in the Year 2009" reflects an optimism in planning and physical development as a tonic for the future that seems almost quaint today.

Planning in Exile

Following Edmund Bacon's retirement from the Philadelphia City Planning Commission in 1970, the city sank into a 37-year planning slumber.[20] City government leaders confronted the impact of white flight, disinvestment in the urban core, shrinking tax base, rise in poverty, crime and drugs, and failing public schools while enduring rolling economic and energy crises. Simultaneously, the public became wary of the big planning ideas of the urban renewal period in which Bacon practiced. Large-scale private property condemnation, displacement of poor and minority communities in the name of progress, and highways that cut neighborhoods in half each caused an urban planning backlash from the citizens of Philadelphia. Most telling was the cancer of surface parking lots that began to creep across the urban landscape—the telltale sign of land clearance, displacement, and unrealized grand projects.

Big-idea planning had bumped up against social, cultural, economic, and global forces.

It is noteworthy that in "Philadelphia in the Year 2009," Bacon predicted the importance of cultural tourism to the region's economy, imagining that a federally funded World's Fair in 1976 would not only transform Philadelphia but establish the city as a leader in this rising economic sector. In actuality, the Fair never happened, and the Bicentennial celebration of 1976 was an anemic summer of tall ships, fireworks, and a giant cake donated by Sara Lee at Memorial Hall in Fairmount Park—a far cry from the transformative urban planning makeover that Bacon hoped for. And yet, ironically, it would be cultural tourism that Mayor Edward G. Rendell would use to attempt to save the city from bankruptcy in the 1990s. In doing so, he began to dismantle the city's fabled planning heritage.

As creative and tenacious as Rendell was in bringing Philadelphia fiscally and psychologically back from the edge of disaster, he often acted impulsively at the expense of the city's physical form.[21] Evidence includes the never built Simon Property Group's enclosed entertainment center, shopping mall, parking garage, and children's museum complex crammed onto Penn's Landing—topped with an ill-conceived river tram to Camden that was more marketing gimmick than urban transportation. Also, consider the Wal-Mart and Lowe's big box stores that *were* built on the Delaware River and the failed DisneyQuest project for an indoor theme park that left a gaping hole at Eighth and Market Streets (ironically, it was the site of the old Gimbels Department Store where the Better Philadelphia Exhibition was held). Each of these is an example of how economic development goals, in a desperate attempt to attract tourism dollars, repeatedly trumped comprehensive, thoughtful, and holistic physical planning.

The Kimmel Center for the Performing Arts at Broad and Spruce Streets, viewed by many as Rendell's crowning architectural achievement as mayor, suffers from a lack of cohesive planning and urban design principles. It does not contribute to its urban context with either human scale or civic gravitas. Rather, the Kimmel Center is a monument to political expediency and hubris. Eschewing the native design talent of Robert Venturi and Denise Scott Brown, who had been commissioned in 1987 to design a new home for the Philadelphia Orchestra, Rendell wrested the project from them when lead donor Sidney Kimmel objected to their design and brought in Argentine-born architect Rafael Viñoly. In 2001 Viñoly delivered a quarter-billion-dollar impenetrable, faceless, poorly built architectural folly that functions badly, both civically and acoustically. Indeed, the Kimmel Center, having finally retired its long-simmering construction debt in the summer of 2008, is now

Figure 22. Sara Lee Bicentennial cake, 1976. Photo by Harris Steinberg.
Courtesy of Harris Steinberg.

poised, only seven years after completion, to undergo a master planning makeover to better integrate it into the public life of the city.[22]

The impact of the Ed Rendell–John Street (Rendell's successor in the mayor's office) planning legacy is instructive. For while the two administrations (1991–2007) tried to advance projects designed to stimulate economic development, the projects were not planned within a larger context that accounted for the impact of development on traffic, transportation, pedestrians, stormwater management, or other urban, cultural, or natural systems. Public good was often sacrificed for private gain in the name of economic development. An outdated zoning code became the vehicle for bypassing the Philadelphia City Planning Commission, and so began the practice of Philadelphia City Council becoming the gatekeeper for development through a practice commonly referred to as "spot zoning," while the Zoning Board of Adjustment became the de facto planning authority.[23] Indeed, the reign of David Auspitz, best known for making cookies at the Reading Terminal Market, as chair of the Zoning Board under Mayor Street epitomized the depths to which public planning had devolved in Philadelphia by the turn of the twenty-first century. Auspitz, with no training in design or planning, repeatedly overstepped the bounds of his office and negotiated zoning agreements between developers and neighborhood groups that dictated choice of materials, heights of buildings, signage, and other amenities of the public realm that flew in the face of best planning practices.

During this time, the city's Historical Commission, the agency that oversees buildings placed on the Philadelphia Register of Historic Places, was used to advance questionable economic development projects and demolish historic fabric. Time and again, projects such as the demolition in 2000 of a row of important, historic townhouses on the 1600 block of Sansom Street highlight the precarious world of historic preservation during the Rendell and Street years. The developer of the Sansom Street project was *also* the chairman of the Historical Commission at the time—testament to a breach of ethical boundaries between government and the development community. And, despite the developer's promise to build a state-of-the-art automated parking garage on the site, the site remains today a ghostly surface parking lot.[24] Rendell and Street were killing the proverbial golden goose as they were destroying Philadelphia's ineffable sense of place and historic quality in the name of progress. In an attempt to save us, the mayors were demolishing a significant part of Philadelphia's character.

We Americans are noted for our voluntary civic associations, which we often create as ballast to the potential abuse of power. In early Philadelphia, voluntary public associations built Pennsylvania Hospital, created the first fire companies, and raised funds for the erection of the steeple of Christ Church. So it was at the end of the twentieth century, as Philadelphia struggled economically and socially to redefine itself within the challenges of a rapidly changing suburban age, that a number of forces conspired to provide counterweight to diminished city services and the shrinking reliance on physical planning as a tool for healthy city making.

As early as 1974, Philadelphia Green, a program of the Pennsylvania Horticultural Society, started a comprehensive urban greening program that developed and maintained community gardens and parks. It remains a national model in the urban revitalization movement. In the 1980s, groups like the Market Street East Improvement Association, a privately funded business improvement district headed by department store patriarch G. Stockton Strawbridge, and the Foundation for Architecture, which engaged in public education and advocacy for the built environment, helped focus attention on the need for oversight and protection of Philadelphia's public spaces and buildings. These groups, which were created and organized by civic and professional leaders, drew volunteers, advocates, and citizens into participating in the protection and enhancement of the public realm.

The Mural Arts Program, a model community development program with roots in an anti-graffiti network from 1984, has helped address the blight and crime that infect neighborhoods through arts education and civic engagement. The Reinvestment Fund (TRF), founded in 1985, became a national leader in financing neighborhood revitalization. Using place-based data to drive investments to underserved communities, TRF's pioneering community renewal and investment strategies are today used locally and nationwide.[25] The Center City District (CCD), founded in 1990, built upon the early success of the East Market Street Improvement District to create a Center City-wide business improvement district funded by property owners and dedicated to a clean and safe commercial area. The CCD's reach eventually included urban planning and implementation efforts such as streetscape improvements and visions for the future of the Benjamin Franklin Parkway.

The Design Advocacy Group (DAG) of Philadelphia arose out the ashes of the defunct Foundation for Architecture in 2002 and became a rising voice for civic design and planning excellence. Other important advocacy voices and agencies included the Preservation Alliance for Greater Philadelphia, which promoted responsible adaptive reuse of historic buildings and sites; the Society Created to Reduce Urban Blight (SCRUB), which fought the proliferation of billboards; PennFuture, a statewide environmental and economic advocacy organization; and the Zoning Matters Coalition, which along with the Business Industry Association of Philadelphia, led a successful zoning code reform movement resulting in the creation of the Zoning Code Commission that began an effort to rewrite the city's outdated code in 2007.

These nongovernmental associations were empowered, in part, by declining city services and public resources. From multiple perspectives, they saw a threat to the quality of Philadelphia's built environment and organized, with the aid of the local philanthropic and business communities, to help change the public discussion about how we use limited public resources within the public realm. They were joined by a plethora of zoning and development savvy civic associations that were acting as frontline warriors in an increasingly pitched battle with the Rendell and Street administrations and members of City Council, who saw development, any development, as vital to the future of the city. Neighborhood groups were being asked to negotiate with developers for zoning approval, while the City Planning Commission had been largely silenced. Supported by strong opinion and editorial voices in the *Philadelphia Inquirer* and the *Philadelphia Daily News,* this group of planners-in-exile began to frame the civic dialogue around the need for sound planning and sustained urban change.[26] It is perhaps ironic, then, that by this point Ed Bacon himself had joined the legion of voices calling for attention to planning and design—playing an active role in resisting the redesign of Independence Mall and publicly decrying the sanitizing of LOVE Park as the Street administration removed skateboarding from the city center.

Civic Visioning as Public Dialogue: A New Model

PennPraxis was created in 2001 as a nonprofit organization supporting the mission of the University of Pennsylvania School of Design. Established by PennDesign dean Gary Hack, PennPraxis was seen as an umbrella clinical practice that would facilitate faculty and student collaboration on real-world problem solving in the fields of architecture, landscape architecture, city and regional planning, historic preservation, and fine arts. One of its objectives was civic engagement. As the founding director of PennPraxis in early 2002, I walked into a perfect storm of heightened civic interest in the built environment, years of pent-up frustration with failed development proposals, and a politically weakened Philadelphia City Planning Commission.

In late 2002, the Simon Property Group withdrew its proposal to the Penn's Landing Corporation for an entertainment center along the Delaware River at the foot of Market Street, leaving city officials anxious to court new developers. Against the backdrop of, by some accounts, 14 unsuccessful attempts to fully develop Penn's Landing's 39 original acres over 25 years, PennPraxis partnered with the editorial board of the *Philadelphia Inquirer*, the University of Pennsylvania Center for School Study Councils, and the Design Advocacy Group. Together, they designed and produced a series of public forums to focus attention on the future of Penn's Landing. The 2003 Penn's Landing Forums provided a forum for civic visioning, as they sought to educate the citizens of Philadelphia as to what was possible in waterfront planning, create principles that would guide development, and put forth design images based on those principles.[27]

The Penn's Landing Forums were successful. They halted the typical "pay-to-play" politics of Philadelphia development and raised public awareness about achieving world-class excellence on the waterfront. They demonstrated that cities around the world were reclaiming their waterfronts with a rich array of public spaces balancing public good and private gain. The forums also highlighted Philadelphia's potential to become a city of choice in the burgeoning knowledge economy. Modeled, in part, on the 2002 "Listening to the City" forums in New York City in the wake of the September 11, 2001, attack on the World Trade Center, the Penn's Landing Forums tapped into a public thirst for creating a public conversation about the future of Philadelphia's physical form. The success of the forums created the model for subsequent collaborations led by PennPraxis around often-contentious planning and urban design topics such as public school design and casinos in Philadelphia.

The Penn's Landing process was based on respectful public dialogue between citizens, experts, and elected officials, and leveraged the power of the press as a means for open and transparent public discussion about development in the city. Harris Sokoloff, director of the University of Pennsylvania's Center for School Study Councils, provided the expertise in trained public deliberation. Chris Satullo, then editorial board editor of the *Philadelphia Inquirer*, ensured that the editorial and commentary pages of the paper were engaged. Citizens, experts, policy makers, and implementers worked together to craft a vision for the future. This was new for Philadelphia.

Development pressures along the Delaware River in the areas abutting Center City continued to mount. While public Philadelphia had put significant energy into trying to develop a largely inaccessible Penn's Landing, a sliver of public land across 380-feet of interstate highway and city streets, the market was beginning to tell a different story. While much fine-grained residential rehabilitation had been taking place in areas such as Old City, Northern Liberties, Queen Village, and Bella Vista for quite some time, development was now pushing the edges of Center City

north into traditionally working-class Fishtown and south toward Pennsport below Washington Avenue. The city's 1998 ten-year property tax
abatement was expanded in 2000 to include new residential construction. This abatement program, in conjunction with historically low interest rates, was driving a condominium boom in Center City and along the
Delaware Riverfront.

In 2004, the Pennsylvania State Legislature passed the Pennsylvania
Race Horse Development and Gaming Act—Act 71—enabling 14 slot-
machine parlors to be built in the commonwealth. Two 5,000-slot-
machine stand-alone casinos would be located in Philadelphia. With siting of the proposed casinos determined by the state-appointed Gaming
Control Board, the fate of Delaware Riverfront development was once
more a topic of citywide concern. Four developers proposed casinos
along the Delaware from Fishtown to Pennsport. Again, PennPraxis
entered the public discussion, this time with the *Philadelphia Daily News.*
Working with Sandra Shea of the paper's editorial board, PennPraxis
tested the physical implications of Act 71 on Philadelphia, the largest
city in the country to see the impact of gambling on this scale. Respond-
ing to the lack of public input or dialogue about how to integrate these
facilities into the structure of the city, PennPraxis and the *Daily News*
hosted a student-design competition at PennDesign and a series of public forums called "Slots and the City," beginning in February 2005. In
partnership with the Design Advocacy Group and public radio station
WHYY, PennPraxis and the *Daily News* convened a public forum on
casino design at the Pennsylvania Convention Center that drew more
than 600 people in May 2006. The goal was to push the state to adopt
progressive design guidelines for urban casinos.[28]

Against this backdrop—the combined potential threats of the casinos
and unchecked condominium and large-scale big box retail development—local civic organizations became increasingly alarmed at the
pace and quality of development along the central Delaware. Traffic was
worsening along Columbus Boulevard/Delaware Avenue, and communities were experiencing increased stormwater flooding as large parking
lots serving regional retail centers now covered parts of the area. In
2006, Governor Ed Rendell and Pennsylvania State Senator Vincent J.
Fumo proposed a moratorium on riparian development rights along the
Delaware to help alleviate the crush of development. This move was
followed by Philadelphia Councilman Frank DiCicco's call for the
establishment of a new nonprofit entity to guide the planning and development of the central Delaware. While it was clear that planning was
sorely needed for this stretch of the river, the public decried the idea as
yet another old-style, Philadelphia backroom development deal.[29] Seeking a neutral party to convene a citywide planning process for the

central Delaware, Councilman Frank DiCicco's office, whose First Councilmanic District includes much of the historic river wards, approached PennPraxis about leading a planning process for the central Delaware. PennPraxis responded with a project that built on the success of the Penn's Landing Forums and the Slots and the City project.

The aim of the PennPraxis project for the central Delaware was to restore public trust around the design and implementation of a waterfront plan. The project was funded by a $1.6 million grant from the William Penn Foundation. A 46-member advisory group, chaired by executive director of the Philadelphia City Planning Commission Janice Woodcock, provided project oversight with 15 civic associations represented on the advisory group. The project area stretched across seven miles of waterfront from Allegheny Avenue at the north to Oregon Avenue at the south, the river at the east, and I-95 at the west. Covering more than 1,100 acres of largely former industrial land at the river's edge, the project captured the public's imagination because of the importance of the Delaware River in the collective memory of the citizens of Philadelphia, along with the threat of the casinos planned in the project area.

PennPraxis conducted extensive outreach over the next thirteen months with waterfront walks, public forums, presentation of best planning practices from across the country, a design workshop with international architects and planners, and more than 200 public, civic association, and stakeholder meetings. In partnership with the Penn Project for Civic Engagement, PennPraxis worked with over 4,000 Philadelphians in a robust conversation about the future of the central Delaware. The project was the largest public planning process in the history of the city in terms of civic engagement. Nearly 80,000 more participated on-line through a website, PlanPhilly.com, an experiment in alternative new media coverage.[30]

The result was a set of civic principles that became the foundation for the "Civic Vision for the Central Delaware."[31] The principles stated that the vision must reconnect the city to the river's edge by restoring the street grid between the neighborhoods adjoining I-95 and the river. They admonished us to honor the Delaware River as a significant natural regional resource, which plays a vital role in the economic, social, historical, and commercial life of the region. The principles declared that development along the river must be ecologically responsible and sustainable. They promoted a 24-hour livable and walkable community along the river's edge that would create a vibrant civic life. They exhorted public officials to take the long view and not be seduced by short-term gains, but rather create an elegant infrastructure that the city can comfortably grow into over the next fifty years. The principles fur-

Figure 23. Waterfront public forum, Furness High School, 20 February 2007. Photo by Matt Golas/PlanPhilly. Courtesy of PennPraxis.

ther declared that the public good must be protected by ensuring that the riverfront accommodates people from all walks of life. And, finally, they told us to make the vision about Philadelphia and not fall into the trap of importing design solutions from other cities. Philadelphians were tired after years of laboring under "Inner Harbor envy," in which we were told that we had to have a waterfront like Baltimore's in order to be a success.

The civic engagement process was often loud, raucous, and not always polite. During the planning, two casinos were granted gaming licenses for waterfront sites, and the resultant civic backlash threatened to overturn the process at several key junctures. Yet, through the haze of conflicting opinions and, at times, bellicose voices, we were able to arrive at common ground. One such example was the evening of 20 February 2007. That night, more than 300 Philadelphians crowded into the ground floor lunchroom of Furness High School in South Philadelphia.

Many of the people in attendance that evening were members of the International Longshoremen's Association, Local 1291 (ILA). The ILA members were concerned with the future of the Port of Philadelphia and their jobs—fearing that casinos and port uses were antithetical. Members threatened to disrupt a community meeting that was intended to help create civic principles for waterfront development. The union members were angry that Governor Rendell had refused to meet with them in Harrisburg earlier that day, and they used the civic visioning process as a platform to express their anger. With local media present, the union members accused PennPraxis and the process of disrespecting the views of the working port. With the help of Jim Paylor, national vice president of the ILA, and Harris Sokoloff of the Penn Project for Civic Engagement, tempers were leveled and the meeting became productive.[32]

The civic vision we arrived at was shaped by the public's values and principles. The demand was there for an extension of William Penn's signature urban street grid and open space network across the Delaware riverside's industrial lands. It was a process also informed by national and international best practices in urban design, transportation, ecology, and economics.[33] The process itself grew from the public's need for participation in the design, urban planning, and development of the city, while raising concerns among members of the city's development establishment who were accustomed to bending the system to their will.[34] The visioning process described here became a symbol for the growing call to reform a broken planning system in Philadelphia, and it points the way forward as we think about the city's pathway to the future.

A Bridge to the Future

Michael A. Nutter won the Philadelphia mayoral election of 2007 with an ambitious agenda that placed city planning at the heart of his economic development strategy. He hired an accomplished group of planning professionals, starting with Andrew Altman, former planning director of Washington, D.C., as deputy mayor for planning and economic development. Rina Cutler, former deputy secretary of the Pennsylvania Department of Transportation, was made deputy mayor for transportation and infrastructure, and Alan Greenberger, a cofounder of the Design Advocacy Group of Philadelphia, was appointed the new executive director of the Philadelphia City Planning Commission. Nutter also tapped Mark Alan Hughes, a senior fellow at the Fels Institute of Government at the University of Pennsylvania, as director of the Office of Sustainability, an innovative new cross-agency office designed to integrate environmentally sustainable city practices ranging from recycling to land use to transportation.[35] And the Zoning Code Commission, approved by public ballot in 2007 after a successful advocacy campaign by the Zoning Matters Coalition, quickly began the long overdue process of rewriting the city's nearly 50-year-old zoning code. Mayor Nutter pledged to restore openness, transparency, and credibility to government, and it was a favorable time, once again, for planning in Philadelphia.

From where we sit today, Nutter's challenge is to instill confidence in the business and development community that combining planning and economic development under one deputy mayor has real merit. Indeed, the two activities should go hand in hand. Public resources are slim, and the path to success is based on strong mayoral leadership and sustained civic advocacy for sound planning principles. Nutter came to power with significant political capital. He was elected on a reform platform reminiscent of the 1950s reform era, which brought Edmund Bacon's planning leadership to the fore. Nutter's placement of planning and urban design at the heart of his urban agenda recalls the days when Bacon's Philadelphia City Planning Commission was a national model.

However, the differences between the Philadelphia of the 1950s and today are striking.

We have challenges we did not have then. We do not have the economic base, population, or federal resources to engage in the kind of large-scale planning that Bacon led.[36] Nor does the public have an appetite for Bacon's brand of top-down leadership and big-idea planning. We are a pluralistic society facing significant economic, social, and environmental challenges. We have the legacy of misguided urban renewal that led to racial strife. Our taxes hinder economic growth. Construction costs and union labor rates depress the quality of development in Philadelphia. The state of public schools continues to force middle-class citizens to leave the city for the suburbs. Most (80 percent) of the population do not have a college degree. Nearly 25 percent live below the poverty line. The hollowed and blighted postindustrial urban landscape is slow to heal. From a regional perspective, we have failed to understand that the fate of the region and the future of the city are intertwined. Greater Philadelphia is currently a fractured collection of competing counties and municipalities, with a patchwork quilt of inefficient and costly transportation and land use policies. Mayor Nutter has given early indications that he will start a regional dialogue such as Mayor Richard Daley's successful caucus in metropolitan Chicago. This is a healthy sign that is in step with the Brookings Institution's call for a quality-of-life, place-based metropolitan agenda.[37] Projects such as depressing I-95 at Market Street to reconnect the city with its riverfront must be part of a regional agenda for federal investment. These types of transformational projects will ensure that Philadelphia, and its region, are competitive in the innovation economy of the twenty-first century.

On the positive side of the ledger, Philadelphia has unrivaled academic and health care institutions—the "eds and meds" sector—which are significant economic and social assets. The cultural resources of the city are very strong. We have an excellent, albeit traditionally underfunded and poorly-kept, regional public transportation system. We have noteworthy parks and open spaces, which also are underfunded, and we have a walkable downtown that is the envy of other American cities. Residential and commercial urban development is popping up along the Delaware River in traditionally industrial Northern Liberties and the working-class communities of Fishtown and Kensington, while Center City is experiencing a renaissance with young people and empty-nesters flocking back to the city. Car sharing is taking off in Philadelphia and transit ridership is up. We have affordable housing prices and a wealth of sturdy housing stock. We have history and historical building fabric that is second to none. These are assets that Ed Bacon appreciated.

The true test of the Nutter administration will be how successful it is in both molding the current political system to its good-government vision *and* attracting a new breed of politician into the political system. Will we see the end of ward politics and domination by a single-party political machine? Will we see the end of the tradition of councilmanic prerogative, which all too often turns Philadelphia planning efforts over into a land of feudal, zero-sum gains? These are two political stumbling blocks to progressive planning reform that must be tackled in order to ensure that positive political change will stick.

Can we afford to invest in infrastructure that will position Philadelphia as a city of choice in the new millennium? Today we live in a world of shrinking resources with an $11 trillion national debt and a subprime mortgage crisis that has crippled the housing industry and caused the largest federal financial bailout in U.S. history. Crushing energy costs are forcing the imperative to build smartly and sustainably.[38] How will we pay for the public works, mass transportation, parks, and open spaces that are the hallmarks of a thriving city, which act as beacons for private investment and innovation? The real question is this: can Philadelphia afford not to make these investments?

Philadelphia's fortunes were rising from 1682 through the 1950s, in large part because of investments in the physical infrastructure that make Philadelphia a great place today. Our vast park system, public spaces, subway and rail systems, civic buildings, recreational riverfronts, and public works are a legacy that younger cities in this country cannot replicate. We know that cities of the future will attract and retain the workers of the next economy in large part because of the quality of life that these civic amenities afford. Cities that will attract the workers of tomorrow will be the cities with the greatest street life, active waterfronts, excellent cultural opportunities, first-rate public education, world-class transportation systems, and thriving opportunities for career advancement. They will be cities where people can raise families without fleeing to the exurbs for schools or because of crime or lack of green space. They will be cities that smartly invest in people, ecologically responsible infrastructure, sound housing, transportation, and new economies in a constant state of renewal. Smart cities of the future will be regional centers that share with, rather than steal from, neighboring counties and states. Smart and successful cities of tomorrow will be investing in new ideas and new technologies while educating the workforce of tomorrow. Marshaling the federal, state, regional, and local resources to assure continued investment in the public realm is imperative to the future health of the city and the region. A clear and consistent regional message that focuses public resource allocation on maintaining a compact, interconnected city and region is the goal.

Along the Delaware River waterfront, where PennPraxis has spent the last three years working to build both a civic vision and the civic advocacy infrastructure to maintain pressure on public officials, the future looks promising. In June 2006, Mayor Nutter embraced the Civic Vision for the Central Delaware as the city's template for the future riverfront growth.[39] Significantly, the mayor has reformed the Penn's Landing Corporation, the nearly forty-year-old public-benefit corporation that had lost the public trust for developing the waterfront. The Penn's Landing Corporation was reborn on 30 January 2009, as an open and transparent Delaware River Waterfront Corporation entrusted with creating world-class public spaces. Early actions we expect to see along the river include an interim zoning overlay based on the Civic Vision for the Central Delaware, providing public access to the riverfront. Also, a master plan for the seven miles of the Delaware that will establish the new street grid and open space network and long-term zoning that will codify the civic vision are anticipated.[40] This is a picture of a government in service to and in dialogue with the people—the democratic ideal in the form of city planning.

Philadelphia 2059: A New Hope

Today is a moment of profound opportunity to reshape the development and planning environment in Philadelphia. We have the chance to move away from development based on political horse-trading and expediency toward one of holistic, civic value-based planning. It is a chance to engage the citizens of Philadelphia in remaking a city that was planned for far more people than currently inhabit it, stimulate techno-logical and entrepreneurial invention, and reform a broken planning system. The public sector and civic community support for the central Delaware Riverfront civic visioning process proves that there is a strong appetite for positive partnership between the public and government in planning and development reform. Mayor Nutter and his team will be well advised to continue constructive engagement with the citizens of Philadelphia in shaping the future physical form of the city. Creating a healthy and lasting framework for growth need not depend on "big bang" projects such as casinos, convention centers, stadiums, Olympic Games, or world's fairs. It takes smart, long-term economic, social, and infrastructural investments, ensuring the growth of public resources for the city's next generation. In the end, it is about the triumph of a pro-gressive planning process that includes citizens.

The future health of Philadelphia rests on our not being contented.[41] Complacency makes us all complicit in the reality we have inherited. The city has strong physical, civic, cultural, and institutional bones, but has been made sick by a sell-off of the public realm to the highest bidder. While Nutter has promised a "new day and a new way," Philadelphians must remain vigilant and hold the administration accountable. Ongoing and sustained public dialogue is crucial to the decisions we make today, decisions that will determine the future health of the city and region.

It is impossible to know what Philadelphia will be like in 2059, but we do know the challenges:

- Reinventing Philadelphia as a center of technological innovation and entrepreneurialism—creating an economy based on new ideas, welcoming new people and new investments to Philadelphia.
- Investing in education that creates wealth across all sectors of our economy and across all social classes.
- Meeting the moral imperative of our age to design with ecological responsibility in mind.

How we account for shrinking resources like fossil fuels, federal funding, and transportation dollars while also capitalizing on our compact urban form to build a city that is sustainable regionally, economically, socially, culturally, and physically: *this* will be the metric by which future genera-tions will judge us.

To accomplish these goals, we must:

- Create an open and accessible business climate that rewards innovation and capitalizes on the new knowledge and intellectual assets within our world-class universities and health care institutions.
- Make our public schools centers of excellence that prepare students to be contributing members of society.
- Fight the scourges of blight, drugs, crime, and violence that plague our postindustrial urban core and blunt our civic psyche.
- Retain and rebuild the middle class with good jobs, safe neighborhoods, low taxes, and a high level of city services.
- Attract and retain the best and the brightest to continue reinvigorating Philadelphia economically, culturally, and politically.
- Invest in ecologically responsible infrastructure and clean energy that smartly manage stormwater, filters pollutants, reduce greenhouse gases, enhance public transportation, and reduce our dependency on automobiles.
- Position Philadelphia as a thriving regional hub within the dense northeast megalopolis that stretches from Boston to Washington.

To accomplish these goals, we must develop an effective framework for public decision making about the future of the physical city that is drawn from an ongoing civic conversation informed by best practices and lessons learned nationally, internationally, and historically. We must hone our civic visioning skills in order to build capacity for our citizenry to offer informed advice to our elected and appointed officials, as we create a vision for the future based on shared values and intelligent choices. This takes a commitment to sustained and respectful civic dialogue.

Here, then, is my hope and my vision of Philadelphia in 2059—a thriving city within a strong region that places public health, safety, and welfare at the heart of city making.

Philadelphia in 2059 is a healthy city. We have tackled poor air quality through sound public policy, such as allowing ships to plug into electric power sources while at the port. Diminished dependence on fossil fuels was accomplished through strong investment in public transportation and clean, renewable energy. Rising fuel costs spurred ecologically sound development around existing public transportation corridors such as the subway stops at Broad Street and Spring Garden, Fairmount, and Girard Avenues. Automobile dependence was reduced through collecting tolls on the Schuylkill Expressway and I-95, all while investing those funds in a world-class regional transportation system.

We have active and safe commercial street life, as our walkable, people-scaled streets and sidewalks have reinvigorated the neighborhoods around our existing transit hubs. Philadelphia's original electric streetcar suburbs were perfectly positioned for a post-fossil fuel age. We manage stormwater effectively, using gray water to sustain a heat-reducing tree canopy with bio-swales that filter pollutants and keep our rivers and watersheds clean and healthy. New development is held to high-performance design standards, using materials of lasting consequence, green roofs, recycled products, clean energy, and pervious pavement that absorbs rain water. Eschewing fads and fashion, our buildings are designed with adaptive reuse in mind. And our green spaces are part of a working network of green infrastructure that reduces flooding and provides tidal wetlands, absorbing storm surges and rising sea levels along the Schuylkill and Delaware Rivers and their tributaries. We successfully met the moral imperative of the age to design smart and live well within the bounds of natural systems. The Delaware River is part of a 300-mile watershed, and nature knows no political boundaries.

Philadelphia of 2059 is a prosperous city because we are harnessing the tremendous intellectual and economic energies within our world-class institutions, such as the University of Pennsylvania, Drexel University, Temple University, Thomas Jefferson Medical School, and Albert Einstein Medical School, to name just the top tier. Philadelphia's greatness in the ages of William Penn, Benjamin Franklin, and Paul Cret rested on a near-constant influx of new ideas, technologies, and people that fueled our economy through innovation and wealth creation. In 2009, we vowed never to let another ENIAC slip through our grasp, remembering how the electronic age bypassed its birthplace and enriched Boston and Silicon Valley. Instead, the Philadelphia of 2059 is sustained by new companies, with new money in the life sciences, bioengineering, pharmaceuticals, nanotechnologies, information technology, and sustainable design, to name just a few sectors. We have also been pioneers in renewable and clean energy technologies, due to initiatives begun by Governor Ed Rendell in the early years of the twenty-first century. We enjoy a healthy economy that is not dependent on tourism or service sector jobs. Our economy creates real value, adds real knowledge, and produces jobs, which translate into prosperity and wealth for the city and the region.

We are prosperous in 2059 because of serious attention given to place-based, quality-of-life investments made in the early years of the twenty-first century. Federal funding of urban infrastructure, such as the right-sizing of I-95 and the Schuylkill Expressway, including the elimination of portions of these highways, and creation of generous public spaces along the Delaware River over a depressed I-95 at Market Street positioned Philadelphia as a city of choice. A tax system that fosters technological and business entrepreneurialism attracts private investment in Philadelphia. An increased tax base provided public funds to restore our park and open space system with an infusion of capital and operating funds. Public investment created value and provided incentives for the private sector to continue to develop our "green country town" across the 135 square miles of the city in an ecologically responsible manner. Philadelphia once again embodies Penn's principle of the careful balance between public good and private gain as public investment in quality public space has stimulated private investment in high-quality development. The economic development principle that proximity to quality open space yields dividends for private sector development has been proved true.

We have created an excellent mass transportation system that combines the SEPTA and PATCO systems as they were in 2009 into a seamless regional transit network including water taxis, ferries, light rail, and new technologies. Transit expansion has included public transportation and pedestrian improvements along Roosevelt Boulevard that link Bucks County with Center City; additional subway stops along West Market Street; extension of the Broad Street subway to the Naval Business Center and southern New Jersey; a Delaware Riverfront transit system that is both land- and-water borne; and a cross-county transportation system that links the traditional hub and spoke rail system of the nineteenth century.[42] Edmund Bacon's ideas from the last century about the "post-petroleum city" were published and discussed. Regional transportation networks ensure that Philadelphia continues to grow smart, compact, and responsibly in the post-fossil fuel age.

We have density and vibrancy along the Benjamin Franklin Parkway because of the capping of the Vine Street Expressway and construction of apartments, hotels, and commercial development that fill the gaps along the Parkway between the Art Museum and cultural clusters. The Gallery at Market East was torn down and replaced with office, residential, and retail buildings that respect the street grid. Market Street has recaptured its bygone eminence as one of the world's great shopping streets with a rich array of shops, cafes, entertainment venues, and restaurants.[43] Wary of "big ideas" like the Gallery, Philadelphia's public realm flourishes as new development and investment demonstrate the sound urban principles of walkable sidewalks, active commercial uses at street level, and parking and service uses placed discretely away from main thoroughfares. New buildings respect the signature Philadelphia street grid, and historic building fabric is celebrated and integrated into contemporary development.

In 2059, Philadelphia is a welcoming and caring city—attracting and retaining new residents on all rungs of the economic ladder and across all ethnic and social boundaries as we provide humane care for the poor, the elderly, the uneducated, and those left behind. Advancing William Penn's legacy of toleration and compassion, we continue to be a place where differences are celebrated. Philadelphia's neighborhoods in 2059 include a healthy mix of income groups, ethnicities, and ages, with public policy ensuring that the elderly can age gracefully in their neighborhoods amid supportive and trusted surroundings. This is a place where the poor and the disadvantaged can lead quality lives integrated into the great social matrix of cosmopolitan Philadelphia. Philadelphia of 2059 is a city of healthy neighborhoods with strong community and civic organizations continuing to ensure that the city is run for and by the governed, as envisioned by William Penn.

Philadelphia of 2059 is a connected city in which business, cultural, nonprofit, academic, and political leadership join forces to create the atmosphere for dynamic civic and business growth and a plan for mutually supportive advancement. It is a vibrant city connected to a vibrant region through committed regional leadership and shared regional agendas for excellence in transportation, economics, housing, open space preservation, and sustainable design. Regional land use and transportation policies cross political boundaries, making Greater Philadelphia the center of a thriving regional network that stretches from Boston to Washington, with clean, frequent, high-speed train connections, excellent public health, and a dynamic, place-based economy. People flock to Philadelphia to live where an energetic city and region merge into an integrated and sustainable whole.

Philadelphia's political realm has broken the hands-off leadership style of "Quaker Philadelphia" and attracted the best and the brightest to high office, as traditional ward politics long ago gave way to nonpartisan, non-council-district-based governance. It is an artistic city, alive with public art, museums, and cafe life, and new forms of expression tested and spread throughout the city. It is a city that is proud of its past but not bound by it—one in which old Philadelphia buildings sit comfortably by ones that are new and experimental. Philadelphia of 2059 is once again at the forefront of American architecture and planning. Human-scaled design is evident, and plans are based on our local social and cultural values and principles, not abstract, imported planning theories. We use ecologically responsible materials and technologies and methods that come out of research in our great universities.

We have seen the integration of the stadiums along South Broad

Figure 24. Port Richmond railyard imagined as a dense urban extension of Philadelphia to the edge of the Delaware River. Drawing by WRT. Courtesy of PennPraxis.

Street with the Navy Yard and FDR Park as the centerpiece of a new district where Temple University and the University of Pennsylvania have satellite campuses, offering courses in sports medicine and sports management. The sea of surface parking lots in the area is filled in with dense mixed-use development. Pattison Avenue is a great cross-town avenue, linking the former petroleum tank farms on the lower Schuylkill with development along the Delaware—a transformation like the Landscape Park Duisburg Nord by Peter Latz in the Ruhr Valley in Germany. The former Port Richmond rail yards on the Delaware are a bustling, transit-accessible, high-tech business incubator providing green collar jobs for the neighborhoods of Kensington and Port Richmond. And the elevated train viaducts along Lehigh Avenue and the truncated main line of the Reading Railroad at Vine Street have been transformed into raised greenways and bikeways comparable to the Promenade Plantée in Paris and the High Line in New York City. Our vibrant riparian riverfront trails and greenways, stretching from the Poquessing Creek at Bensalem along the Delaware to the Schuylkill at Andorra, are alive with

Figure 25. Penn's Landing reimagined as a world class urban waterfront park. Drawing by WRT. Courtesy of PennPraxis.

marine and plant life that protect and preserve the delicate tidal ecosystems that nourish the city. We benefit today from the considered choices we made in 2009, choices that positioned Philadelphia for fifty years of active, contributing urban growth.

And so we return to 2009, remembering that fifty years is a blink of the eye in the sweep of human history. Human beings are social animals and cities are the fullest flowering expression of our collective human aspirations. In cities, the energies of millions of people collide to create new ideas, new forms of expression, and new knowledge. Cities are clusters of self-propelling energy that build upon strength and interconnectivity between people and institutions across time. They can be places of enormous beauty that uplift the human spirit.

Philadelphians in 2059 will still meet in coffeehouses and cafes as we have throughout our history. We will still walk our Philadelphia-scaled sidewalks and live in our Philadelphia-scaled brick row houses. Technology will make life easier for many and enable government to deliver services more efficiently. Primarily, though, it is up to all of us to imagine a city that is healthy, caring, welcoming, vital, alive, and prosperous, and to commit to ensuring that we achieve it through sound planning. We will not achieve this vision of a prosperous and sustainable future through cutthroat regional competition, small-minded local politics, or submission to a sense of desperation.

To achieve this future, we must adopt a "do-no-harm" policy when it comes to development and check all plans against sound principles of healthy urbanism—ensuring that the public good is balanced by private gain. Creating the atmosphere for innovation and wealth creation along with strong planning, progressive development policy, and enforcement will ensure that Philadelphia has a fighting chance. Philadelphia in 2059 will be prosperous only if we all contribute to making it happen, in a sustained effort to build on our assets and combine our strengths. Our potential lies in our capacity for reasoned dialogue, our history of cultivating new ideas, and the inspiring physical framework that reflects the values and spirit of William Penn. Nowhere is it written that Philadelphia has to be. It is up to all of its citizens to make sure that the city survives and fulfills William Penn's 1684 prayer for Philadelphia:

And Thou Philadelphia the virgin settlement of this province named before thou wert born, what care, what service, what travail have there been to bring thee forth and preserve thee from such as would abuse and defile thee. O that thou mayest be kept from the evil that would overwhelm thee, that faithful to the God of thy mercies in the life of righteousness, thou mayest be preserved to the end. My soul prays to God for thee that thou mayest stand in the day of trial, that thye children may be blest of the Lord and thy people saved by His power.[44]

Afterword

Eugenie L. Birch

The future of Philadelphia will be determined, not by technological advances, but by the character of its leadership and by the strength and quality of the ideas it supports.

—Edmund Bacon, 1959

Edmund Bacon's essay, "Philadelphia in the Year 2009," offers enduring guidance in its first sentence, and it goes on to anticipate a glowing future for the City of Brotherly Love—it provides a vision that centers this book. Bacon's words also exemplify his career—he was a leader and an "idea man."

Like any leader, Bacon was a creature of his education, experiences, and the times. As we know from Gregory Heller, he had studied architecture at Cornell University and a prestigious architectural academy, Cranbrook. But his education went beyond formal instruction; it included the best teachers of all, travel and exposure to places far from everyday American life. Whether it was wandering through Beijing's Forbidden City or parsing Florentine public spaces or soldiering in the Far East during World War II, Bacon was an eager and observant student. He fully experienced the places he studied; he watched how people used a physical space, analyzed its angles, light and shadows, its vistas, and observed how it fit with adjacent areas. The intricacies of urban design always guided his thinking.

As Scott Gabriel Knowles and Guian McKee explain in their chapters, Bacon applied his knowledge in the tug-of-war political arena of postwar Philadelphia. While others may have had the financial know-how or the legislated decision-making responsibilities in the redevelopment arena, Bacon had the ideas, and having the ideas was empowering. Only certain parts of Bacon's vision would come to pass during his lifetime, and some would become obsolete. Philadelphians are still working on parts

Figure 26. Edmund N. Bacon standing in Pennypack Creek in 1994. Photo by
Don Springer. Courtesy of Don Springer.

of the vision, as Harris Steinberg demonstrates in his chapter, highlighting current planning efforts, and the dreams of our possible future.

   Bacon's ideas and leadership have expression in the physical imprint
of specific projects—Penn Center, Society Hill, Eastwick, the Gallery—
that he, along with others, left on the city. They are also found in *Form,*

Design and the City (1963), a landmark film that showcases the work of the Philadelphia City Planning Commission under Bacon's direction, and in *Design of Cities* (1967), his monumental book on urbanism. Here Bacon displays his genius: a systematic appraisal of the features, values, and physical dynamics that define a place, and an ability to synthesize this information into a vision for the future. His strength was in his ability to understand the structural aspects of a city, intuiting how the relationships among streets, open space, and building mass define a place. From this understanding he crafted a comprehensive vision for the twentieth-century city that served as a goal. Then he moved opportunistically, undertaking projects as he could, but always aiming toward the desired end. Brash and wily, he was also single-minded and patient. "What is emerging in Philadelphia," he explained in *Design of Cities*, "is proving that, in the current tempo of things, within a decade there can be achievement on the ground related to the . . . order of design."[1]

"Philadelphia in the Year 2009" is the work of a city-builder displaying his city-building skills. But it is also a work that bears the influence of the times, the United States in the 1950s. As Bacon wrote the piece, President Dwight D. Eisenhower was nearing the end of his second term. The nation had lived through the Korean War and was deep in the Cold War, with the threat of Soviet dominance represented in a massive arms build-up, and, even worse, the launching of Sputnik. The takeover of Cuba by Fidel Castro, and his defiant turning to Russia for support, would heighten international tensions. Domestic affairs were in turmoil. The country was still smarting over Joseph McCarthy's red-baiting, and civil rights battles were heating up. The Supreme Court had outlawed school segregation in *Brown v. Board of Education,* but resistant governors like Orval Faubus of Arkansas had to be met with military force to safeguard the integration of Little Rock High School.

In the realm of city planning, government spending programs were beginning to shape American settlement patterns. Of particular importance was the Federal-Aid Highway Act of 1956 that would support 41,000 miles of new interstate highways and accelerate the central city decline that Bacon was trying to stave off. The Housing Act of 1954 transformed urban renewal, and the subsequent Act of 1964 allowed the use of federal funds for rehabilitation and conservation. In addition, the state of Pennsylvania, a national leader in supporting redevelopment, had allocated almost $200 million (2008 dollars) for downtown improvement. Bacon and his colleagues lined up Philadelphia to take advantage of these funds.[2]

Although Philadelphia's population of two million ranked it as the fourth most populous city in the United States, danger signs were on the horizon in 1959. It had lost more than 3 percent of its population over the decade of the 1950s, while the surrounding area had grown by 46 percent.[3] By all accounts, these trends were continuing. So, in a sense, Bacon's optimistic predictions of a healthy and prosperous future based on energizing redevelopment via the World's Fair celebration were really a plea for help. He and his associates were in a high stakes game. The city was competing with the suburbs for residents and employment. Bacon wanted to win, and the clock was ticking. While the redevelopment successes that would put him on the cover of *Time* five years later were emerging, attacks from all sides were also imminent. Bacon, in fact, showed Jane Jacobs around Philadelphia in the 1950s, and while she loved Rittenhouse Square, she was horrified by nearby public housing developments.[4] Jacobs (*The Death and Life of Great American Cities*, 1961), Herbert Gans (*The Urban Villagers*, 1962), and Martin Anderson (*The Federal Bulldozer*, 1964) were in the midst of their research and writing. Many of these vocal critics attended the Penn-Rockefeller Conference on Urban Design Criticism in 1958 that would serve as a catalyst for a number of the landmark books of the era critical of postwar American urban planning.[5] In this context, "Philadelphia in the Year 2009" is also a battle cry. Conflict and criticism were part of the reality that planners operating at such a high level faced. Today's urban historians discredit "great man" interpretations of city development, correctly noting that men like Bacon, Ed Logue in Boston, and Robert Moses in New York City were members of a larger cast of city-building characters. Nevertheless, like his famous contemporaries—though with considerably less authority—Bacon had not only a comprehensive vision of how to make Philadelphia a modern, twenty-first century city but also the savvy ability to make it happen.

So now we come to the present day. Who will envision and build the twenty-first-century city—what ideas will prevail? We probably will not see the type of leader that Bacon represented or the types of programs that involved him. Harris Steinberg's chapter gives evidence of some of the changes, particularly in the area of citizen engagement, that have occurred since 1959. Citizens, design professionals, public and private sector professionals will work collaboratively to forge and execute a vision for their city. Some entity may facilitate their efforts—a neutral party like PennPraxis, government leadership, or community-based initiatives will emerge.

Conditions have changed dramatically as well. Large-scale federally funded redevelopment is a relic of the past, as is the massive federal highway construction program of the 1950s. In exchange came public policy that favored people-based over place-based approaches. One unintended effect of this philosophy was that it fueled market-driven development that favored greenfields over cities because of the pure economics of the deals. The suburban growth that Bacon feared occurred, leaving abandoned property and buildings behind. At the same time, the deindustrialization that overtook the nation hit the northeast especially hard. Central cities, especially those that have no ability to increase their land areas, have suffered demographically and fiscally. Philadelphia has been overtaken by Phoenix and Houston in population, a catastrophic decline to 1.4 million that the last century's improvements in Center City, Society Hill, University City, Eastwick, the Gallery, and the Far Northeast simply could not arrest.

However, through the work of the Brookings Institution, America 2050, Urban Land Institute, and American Planning Association, many of these conditions may change. Federal expenditures on infrastructure, housing, education, and other place-based projects are now in order. Leaders will be challenged to choose those investments that will not only repair obsolete facilities but also position places for the future, and to address questions of equity and of economic competitiveness. If handled wisely, these investments can feed into a vision for Philadelphia in 2059 that addresses structural issues, especially the reality of a declining population, and the new threats of global warming and energy shortages. Most likely, the ideas we generate today will not be so detailed as Bacon's were for 2009. Planning for the Philadelphia of 2059 will likely be driven by a set of principles whose details will be worked out later. Three principles come to mind: (1) promoting socially inclusive economic growth; (2) increasing resilience in the face of natural and human-made disasters; and (3) fostering sustainability in order to reduce greenhouse gas emissions. In essence, Philadelphia will need to reinvent itself to meet the demands of the twenty-first century.

Notes

Introduction: Revisiting Edmund Bacon's Vision for the City

1. "Philadelphia in the Year 2009" was the title of Bacon's essay in its unpublished draft form. See Edmund N. Bacon, "Philadelphia in the Year 2009," Edmund Bacon Collection, Box 095.150–095.278, "Bacon Writings—1950s," Architectural Archives of the University of Pennsylvania. The essay was later published as Edmund N. Bacon, "Tomorrow: A Fair Can Pace It," *Greater Philadelphia Magazine* (October 1959). For the sake of consistency throughout this book we refer to the "Philadelphia in the Year 2009" essay text, as reprinted in Chapter One. The unpublished essay version offers slightly more to us today than does the published version, as the magazine's editors cut a few key phrases here and there (as editors will do).

Chapter 2. Salesman of Ideas: The Life Experiences That Shaped Edmund Bacon

I would like to thank the following people for their support and assistance on this project: Karin, Elinor, Hilda, Michael, Kira, and Kevin Bacon; William Whitaker and Nancy Thorne at the University of Pennsylvania Architectural Archives; Daniel Brook; Andrew Dalzell; Annie Juergens Behr; and my wonderful, loving, and supportive family.

1. "The City: Under the Knife, or All for Their Own Good," *Time* 84, 19 (6 November 1964).

2. James Reichley, "Philadelphia Does It: The Battle for Penn Center," *Harper's* (31 January 1957): 49–56, 51.

3. Ibid.

4. Author interview, Richard Huffman, 10 September 2008, personal collection of Gregory Heller.

5. For examples of Bacon's writing about planning with communities, see Edmund Bacon (hereafter EB), "Notes on 'Civic Education in Planning,' Report of AIP Subcommittee on Civic Education," 29 January 1952, Coll. 095, Architectural Archives of the University of Pennsylvania (hereafter AAUP); EB, "What the Building Products Executives Can Do About City Planning," talk at Building Products Executive Conference, Washington, D.C., 17 October 1967, Box A-2928, Folder "Mr. Bacon's Correspondence September–December 1967," Philadelphia City Archives (hereafter PCA); EB, "The Role of Planning in Our Changing Society," 29th World Congress International Federation for Housing and Planning (Philadelphia), 30 June 1968, 095, Box 427, AAUP. For discussion of democratic feedback, see EB, *Design of Cities* (New York: Penguin, 1974), 258–62; also EB, Correspondence to William A. Doebele, Jr., 11 May 1965, 095, Box.285, AAUP.

6. See, for example, Nancy Love, "Paradise Lost," *Philadelphia* (July 1968): 96.

7. See John B. Atkinson, *The Atkinsons of New Jersey from the Records of Friends Meetings and from Offices of Record in the State*, Gen At1:2, Historical Society of Pennsylvania. See also George Norwood Comly, *Comly Family in America* (Philadelphia: J.B. Lippincott, 1939), Fa 929.2 C734c, Historical Society of Pennsylvania. See also *John Comly's Journal*, EB, 292 Box 47, AAUP.

8. See George E. Thomas, *William L. Price: Arts and Crafts to Modern Design* (New York: Princeton Architectural Press, 2000).

9. David B. Brownlee, *Building the City Beautiful: The Benjamin Franklin Parkway and the Philadelphia Museum of Art* (Philadelphia: Philadelphia Museum of Art, 1990), 86.

10. For a discussion of early American suburbs, see David Gosling, *The Evolution of American Urban Design* (Chichester: John Wiley, 2003). For a good discussion specifically of the Radburn design concept, see Alexander Garvin, *The American City: What Works, What Doesn't* (New York: McGraw-Hill, 2002).

11. For more on Murphy's life and career, see Jeffrey W. Cody, *Building in China: Henry K. Murphy's "Adaptive Architecture," 1914–1935* (Hong Kong: Chinese University Press, 2001).

12. Bacon wrote to his parents, "Peking is so brilliant that it rather blots out everything else temporarily." EB, Correspondence to Mother and Dad, 30 May 1934, personal collection of Elinor Bacon.

13. For more information on W. Pope Barney, see American Architects and Buildings database, www.philadelphiabuildings.org.

14. See Richard Pommer, "The Architecture of Urban Housing in the United States During the Early 1930s," *Journal of the Society of Architectural Historians* 37, 4 (December 1978): 235–64.

15. For more on Catherine Bauer and Lewis Mumford, see H. Peter Oberlander and Eva Newbrun, *Houser: The Life and Work of Catherine Bauer* (Vancouver: University of British Columbia Press, 1999).

16. Correspondence from EB to Eliel Saarinen, 27 September 1935, Correspondence Boxes, EB, AAUP.

17. Eliel Saarinen, *The City: Its Growth, Its Decay, Its Future* (New York: Reinhold, 1943), 2.

18. Ibid., 4.

19. Ibid., 23.

20. For a discussion of Flint's planning program, see Madeline L. Cohen, "Postwar City Planning in Philadelphia: Edmund Bacon and the Design of Washington Square East" (Ph.D. dissertation, University of Pennsylvania, 1991). For Flint's planning program, see *Reports of the Flint Institute of Research and Planning* (Flint, Mich.: Flint Public Library), 977.437/Fl.

21. Information on Bacon's years in Flint comes from Bacon's correspondence in Papers of EB, AAUP, Correspondence Boxes, 1936–1939.

22. Correspondence from EB to his parents, 16 March 1937, 292, Correspondence Boxes, AAUP.

23. EB, Correspondence to Parents, 28 April 1937, 292, Correspondence Boxes, AAUP.

24. Correspondence from Paul Opperman to EB, 7 February 1938, 293, Correspondence Boxes, AAUP.

25. See Oberlander and Newbrun, *Houser*, 159, 161.

26. Taped interview with EB by Madeline L. Cohen, AAUP, Bacon Tape 2, 19 January 1988, 278.III.A.22.

27. "Sarvis Resigns Housing Position," *Flint Journal*, 2 April 1939; "Will Discontinue Institute of Planning," *Flint Journal*, 29 January 1939; microfilm, Flint Public Library.

28. Ibid.

29. Ibid.

30. Michael A. Gorman, Correspondence to Richard P. Raseman (28 February 1939), Cranbrook Academy of Art Archives, CAA Alumni Records—EB.

31. Flint City Commission Proceedings (2 June 1939), vol. 7, 14 November 1938–23 April 1940, Flint Public Library, 307.121 Fl.

32. Jack Bell, "Housing and Pay Boost Plans Lose: Commission Members Submit Resignations; Vote Exceeds 16,000," *Flint Journal*, 3 July 1939; microfilm, Flint Public Library.

33. EB quoted in Gerald McKelvey, "Philadelphia Urban Planning: Looking Back, Forward," *Philadelphia Inquirer*, 3 May 1970.

34. EB, "A Diagnosis and Suggested Treatment of an Urban Community's Land Problems (Flint, Michigan)," *Journal of Land and Public Utility Economics* 16, 1 (February 1940): 71–88.

35. EB, "Tax-Delinquent Subdivisions: A Liability That Might Become a Municipal Asset," *American City* 55, 4 (April 1940): 86–87.

36. See Emily Lewis Jones and Hans Knight, eds., *Walter M. Phillips: Philadelphia Gentleman Activist*, Portraits on Tape (Bryn Mawr, Pa.: Dorrance & Company, 1987), 23.

37. See "Men and Things: Housing Oases Brighten City's Blighted Areas," *Philadelphia Evening Bulletin*, 1 January 1942, 8C.

38. Brownlee, *Building the City Beautiful*, 13.

39. John Andrew Gallery, *The Planning of Center City Philadelphia* (Philadelphia: Center for Architecture, 2007), 27.

40. Ibid.

41. "Proper City Planning Would Save Philadelphia Money, Says Expert," *Philadelphia Evening Bulletin*, 17 May 1941, City Planning Supplement, 1.

42. See "Philadelphia's Hole," *Time* 35, 2 (8 January 1940): 17.

43. Digby Baltzell wrote, "Edward Hopkinson, Jr. . . . after the death of Thomas Gates in 1948 became the most influential member of the upper class in the city." E. Digby Baltzell, *Philadelphia Gentlemen: The Making of a National Upper Class* (Philadelphia: University of Pennsylvania Press, 1979), 372.

44. The critical committee hearing with the vast public support and Hopkinson was on 1 December 1942. It was read before the full Council on 3 December and passed on 10 December; *Journal of City Council*, PCA (10 December 1942). See also EB, "How City Planning Came to Philadelphia," *American City* 58, 2 (February 1943): 62.

45. Action Committee on City Planning, "Memorandum: Suggested Organization of Citizens' Council on City Planning," 12 March 1943, Walter M. Phillips Papers, Box 13, Folder "City Planning: Joint Committee on City Planning, 1941–42," Temple University Urban Archives.

46. Citizens' Council on City Planning. Newsletter, July 1943, Walter M. Phillips Papers (Coll 527). Temple University Urban Archives, Box 11, Folder "City Planning: CCCP—Newsletter, 1943, 1945–49, 1960."

47. Bacon's correspondence from his time in the navy is housed in his papers at the AAUP, Correspondence Boxes, 1943–1945.

48. For information on the Better Philadelphia Exhibition, see "Philadelphia Plans Again," *Architectural Forum* (December 1947): 66–87; also David Clow,

"The Show That Got Philadelphia Going," *Philadelphia* (May 1985): 111–18; and EB, "Are Exhibitions Useful? A Postscript to the Philadelphia Show," *Journal of the American Institute of Planners* (Spring 1948): 23–28.

49. See Clow, "The Show That Got Philadelphia Going"; "Philadelphia Plans Again"; and "The Better Philadelphia Exhibition: What City Planning Means to You," official exhibition program, 1947, AAUP, 292–93.

50. In his "2009" essay, Bacon rounds this estimated attendance figure up to 400,000.

51. Cyril B. Roseman, "Public-Private Co-Operation and Negotiation in Downtown Redevelopment; A Study of the Decision Process in Philadelphia" (Ph.D. dissertation, Princeton University, 1963), 54.

52. See Peter Shedd Reed, "Toward Form: Louis I. Kahn's Urban Designs for Philadelphia, 1939–1962" (Ph.D. dissertation, University of Pennsylvania, 1989).

53. Reed, "Toward Form."

54. See "Capital Program 1946–1951," Box A-193, PCA; also see Annual Reports 1943, 1946–1947, Box A-1620; and "A Progress Report on the Survey of the Planning Work that Has Been Done in the City of Philadelphia and Vicinity," Institute of Local and State Government, University of Pennsylvania, For the Philadelphia City Planning Commission, April 1943, Box A-1606, PCA.

55. Formed in December 1948 by Harry Batten and Robert T. McCracken. See Jeanne R. Lowe, *Cities in a Race with Time* (New York: Vintage, 1968), 325.

56. The "Lord Home Rule Bill" was signed by Governor James H. Duff on 21 April 1949. For more on the Home Rule Charter, see Russell F. Weigley, ed., *Philadelphia: A 300-Year History* (New York: Norton, 1982), 654–55.

57. Statement by EB (6 September 1963), Box A-2918, "City Planning Commission Files, Mr. Bacon's Correspondence, September 1963," PCA.

58. EB, "Urban Redevelopment," reprinted from *Planning* (1949): 18–25.

59. Ibid, 20–22.

60. Ibid, 22.

61. EB, "Urban Designs of Today: Philadelphia," *Progressive Architecture* 37, 8 (August 1956): 108–9.

62. Philadelphia City Planning Commission (hereafter PCPC), *East Poplar Redevelopment Area Plan*, 31 July 1948, Box A-1607, "City Planning Commission Reports, 1948–1949, Redevelopment," PCA, PCPC Papers; David M. Wallace, "Renaissancemanship," *Journal of the American Institute of Planners* 26, 3 (1960): 160–61.

63. "The Philadelphia Cure: Clearing Slums with Penicillin, Not Surgery," *Architectural Forum* (April 1952): 112–19.

64. Wallace, "Renaissancemanship," 160–61; Kirk R. Petshek, *The Challenge of Urban Reform: Policies and Programs in Philadelphia* (Philadelphia: Temple University Press, 1973), 136.

65. Correspondence from David M. Walker, administrative secretary, RDA, to EB, 5 August 1949, Eastwick, Box A-2913, Folder "Redevelopment—Eastwick, Correspondence, 1948–September 1952," PCA.

66. Guian A. McKee, "Liberal Ends Through Illiberal Means: Race, Urban Renewal, and Community in the Eastwick Section of Philadelphia, 1949–1990," *Journal of Urban History* 27, 5 (July 2001): 547–83.

67. Ibid.

68. Wallace, "Renaissancemanship," 171.

69. For a discussion of CURA, see Wallace, "Renaissancemanship," 160–63.

70. Petshek, *The Challenge of Urban Reform*, 134.

71. See William Pope Barney, "The Architecture of Business Streets," *T-Square Club Journal* 1, 7 (June 1931): 14–17.

72. See Associated City Planners, *Report on the Redevelopment of "The Triangle"*, 19 January 1948, PCPC office library.

73. "Kahn," typed manuscript, 14 March 1991, Alphabet Files Box 4, "Kahn" Folder, AAUP.

74. Henry S. Churchill, "City Redevelopment," *Architectural Forum* (December 1950); discussed in Reed, "Toward Form," 85–86.

75. "Kahn," typed manuscript , 14 March 1991, AAUP Alphabet Files, Box 4, "Kahn" folder.

76. Author's interview with EB, 19 March, personal collection of GH.

77. See EB, "Urban Designs of Today: Philadelphia," *Progressive Architecture* 37, 8 (August 1956): 108–9.

78. Taped discussion with EB, Vincent G. Kling, and GH at the home of Vincent G. Kling (Chester Heights, Pa.), 2 November 2002, personal collection of GH.

79. Ibid.; Roseman, "Public-Private Co-Operation," 145.

80. EB and Kling later discussed their meetings with Symes in the taped discussion on 2 November 2002. For biographical information on Robert Dowling, see Roseman, "Public-Private Co-Operation," 146–47.

81. EB, memo to files, 3 January 1952, Box A-2913, Folder "Penn Center 1951–1952," PCA, PCPC Papers.

82. John C. Phillips, notice from CCCP, 18 January 1952, Box A-2913, Folder "Penn Center, 1951–1952," PCA, PCPC Papers.

83. EB, "Statement on Penn Center Plan," address at Luncheon of the Citizens' Council on City Planning, 21 February 1952, Box A-2913, Folder "Penn Center, 1951–1952," PCA, PCPC Papers.

84. PCPC, 1952 Annual Report, 1 March 1953, Box A-1620, PCA, PCPC Papers.

85. EB, "Talk at Cornell Reception," 1 May 1993, 229, Box II.D.306, AAUP; Ralph W. Olmstead, Correspondence to EB, 9 April 1952, Box A-2913, Folder "Penn Center 1951–1952," PCA, PCPC Papers.

86. See "Bob Dowling Climbs Philadelphia's Chinese Wall," *Architectural Forum* (April 1953): 149–51.

87. Ibid.

88. Memo, 8 August 1953, Box A-2913, Folder "Penn Center, 1953," PCA, PCPC Papers.

89. Douglas Haskell, "Architecture: Stepchild or Fashioner of Cities?" *Architectural Forum* (December 1953): 117.

90. Roseman, "Public-Private Co-Operation," 157.

91. John. S. Shultz, Correspondence to Mayor Joseph S. Clark, 10 October 1952, Box A-2933, Folder "Zoning—Revision of Text—C-1 Residential 1952–1955," PCA, PCPC Papers.

92. EN, Statement, Subject: "Concerning Proposed 'C-1' Residential Zoning," 11 February 1953, Box A-2933, Folder "Zoning—Revision of Text—C-1 Residential, 1952–1955," PCA, PCPC Papers.

93. This plan relied on the planning commission's stronger role in subdivision planning afforded by the Home Rule Charter. The planning commission produced the city's Subdivision Ordinance in 1954; see Appendix 241, 21 April 1954, *Appendix to the Journal of Council*, PCA.

94. William H. Whyte, *The Last Landscape* (New York: Doubleday, 1968);

reprint with Foreword by Tony Hiss (Philadelphia: University of Pennsylvania Press, 2002).

95. For "design idea," see EB, *Design of Cities* (New York: Viking, 1967), 13. He used the term "organizing concept," and sometimes "controlling concept" later in life; for example, tape-recorded interview with EB by GH, 15 August 2003, personal collection of GH.

96. EB interview, 15 August 2003.

97. The neighborhood's historical name was revived as part of its 1950s redevelopment. The first reference I can find to Bacon using the name was in June 1950. See "Project Started to Restore Society Hill Area Near Shrine," *Philadelphia Evening Bulletin*, 9 June 1950.

98. Interview with Stanhope and Libby Browne et al., 24 June 2006, filmed by Charles Cook, copy in personal collection of GH.

99. For more on the Dock Street Market, see Roseman, "Public-Private Co-Operation." For more on Independence Mall, see Constance M. Greiff, *Independence: The Creation of a National Park* (Philadelphia: University of Pennsylvania Press, 1987).

100. PCPC release, 8 June 1950, Subject: Society Hill, Box A-2914, Folder "Redevelopment—Old City, 1946–1953," PCA, PCPC Papers.

101. PCPC, "Report on Design for Redevelopment of Old City Area (south)," Eugene H. Klaber, Consultant, 9 February 1950, Box A-2914, Folder "Redevelopment—Old City, 1946–1953," PCA, PCPC Papers.

102. Ibid.

103. N. S. Keith, Correspondence to David M. Walker, 22 September 1950, attached to correspondence from Francis J. Lammer to EB, 30 April 1970, EB, 292, Series II.A.3.a (General Corr.), 1970–July 1973, Folder 292.II.A.3.2, AAUP..

104. Roseman, "Public-Private Co-Operation," 121.

105. For more on the RDA Society Hill competition, see Stephen G. Thompson, "Philadelphia's Design Sweepstakes," *Architectural Forum* 109, 12 (December 1958): 94–99.

106. "Bacon's Foresight Led to Hill Towers," *Sunday Bulletin*, 24 May 1970, Sect. 2, 6.

107. EB, "PCPC Report to RDA," 18 November 1958, included in Weekly Reports to the Mayor, 24 November 1958, EB AAUP.

108. For a discussion of the demographics and displacement in Society Hill, see Cohen, "Postwar City Planning in Philadelphia," 530.

109. See, for example, "Society Hill a Nightmare, Park Aid Says," *Sunday Bulletin*, 14 January 1962, Sect. 1, 9.

110. See, for example, Lowe, *Cities in a Race with Time*, 351–52.

111. For an overview of early shopping mall development, see Joshua Olsen, *Better Places, Better Lives: A Biography of James Rouse* (Washington, D.C.: Urban Land Institute, 2003), 78–79.

112. PCPC, "Market East Plaza," May 1958, Box A-1612, PCA.

113. "A Study of Practicalities," *Philadelphia Inquirer*, Editorial, 31 April 1958, d6.

114. "$100 Million Midcity Job Okd by Planning Board," *Philadelphia Inquirer*, 2 April 1958, 1.

115. PCPC, *Comprehensive Plan for the City of Philadelphia*, 1960, EB, 292 Box 44, AAUP.

116. Author interview with EB, 5 January 2002, personal collection of GH.

117. PCPC, *Center City Philadelphia: Major Elements of the Physical Development Plan for Center City*, May 1960, EB 292, AAUP).

118. Louis Kahn had espoused the Chestnut Street idea in 1955, for example, and the waterfront concept was shown in the Better Philadelphia Exhibition. See Reed, "Toward Form," 228; also PCPC, *Center City Philadelphia: Major Elements.*

119. EB, "A Fair Can Pace It," *Greater Philadelphia Magazine* (October 1959): 242.

120. Warren Eiseberg, "Enter the Age of Tate," *Greater Philadelphia Magazine* (January 1964).

121. "City Planners Are Not Impressed By Idea of 'New' Towns in Suburbs," *Philadelphia Sunday Bulletin*, 8 October 1967, Sect. 1, 12.

122. EB, Weekly Reports to the Mayor, 12 September 1968, EB, AAUP.

123. EB, Weekly Reports to the Mayor, 10 March 1966, EB, AAUP.

124. Bacon discussed his pitching the program to Dilworth in a taped interview with GH, 24 September 2002, personal collection of GH; Bacon discussed his negotiation with Isard in EB, Weekly Reports to the Mayor, 6 June 1963, EB, AAUP; also see Weekly Reports, 13 June 1963.

125. John F. Bauman, *Public Housing, Race and Renewal: Urban Planning in Philadelphia, 1920–1974* (Philadelphia: Temple University Press, 1987), 195.

126. Untitled draft of article by Alexander L. Crosby, 13 March 1963, Box A-2918, Folder "Mr. Bacon's Correspondence March–April 1963," PCA.

127. See Jeanne R. Lowe, *Cities in a Race with Time* (New York: Vintage, 1968), 359; also Gerald McKelvey, "The Tate Regime: How Crisis Piles on Crisis," *Philadelphia Inquirer*, 1 March 1970, Today's World section, 1.

128. Love, "Paradise Lost," *Philadelphia* (July 1968).

129. Browne et al. interview.

130. See, for example, EB, Weekly Reports to the Mayor, 25 March 1965, EB, AAUP.

131. Reed, "Toward Form," 116; for Bacon's concept, see PCPC, *Center City Philadelphia*, 8 January 1963, Box A-1605, PCA.

132. Phil Willon and Ed Smith interview with EB, 1966, Box A-2928, Folder "Mr. Bacon's Correspondence, September–December 1966," PCA, PCPC Papers.

133. ENB, "Philadelphia—Tradition or Progress," Speech to Fairmount Park Art Association, in FPAA Annual Report of the Board of Trustees, 1976.

134. See, for example, ENB, "Clear Air, No Gangs, No Private Cars," *Philadelphia Daily News*, 14 April 1975, 24.

135. The best example is PCPC, *Center City Philadelphia.*

136. PCPC, *Center City Philadelphia.*

137. "Transit Has Key Role in Philadelphia Planning Processes," *Railway Age* (4 March 1968), copy of reprint available in EB, 292, Box II.D.314, AAUP.

138. "Bacon Predicts Business Hub at 30th-Market," *Philadelphia Evening Bulletin*, 24 September 1965, 1.

139. McKelvey, "The Tate Regime."

140. EB quoted in McKelvey, "Philadelphia Urban Planning."

141. Adrian I. Lee, "Bacon's Battle Against the Bulldozer," *Philadelphia Evening Bulletin*, 27 February 1970, 18.

142. "Bacon Quits Both Jobs After 20 Years with City," *Philadelphia Evening Bulletin*, 20 February 1970, 1.

143. Author interview, Walt D'Alessio, 19 March 2009, personal collection of GH.

Chapter 3. A Utopian, a Utopianist, or Whatever the Heck It Is: Edmund Bacon and the Complexity of the City

The author would like to thank Scott Knowles and Greg Heller for their detailed comments on earlier drafts of this essay, and to add a particular note of thanks to Scott for his assistance in locating illustrations.

1. "CCCP Luncheon," 4 February 1965, Kirk R. Petshek Papers (hereafter KRPP), Accession 202, Box 2, Folder Urban Renewal, Temple University Urban Archives (TUUA); "Under the Knife, or All for Their Own Good," *Time* (6 November 1964). In his own work, Davidoff had begun to develop what would become an influential theory of "advocacy planning" that called on planners to seek out and represent the interests and preferences of low-income neighborhoods. Paul Davidoff, "Advocacy and Pluralism in Planning," *Journal of the American Institute of Planners* 31, 4 (1965): 331–38; Barry Checkoway, "Paul Davidoff and Advocacy Planning in Retrospect," *Journal of the American Planning Association* 60, 2 (June 1994): 139–43.

2. Philip Herrera, "Philadelphia: How Far Can Renewal Go?" *Architectural Forum* 121, 2 (August–September 1964): 192.

3. Sidney Hopkins, "Requiem for a Renaissance," *Greater Philadelphia Magazine* (November 1964): 32, 34, 59.

4. Doug Hassebroek, "Philadelphia's Postwar Moment," *Perspecta* 30 (1999): 89–90; Howard Altman, "LOVE Burns Bacon: The Man Who Planned LOVE Park Gets on Board to Protest the Skater Ban," *Philadelphia Weekly*, 31 October–6 November 2002; Robin Pogrebin, "Edmund Bacon, 95, Urban Planner of Philadelphia, Dies," *New York Times*, 18 October 2005; Suzanne Stephens, "A Look Back: Planner Ed Bacon," *Architectural Record News* (22 November 2005), http://archrecord.construction.com/news/daily/archives/051122bacon.asp.

5. Alexander Garvin, *The American City: What Works, What Doesn't* (New York: McGraw-Hill, 1996), 454; Hassebroek, "Philadelphia's Postwar Moment," 84–85; Pogrebin, "Edmund Bacon, 95"; Stephens, "A Look Back."

6. Bacon, "What Was Attempted—II; The Planning Story," in *The Politics of Utopia: Towards America's 3d Century*, ed. Stanley Newman (Philadelphia: Temple University Political Science Department, 1975), 3.

7. Kirk R. Petshek, *The Challenge of Urban Reform: Policies and Programs in Philadelphia* (Philadelphia: Temple University Press, 1973), 96–98; David A. Wallace, "Renaissancemanship," *Journal of the American Institute of Planners* 26, 3 (August 1960): 161; "William L. Rafsky—Civil Servant, 81," *New York Times*, 29 June 2001.

8. David Wallace, interview by Kirk R. Petshek, 9 November 1964, transcript, KRPP, Accession 202, Box 5, Folder [Interviews], TUUA, 2–3; Paul Croley, interview by Kirk R. Petshek, 10 December [1964], ibid., 7–9; Richardson H. Dilworth, interview by Kirk R. Petshek, 21 March 1965, ibid., 4; Joseph Turchi, interview by Kirk R. Petshek, 16 December 1964, transcript, ibid., 3; Harold Wise, interview by Kirk R. Petshek, 1 November 1964, transcript, KRPP, Accession 202, Box 5, Folder [Interviews], TUUA, 10; Petshek, *The Challenge of Urban Reform*, 91–99, 140–44, 220–23.

9. This view was based on Clark's perception that the Better Philadelphia Exhibition, a major planning exhibit held at the Gimbels department store in October 1947, had helped Republican Mayor Bernard Samuel win reelection over Clark's reform partner Richardson Dilworth. Bacon had played an important part in organizing the exhibition. Phillips indicated that the relationship never improved: "Joe Clark does not like Ed Bacon even today." Edmund N.

Bacon, interview by Walter M. Phillips, 13 November 1974 (part 2), transcript, Walter M. Phillips Oral History Project (hereafter WMPOHP), Box 1, Folder Edmund Bacon, 10; Walter M. Phillips, interview by Kirk R. Petshek, 24 March 1965, transcript, KRPP, Accession 202, Box 5, Folder [Interviews], TUUA, 9.

10. Dilworth, interview by Petshek, 3–4; Petshek, *The Challenge of Urban Reform*, 102–3.

11. In a 1975 speech, Bacon even referred to Tate as "my mayor." Edmund N. Bacon, "Planning, Architecture, and Politics in Philadelphia," Russell Van Nest Black Memorial Lecture, Cornell University, 24 April 1973, WMPOHP), Box 1, Folder Edmund Bacon, [17]. See also Bacon, interview by Phillips, 13 November 1974 (part 2), 11–13; Petshek, *The Challenge of Urban Reform*, 103.

12. The state law, in turn, reflected the 1935 case *United States v. Certain Lands in the City of Louisville*, which established that the federal government could not employ eminent domain to acquire land for the construction of housing. This decision left such authority with the states, which in turn could delegate such powers to local municipal authorities. This reliance on designated local redevelopment authorities was reflected in the 1937 and 1949 U.S. Housing Acts. Kenneth T. Jackson, *Crabgrass Frontier: The Suburbanization of the United States* (New York: Oxford University Press, 1985), 224. On Pennsylvania's law, see "The Philadelphia Cure: Clearing Slums with Penicillin, Not Surgery," *Architectural Forum* 96, 4 (April 1952): 115; John F. Bauman, *Public Housing, Race, and Renewal: Urban Planning in Philadelphia, 1920–1974* (Philadelphia: Temple University Press, 1987), 97–101.

13. At least one of Bacon's colleagues at the PCPC felt that the coordinator's position would have vastly increased Bacon's influence (and argued that it should have been given to him). Croley, interview by Petshek, 8–10.

14. Bacon, "What Was Attempted—II," 4.

15. Arnold Hirsch, *Making the Second Ghetto: Race and Housing in Chicago, 1940–1960* (New York: Cambridge University Press, 1983); Jon Teaford, *The Rough Road to Renaissance: Urban Revitalization in America, 1940–1985* (Baltimore: Johns Hopkins University Press, 1990).

16. "The Philadelphia Cure," 114.

17. "The Philadelphia Cure," 112–19; David Wallace, interview by Kirk R. Petshek, 16 November 1964, transcript, KRPP, Accession 202, Box 5, Folder [Interviews], TUUA, 3; Wallace, "Renaissancemanship," 160; Bauman, *Public Housing, Race, and Renewal*, 108–11.

18. Nathaniel Burt, "Race and Renaissance in Philadelphia," *Harper's* 229, 1372 (September 1964): 69.

19. Bacon, "What Was Attempted—II," 7–8; Wallace, interview by Petshek, 1; "The Philadelphia Cure," 113.

20. Hopkins, "Requiem for a Renaissance," 34; Wallace, "Renaissancemanship," 160. For Bacon's support of Eastwick as a rehousing site for African Americans, see David M. Walker to Edmund N. Bacon, 5 August 1949, Philadelphia City Planning Commission (CPC) Records, RG 145.2, Box A-2898, Folder Eastwick Correspondence 1948–1952, Philadelphia City Archives (hereafter PCA); Edmund N. Bacon to David M. Walker, March 9, 1950, ibid. For the author's examination of the Eastwick project, see Guian A. McKee, "Liberal Ends Through Illiberal Means: Race, Urban Renewal, and Community in the Eastwick Section of Philadelphia, 1949–1990," *Journal of Urban History* 27, 5 (July 2001): 547–83.

21. Bauman, *Public Housing, Race, and Renewal*, 149–86.

22. Development Committee, "Interim Report; To: Philadelphia Redevelopment Authority," KRPP, Accession 202, Box 2, R.A. Development Areas, TUUA, 3.

23. William L. Rafsky, "What Was Attempted—I; Urban Renewal in Philadelphia," in *The Politics of Utopia*, 8.

24. Redevelopment Authority of the City of Philadelphia (hereafter cited as RDA), "Summary Statement on Urban Renewal Policy and Program (Draft)," no date, KRPP, Accession 202, Box 2, Folder Urban Renewal, TUUA, 1.

25. Bacon, "Planning, Architecture, and Politics in Philadelphia," [10].

26. Walter H. Blucher, "The Philadelphia City Planning Commission: An Appraisal," 1954, Albert M. Greenfield (AMG) Papers, Box 258, Folder 4, Historical Society of Pennsylvania (hereafter HSP), 8–9.

27. Ibid., 8; Walter H. Blucher, "Summary of Report Regarding Functions, Staff and Salary Scale Philadelphia City Planning Commission," 3 November 1954, 8–10, CPC Records, RG 145.2, Box A-2416, PCA, 10–11; Petshek, *The Challenge of Urban Reform*, 24.

28. Joseph S. Clark Jr. to Edward Hopkinson Jr., July 22, 1954, Mayor's Correspondence 1952–1954, RG 60–2.3 (Clark), Box A-473, Folder City Planning Commission 1955—1 July to December, PCA; Wallace, "Renaissancemanship," 159, 164.

29. Lennox Moak, interview by Kirk R. Petshek, n.d., transcript, Moak interview #1, KRPP, Accession 202, Box 5, Folder [Interviews], TUUA, 5; Wallace, "Renaissancemanship," 164.

30. Wallace, interview by Petshek, 9 November 1964, 2–3. See also Petshek, *The Challenge of Urban Reform*, 24.

31. RDA, "Summary Statement on Urban Renewal Policy and Program," 1; RDA, Planning Division, *Summary Report on the Central Urban Renewal Area (C.U.R.A.)* (Philadelphia: City of Philadelphia, March 1956, rev. April 1956), 46–85.

32. Rafsky, "What Was Attempted—I," 8.

33. RDA, "Summary Statement on Urban Renewal Policy and Program," 1; William L. Rafsky, "Memo to Mayor Joseph S. Clark on Progress of Evaluation of the City's Redevelopment Program," 22 July 1955, MCF, RG 60–2.3, Box A-478, Folder 41D, PCA; Philadelphia City Planning Commission, Comprehensive Planning Division, "Summary Report on the Central Urban Renewal Area (Preliminary Draft)," February 1956, Housing Association of the Delaware Valley, Neighborhoods and Urban Renewal Area Files (HADV NURA), Accession 781, Box 1, Folder 12, TUUA.

34. Office of the Development Coordinator, "A New Approach to Urban Renewal for Philadelphia," March 1957, GPC 529–3, TUUA, 1–2; RDA, Planning Division, *Summary Report on the Central Urban Renewal Area*, 46–62.

35. Public housing would "be constructed in small scattered clusters of units wherever it fits in with the neighborhood plan and can help with the improvement program." Office of the Development Coordinator, "A New Approach to Urban Renewal," 1–6; RDA, Planning Division, *Summary Report on the Central Urban Renewal Area*, 72–85; RDA, "Summary Statement on Urban Renewal Policy and Program (Draft)," 1–4; William L. Rafsky to Henry C. Beerits, May 9, 1957, KRPP, Accession 202, Box 2, Urban Renewal, 1–5; Wallace, "Renaissancemanship," 160–61.

36. RDA, "Summary Statement on Urban Renewal Policy and Program," 4.

37. For urban renewal in West Philadelphia, see Margaret Pugh O'Mara,

Cities of Knowledge: Cold War Science and the Search for the Next Silicon Valley (Princeton, N.J.: Princeton University Press, 2004).

38. Wallace, interview by Petshek, 9 November 1964, 2–3.

39. George Tucker, interview by Kirk R. Petshek, 25 January 1965, transcript, KRPP, Accession 202, Box 5, Folder [Interviews], TUUA, 1.

40. Wallace, "Renaissancemanship," 161; Wallace, interview by Petshek, 9 November 1964, 3.

41. Philadelphia City Planning Commission Staff, "A Suggested Approach to the Problem of Urban Renewal," January 1957, KRPP, Accession 202, Box 2, Folder Urban Renewal, TUUA, 7; Wallace, "Renaissancemanship," 161.

42. In making these proposals, the commission staff accepted CURA's conservation program in the "C" areas. PCPC Staff, "A Suggested Approach to the Problem of Urban Renewal," January 1957, 8–10.

43. Although innovative, the used-house program produced disappointing results. Bauman, *Public Housing, Race, and Renewal*, 180–81, 195–97; Bacon, "Planning, Architecture, and Politics in Philadelphia," 16–17.

44. Kirk R. Petshek, "Memo to Walter M. Phillips; Subject: The City's Economic Problems," 22 November 1955, MD-FC, RG 61.2, Box A-710, Folder Confidential—Cabinet Meetings 1954, PCA, 1–2.

45. Kirk R. Petshek, "Memo to Walter M. Phillips; Subject: Unemployment," 25 July 1955, MD-FC, RG 61.2, Box A-710, Folder Confidential—Cabinet Meetings 1954, PCA, 3.

46. Walter M. Phillips, "A Proposal for Using City-Owned Land in Strengthening Philadelphia's Industrial Base," 19 December 1953; and "Recommended Method for Assuring Availability of Land for Industrial Development in Philadelphia," 3 June 1954, WMPOHP, Accession 527, Box 17, Industrial Development Memos, 1953–54, TUUA; Phillips, "A Program For Industrial Land Development Within the Corporate Limits of Philadelphia," 20 September 1954, MCF, RG 60–2.5, Box A-490, Industrial Land Development, PCA; Walter A. Phillips, "Memo to Joseph S. Clark, Jr.; Subject: Budget Message," 7 September 1955, Mayor's Correspondence 1956 (Richardson H. Dilworth), RG 60–2.4, Box A-473, Folder 10 Budget For 1956, PCA; Walter M. Phillips, interview by Kirk R. Petshek, 24 March 1965, transcript, KRPP, Accession 202, Box 5, TUUA, 1; "Chronology of Industrial Development Program Activities," December 1955, Phillips Papers, Accession 527, Box 17, Folder Industrial Land Documents, 1952–56; 1961; 1964, TUUA, 3–8.

47. Edmund N. Bacon to Walter M. Phillips, 8 June 1954, CPC-Files, RG 145.2, Box A-6390, Folder Land Use—Industrial, 1952–1956, PCA.

48. Walter M. Phillips to Edmund N. Bacon, 25 June 1954, CPC-Files, RG 145.2, Box A-6390, Folder Land Use—Industrial, 1952–1956, PCA.

49. For a more complete assessment of Philadelphia's industrial renewal program, see Guian A. McKee, *The Problem of Jobs: Liberalism, Race, and Deindustrialization in Philadelphia* (Chicago: University of Chicago Press, 2008), chaps. 1–2.

50. Walter M. Phillips to Edmund N. Bacon, 21 January 1955, MD-FC, RG 61.2, Box A-709, Folder City Planning Commission 1955, PCA, 1–4; CPC, *Preliminary Far Northeast Physical Development Plan* (Philadelphia: City of Philadelphia, January 1955).

51. Ibid., 8; Paul A. Wilhelm, "Statement of the Department of Commerce Regarding Preliminary Far Northeast Physical Development Plan," 28 February 1955, Mayor's Correspondence 1956 (Richardson H. Dilworth), RG 60–2.5, Box A-490, Folder Industrial Land Development, PCA.

52. For a summaries of the Department of Commerce's position, see Wilhelm, ibid.; and Paul A. Wilhelm to Comprehensive Planning Committee of the Citizens Council on City Planning, 28 February 1955, Mayor's Correspondence 1956 (Richardson H. Dilworth), RG 60–2.4, Box A-490, Folder Industrial Land Development, PCA.

53. Phillips was not alone in raising questions about the Far Northeast plan. In July, Britton Harris, Director of the Institute of Urban Studies ongoing study of Philadelphia's industrial base, informed Bacon that the preliminary findings of his study supported Phillips's position. Britton Harris, "Memo to Edmund Bacon; Subject: Industrial Expansion in the Northeast," 8 July 1955, CPC Files, RG 145–2, Box A-6390, Folder Land Use—Industrial, July 1955–Oct. 1957, PCA.

54. Walter M. Phillips, "Weekly Report to the Mayor," 4 February 1955, MD-FC, RG 61.2, Box A-713, Folder: Confidential—Weekly Reports, City Representative, 1955, PCA, 1; William L. Rafsky, "Memo to Peter Schauffler," 8 February 1955, Mayor's Correspondence 1955 (Joseph S. Clark), RG 60–2.3, Box A-473, Folder 18 City Planning Commission 1955, PCA.

55. CPC, *1955 Annual Report*, 27–28; "Chronology of Industrial Development Program Activities," 10.

56. McKee, *The Problem of Jobs*, chap. 2.

57. Wise, interview by Petshek, 1 November 1964, 10–11; Elizabeth Deuterman, interview by Kirk R. Petshek, 10 November 1964, transcript, KRPP, Accession 202, Box 5, Folder [Interviews], TUUA, 2; Phillips, interview by Petshek, 9; Richard McConnell, interview by Kirk R. Petshek, 11 November 1964[?], transcript, KRPP, Accession 202, Box 5, Folder [Interviews], TUUA.

58. This idea is explored in Edmund Bacon, *Design of Cities* (New York: Penguin, 1967), 32–65, 252–53.

59. Hassebroek, "Philadelphia's Postwar Moment," 30; Jonathan Barnett and Nory Miller, "Edmund Bacon: A Retrospective," *Planning* 49, 11 (December 1983): 9–10.

60. For displacement in Society Hill, see Neil Smith, *The New Urban Frontier: Gentrification and the Revanchist City* (New York: Routledge, 1996), 119–39.

61. CPC, *Philadelphia's Comprehensive Plan for Expressways* (Philadelphia: CPC, 1966); CPC, *Center City, Philadelphia: Major Elements of the Physical Development Plan for Center City* (Philadelphia: CPC, 1960), 3, 8–9; Michelle Osborne, "A History of the Ups and Downs That Finally Resulted in the Defeat of the Expressway," *Architectural Forum* 135, 3 (October 1971): 38–41.

62. Bacon quoted in Madeline L. Cohen, "Postwar City Planning in Philadelphia: Edmund N. Bacon and the Design of Washington Square East" (Ph.D. dissertation, University of Pennsylvania, 1991), 567. See also *Report of the Interdepartmental Task Force on the Delaware Expressway in Philadelphia, Pennsylvania* (Washington, D.C., May 1967); "The Expressway Dilemma," *Greater Philadelphia Magazine* (April 1965): 91–97.

63. For these early models, see Bacon, *Design of Cities*, 265–71. In this work, Bacon articulated the functionalist, urban system-based view of the highway when he commented that I. M. Pei's Society Hill Towers "serve as a powerful articulation point in relation to the fast movement on the Delaware Expressway," ibid., 264. For Bacon's positions, see Cohen, "Postwar City Planning in Philadelphia," 567–68.

64. Ibid., 95.

65. "Philadelphia Road Plan Spurs Closer U.S. Ties with Cities," *New York Times*, 29 May 1967; Donald Janson, "Expressway Construction Lags as Officials Heed Urban Outcry," *New York Times*, 15 February 1970.

66. Nancy Love, "Paradise Lost," *Philadelphia Magazine* 59, 7 (July 1968): 72–75, 87–88, 94–99.

67. Deuterman, interview by Petshek, 2.

68. Petshek, *The Challenge of Urban Reform*, 173–74.

69. Bacon, "What Was Attempted—II," 8–9.

70. Bacon, "Planning, Architecture, and Politics in Philadelphia," 10.

71. Ibid., 14.

Chapter 4. Staying Too Long at the Fair: Philadelphia Planning and the Debacle of 1976

I dedicate this chapter to Gabriel and the next generation of urban visionaries. Julia Meurling provided unlimited understanding and support throughout. I wish to thank the following for their assistance in the research and writing of this chapter: Stanhope Browne, Catherine Susan Leslie Craig, Greg Downey, John Andrew Gallery, Kali Gross, Gregory Heller, Bruce J. Hunt, Anthony Lame, Guian McKee, Walter Palmer, Carl Smith, and Harris Steinberg.

1. Guian A. McKee, *The Problem of Jobs: Liberalism, Race, and Deindustrialization in Philadelphia* (Chicago: University of Chicago Press, 2008), 22–26.

2. U.S. Bureau of the Census, "Population of the 100 Largest Cities and Other Urban Places in the United States, 1790 to 1990," Tables 19, 20, 1998, http://www.census.gov/population/www/documentation/twps0027/twps0027 .html (accessed 2 April 2009).

3. For an overview of this time period in Philadelphia, see Joseph S. Clark, Jr., and Dennis J. Clark, "Rally and Relapse, 1946–1968," and Stephanie G. Wolf, "The Bicentennial City, 1968–1982," in *Philadelphia: A 300-Year History*, ed. Russell F. Weigley (New York: Norton, 1982), 649–703, 704–34.

4. For historical analyses of postwar urban renewal and deindustrialization, see Howard Gillette, Jr., *Camden After the Fall: Decline and Renewal in a Post-Industrial City* (Philadelphia: University of Pennsylvania Press, 2005); and Thomas J. Sugrue, *The Origins of the Urban Crisis: Race and Inequality in Postwar Detroit* (Princeton, N.J.: Princeton University Press, 1998).

5. Robert W. Rydell, *World of Fairs: The Century-of-Progress Expositions* (Chicago: University of Chicago Press, 1993), 5.

6. Robert W. Rydell, John E. Findling, and Kimberly D. Pelle, *Fair America: World's Fairs in the United States* (Washington, D.C.: Smithsonian Institution Press, 2000), 5–7. On world's fairs see also David E. Nye, *Electrifying America: Social Meanings of a New Technology* (Cambridge, Mass.: MIT Press, 1997), 29–84; and Robert W. Rydell, *All the World's a Fair: Visions of Empire at American International Expositions, 1876–1916* (Chicago: University of Chicago Press, 1985).

7. Neil Harris, *Building Lives: Constructing Rites and Passages* (New Haven, Conn.: Yale University Press, 1999), 164. See also Neil Harris, "Memory and the White City," in Harris et al., *Grand Illusions: Chicago's World's Fair of 1893* (Chicago: Chicago Historical Society, 1993), 1–32.

8. Alison Sky and Michelle Stone, *Unbuilt America: Forgotten Architecture in the United States from Thomas Jefferson to the Space Age* (New York: McGraw-Hill, 1976), 1.

9. Edmund N. Bacon, "Understanding Cities. Part IV. The American Urban Experience," 19 July 1979, 3, Papers of Edmund Bacon (hereafter EB), 292 Box 47, Architectural Archives of the University of Pennsylvania (hereafter AAUP),

10. John Henry Hepp, IV, *The Middle-Class City: Transforming Space and Time in Philadelphia, 1876–1926* (Philadelphia: University of Pennsylvania Press, 2003),

21–24. For a view from the time period see *Magee's Centennial Guide of Philadelphia and the Exhibition* (Philadelphia: Richard Magee and Son, 1876; reprinted New York: Nathan Cohen, 1975).

11. Dorothy Gondos Beers, "The Centennial City: 1865–1876," in Weigley, ed., 461, 459–70.

12. "Centennial Exhibition Digital Collection," Free Library of Philadelphia, http://libwww.library.phila.gov/CenCol/ (accessed 8 April 2009); "Transformation of the Landscape," http://www.fairmountpark.org/HistoryPart3.asp (accessed 8 April 2009).

13. Bacon, "Understanding Cities," 3.

14. EB, "Urban Productions: Understanding Cities," n.d., EB, 292 Box 47, AAUP.

15. Thomas S. Hines, *Burnham of Chicago: Architect and Planner* (New York: Oxford University Press, 1974), 77.

16. Ibid., 79.

17. Carl Smith, *The Plan of Chicago: Daniel Burnham and the Remaking of the American City* (Chicago: University of Chicago Press, 2006), 30–31.

18. Daniel H. Burnham and Edward H. Bennett, *Plan of Chicago*, ed. Charles Moore (New York: Princeton Architectural Press, 1993), 4.

19. Ibid., 6.

20. Ibid., 121. For an overview of the *Plan of Chicago* and its effects on the city, see "Encyclopedia of Chicago," http://www.encyclopedia.chicagohistory.org/pages/10537.html (accessed 9 April 2009).

21. Bacon, "Understanding Cities," 3–4.

22. Peter Hall, *Cities of Tomorrow* (Oxford: Blackwell, 1996), 183.

23. Eugene A. Santomasso, "The Design of Reason: Architecture and Planning at the 1939/1940 New York World's Fair," in *Dawn of a New Day: The New York World's Fair, 1939/40*, ed. Helen A. Harrison (New York: Queens Museum/NYU Press, 1980), 30–31.

24. "Flushing Meadow Park to Become Versailles of America after Fair," *Flushing Meadow Improvement*, October 1936, 1.

25. Robert Caro, *The Power Broker: Robert Moses and the Fall of New York* (New York: Vintage, 1975).

26. Santomasso, "The Design of Reason," 30–31.

27. Rydell, *World of Fairs*, 133–35; Lawrence R. Samuel, *The End of the Innocence: The 1964–1965 New York World's Fair* (Syracuse, N.Y.: Syracuse University Press, 2007), 9.

28. Samuel, *The End of the Innocence*, 4.

29. Arthur P. Dudden, "The City Embraces Normalcy," in Weigley, ed., *Philadelphia: A 300-Year History*, 571–75.

30. "The Better Philadelphia Exhibition: What City Planning Means to You," 1947, General Pamphlets, Box 521, Temple University Urban Archives (hereafter TUUA).

31. "Youth Shares in Planning a Better Philadelphia, Philadelphia Public Schools," 1947, EB, 292 Box 93, AAUP.

32. "Philadelphia Plans Again," *Architectural Forum* (December 1947): 1.

33. Ibid., 4.

34. Ibid., 8–10.

35. Ibid., 22.

36. Edmund N. Bacon, "Are Exhibitions Useful? A Postscript to the Philadelphia Show," *Journal of the American Institute of Planners* (Spring 1948): 23–28, 23.

37. Ibid., 26.

38. Oskar Stonorov, "Phila World's Fair," 31 December 1947, EB, AAUP.

39. Ibid.

40. "Weekly Report to the Mayor, City Planning Commission, 11 August 1960," Weekly Reports to the Mayor, EB, AAUP.

41. "Confidential Report to the Mayor, City Planning Commission, 14 July 1960," EB, AAUP.

42. "The New Face of Philadelphia," *Philadelphia Inquirer Magazine*, 10 September 1961, 23.

43. Ibid., 11.

44. "Weekly Report to the Mayor, City Planning Commission, July 12, 1962," Weekly Reports to the Mayor, EB, AAUP.

45. Philadelphia City Planning Commission (hereafter PCPC), 7 April 1964, *United States of America Bicentennial: Philadelphia, 1976*, 6, Box A-7331, Philadelphia City Archives (hereafter PCA).

46. Ibid., 8.

47. Ibid., 16.

48. Ibid., 19.

49. Samuel, *The End of the Innocence*, 244–48.

50. "Weekly Report to the Mayor, City Planning Commission, July 15, 1965," Weekly Reports to the Mayor, EB, AAUP.

51. "Olympic View of Philadelphia: Report to the United States Olympic Committee by the City of Philadelphia Documenting Why Philadelphia Is the Outstanding Choice in the United States for the XX Olympiad, 1972," Box A-4522, 2–3, 4, PCA.

52. "Communication from the President of the United States, Transmitting a Draft of a Joint Resolution to Establish the American Revolution Bicentennial Commission and for Other Purposes" (Washington, D.C.: U.S. Government Printing Office, 1966).

53. Richard Saul Wurman graduated from the University of Pennsylvania in architecture and was closely associated with Louis I. Kahn. After leaving Philadelphia he founded the Access Guides and the Technology, Entertainment, Design (TED) conference. For more on Wurman's life and work, see Patricia Leigh Brown, "A Designer in Untrod Byways," *New York Times*, 19 November 1987, C1; Patricia Leigh Brown, "3 Days in the Future," *New York Times*, 28 February 2002, F1; and Stephen J. McGovern, "Evolving Visions of Waterfront Development in Postindustrial Philadelphia: The Formative Role of Elite Ideologies," *Journal of Planning History* (2008): 295–326, 304–5.

54. Richard Saul Wurman to Lyndon Baines Johnson, 26 January 1966, EB, 292 Box 97, AAUP.

55. EB to Richard Saul Wurman, 16 March 1966, EB, 292 Box 97, AAUP.

56. Richard Saul Wurman to EB, 17 March 1966, EB, 292 Box 97, AAUP.

57. "Plan '67 for Philadelphia '76," Franklin Institute Research Laboratories, April 1967, iii, Pamphlets, Box 513, TUAA; for discussion on the life and work of Joel N. Bloom, see Lucinda Fleeson, "Unplugging Himself Joel Bloom Took Over the Aging Franklin Institute in 1969 and Steered It into the Future—and Ultimately to the Futures Center," *Philadelphia Inquirer*, 17 December 1990, E1.

58. "Fair Without Walls . . . Showcase for Freedom," Franklin Institute Research Laboratories, 8 February 1967, 1, EB, 292 Box 97, AAUP.

59. Ibid., 2.

60. Arlen Specter, "Arlen Specter's Blueprints for a Better Philadelphia. No.

10: 1976 Bicentennial," September 1967, 1–18, Box A-7305, "Bicentennial Miscellaneous," PCA.

61. Author interview with Stanhope Browne, 27 February 2009. For more on Browne see: "A Long View of the Penn's Landing Corp.," PlanPhilly, 22 December 2008, http://www.planphilly.com/node/5469 (accessed 2 April 2009).

62. "Crosstown Expressway," Phillyroads.com, http://www.phillyroads.com/roads/crosstown/ (accessed 2 April 2009).

63. Stanhope Browne to Henderson Supplee, 17 August 1967, Box A-7305, "Young Professionals," PCA.

64. Browne interview, 2009; author interview with John Andrew Gallery, 21 November 2008; Philadelphia 1976 Bicentennial Corporation (hereafter BC), "Toward a Meaningful Bicentennial" (presentation), 1969, Pamphlets Box 513, TUUA, 60.

65. "A Proposal for an International Exposition in Philadelphia in 1976," 1967, 1–4, EB, 292 Box 97, AAUP.

66. Catherine Drinker Bowen to EB, 8 March 1968, EB, 292 Box 97, AAUP.

67. EB to Ewen Dingwall, 15 January 1968, EB, 292 Box 97, AAUP.

68. For example, see BC, "The Philadelphia Plan: A Proposal for the Bicentennial Celebration of the United States and an International Exposition in Philadelphia in 1976," 27 March 1968, Box A-7331, PCA.

69. Browne interview, 2009.

70. Gallery interview, 2008.

71. "Weekly Report to the Mayor, City Planning Commission, April 1, 1970," Weekly Reports to the Mayor, EB, AAUP.

72. BC, "Toward a Meaningful Bicentennial," 4–5, 17, 28–32, 54–59.

73. BC, "Projection: 1976, A Forward Look at a Forward-Looking city: Philadelphia . . . The Bicentennial City," EB, 292 Box 97, AAUP.

74. PCPC, "Mantua Community Plan," 6–7, December 2005, http://www.philaplanning.org/cpdiv/Neighborhood_Plans/Mantua.html. For Powelton Village history see http://www.poweltonvillage.org/history.html.

75. Browne interview, 2009.

76. BC, "Toward a Meaningful Bicentennial."

77. Ibid., 11–12.

78. Author interview with Catherine Susan Leslie Craig (hereafter CSLC), 18 March 2009.

79. For a full discussion of African American community organizing, civil rights movements, Black Power, and political development in these years see: Matthew J. Countryman, *Up South: Civil Rights and Black Power in Philadelphia* (Philadelphia: University of Pennsylvania Press, 2006).

80. CSLC interview, 2009.

81. Ibid.

82. "Homeowners Withdraw Endorsement of Bicentennial Site, *Powelton Quarterly* (Spring 1970), 1–3.

83. For a complete timeline of the World's Fair planning period see: "Bicentennial Chronology," n.d. (c. 1976) Box A-7640, Phila. '76 Inc. Final Reports of Different Units, PCA.

84. "The Mayor's Fiscal 1970 Operating Budget and Programs," City of Philadelphia, 2–3, Box A-2896, FY 1970 folder, PCA.

85. For a complete review of the conflicts swirling around the Fair in 1970, racial and otherwise, see: Nancy Love, "Which Way to the Fair," *Philadelphia Magazine* (December 1970); and Mimi Reimel, "It was the day the sky fell in," *Philly Talk* (1970), Box A-7318, "Agenda for Action," PCA.

86. CSLC interview, 2009.

87. "As We See It!," *Philly Talk* (1970), Box A-7318, "Agenda for Action," PCA.

88. Mike Willmann, "$1.2 Billion Bicentennial Approved at Stormy Meeting," *Philadelphia Inquirer*, 24 October 1970, A1.

89. "Bicentennial Chronology."

90. Sky and Stone, *Unbuilt America*, 260.

91. "Public Hearing on Shall the Philadelphia Metropolitan Region Host a US World Exposition in 1976?" 18 June 1971, 378–79, Box A-7335, PCA.

92. Desmond Ryan and Gerald McKelvey, "I Wouldn't Pay $8 for Bicen. Symbol—Rizzo," *Philadelphia Inquirer*, 17 December 1971.

93. S. A. Paolantonio, *Rizzo: The Last Big Man in Big City America* (Philadelphia: Camino Books, 1993), 143–56.

94. For discussion of urban planning conflicts continuing through the Bicentennial, see Andrew Feffer, "Show Down in Center City: Staging Redevelopment and Citizenship in Bicentennial Philadelphia, 1974–1977," *Journal of Urban History* 30, 6 (September 2004): 791–825.

95. Hall, *Cities of Tomorrow*, 334.

96. John Friedmann, *Planning in the Public Domain: From Knowledge to Action* (Princeton, N.J.: Princeton University Press, 1987), 34, 400–401.

Chapter 5. Philadelphia in the Year 2059

I'd like to thank Shawn McCaney, Michael Greenle and Jane Steinberg for reading and critiquing my chapter as I refined its message and voice. I'd also like to acknowledge Scott Knowles's editing and leadership skills in bringing this volume to light.

1. Gary Nash, *First City: Philadelphia and the Forging of Historical Memory* (Philadelphia: University of Pennsylvania Press, 2002), 261.

2. Mayor John Street launched the Neighborhood Transformation Initiative in 2001 to leverage $250 million in bond funds to acquire and prepare abandoned and blighted properties for private development. See Stephen J. McGovern, "Philadelphia's Neighborhood Transformation Initiative: A Case Study of Mayoral Leadership, Bold Planning, and Conflict," Fannie Mae Foundation, Housing Policy Debate, 17, no. 3, Haverford College, 2006, http://www.fannie maefoundation.org/programs/hpd/pdf/hpd_1703_mcgovern.pdf (accessed 4 October 2008).

3. Anthony N. B. Garvan, *Philadelphia's Urban Image in Painting and Architecture*, City Chronicles (Philadelphia: Philadelphia '76, 1976), 5–6.

4. Edmund Bacon (hereafter EB), "Philadelphia in the Year 2009."

5. "EB, 95, Urban Planner of Philadelphia, Dies," *New York Times*, 18 October 2005.

6. Elizabeth Milroy, "For the Like Uses, as the Moore-fields: The Politics of Penn's Squares," http://www.historycooperative.org/cgibin/justtop.cgi?act= justtop&url=http://www.historycooperative.org/journals/pmh/130.3/milroy .html (accessed 11 August 2008).

7. "Excerpts from the Frame of Government of Pennsylvania by William Penn 1682," http://www.constitution.org/bcp/frampenn.htm (accessed 11 August 2008).

8. Richard Thom and John Farnham, "Streets, Roads, and Highways," pre-

sentation to Philadelphia Bar Institute Law of Historic Preservation Program, December, 2004.

9. The Pennsylvania Supreme Court restored Philadelphia's land use prerogative, but as of this writing the fate of the two riverfront casinos remains undecided. The Gallery at Market East has been discussed as a possible site for one of them while the state Supreme Court has installed a special master to oversee the construction of the other.

10. John L. Cotter, Daniel G. Roberts, and Michael Parrington, *The Buried Past: An Archaeological History of Philadelphia* (Philadelphia: University of Pennsylvania Press, 1994), 42–44.

11. Benjamin Franklin, *Proposals Relating to the Education of Youth in Pensilvania*, 1749; Appendix to *The Autobiography of Benjamin Franklin*, Penn Reading Project Edition (Philadelphia: University of Pennsylvania Press, 2005), 165–70, http://www.archives.upenn.edu/primdocs/1749proposals.html (accessed 26 August 2008).

12. For example, note the September 2007 commission for the Barnes Foundation's new home on the Benjamin Franklin Parkway being given to New York architects Tod Williams and Billie Tsien.

13. As observed by Bruce Laverty, curator of architecture, Athenaeum of Philadelphia, during a summer 2006 gallery talk for the exhibition "Modern Classics: Sections from the Paul Phillipe Cret Collection." The exhibition ran 7 February–25 August 2006.

14. Cret provided early planning drawings for the Benjamin Franklin Parkway, but the current design is attributed to the French landscape architect Jacques Gréber.

15. Cret's Wissahickon Memorial Bridge stands in stark contrast to the current Philadelphia Streets Department redesign of his South Street Bridge. See Inga Saffron, "South Street Bridge: Philadelphia Deserves Better," *Philadelphia Inquirer,* 9 February 2007, E1. Local community and design activists have helped push for a redesign of the bridge.

16. "Under the Knife, or All for Their Own Good" *Time* (6 November 1964), http://www.time.com/time/magazine/article/0,9171,876419-2,00.html (accessed August 21, 2008).

17. Jan Rowan, "Wanting to Be: The Philadelphia School," *Progressive Architecture* 42, no. 4 (April 1961): 150–54.

18. Quote is attributed to Anthony N. B. Garvan during a spring 1978 walking tour of Philadelphia for his American Civilization class at the University of Pennsylvania on Philadelphia art and architecture.

19. Christopher Klemek, "Modernist Planning and the Crisis of Urban Liberalism in Europe and North America: 1945–1975" (Ph.D. dissertation, University of Pennsylvania, 2004).

20. The Philadelphia City Planning Commission "Plan for Center City" created in 1988 in reaction to One Liberty Place breaking the 491-foot height limit of City Hall Tower, being a notable exception.

21. Recall that Rendell's predecessor, W. Wilson Goode, the city's first African American mayor, had bombed a portion of West Philadelphia in a stand-off with the radical group MOVE.

22. PennPraxis, along with the Penn Project for Civic Engagement, conducted a civic engagement and design process for the Kimmel Center in early 2008 to determine how the Kimmel might engage better with the city. See http://www.planphilly.com/kimmel.

23. See "Citizens Agenda on Planning and Zoning," 2007 Great Expectations Project of the *Philadelphia Inquirer* and the Penn Project for Civic Engagement, http://www.greatexpectationsnow.com/content/citizens-agenda-planning-and-zoning-0 (accessed 2 October 2008); Inga Saffron, "Zoning Board Thumbs Its Nose at Laws," *Philadelphia Inquirer*, 12 January 2007, E1; and Harris Steinberg, "Spot Zoning Fails to Accommodate the Greater Good," *Philadelphia Inquirer*, 7 February 2007, B2.

24. See Inga Safffron, "RIP: Minar Palace on Sansom Street," http://changingskyline.blogspot.com/2006/09/rip-minar-palace-on-sansom-street.html (accessed 4 October 2008).

25. TRF's Market Value Analysis (MVA) served as the statistical underpinnings for Mayor Street's 2001 Neighborhood Transformation Initiative (NTI), http://www.trfund.com/planning/market-phila.html (accessed 4 October 2008).

26. Simultaneously, Judith Rodin, president of the University of Pennsylvania, and her team of administrators were reshaping University City through the West Philadelphia Initiative—a five-pronged approach to neighborhood revitalization that placed Penn at the center of healthy city making. The West Philadelphia Initiative would become a national model for the role of anchor institutions in local economies, planning, and design. See Lucy Kerman and John Kromer, "West Philadelphia Initiatives: A Case Study in Urban Revitalization" (2004), http://www.upenn.edu/campus/westphilly/casestudy.pdf (accessed 5 October 2008).

27. See Harris Sokoloff and Harris Steinberg, "Deliberative City Planning on the Philadelphia Waterfront" in *The Deliberative Democracy Handbook: Strategies for Effective Civic Engagement in the Twenty-First Century*, ed. John Gastil and Peter Levine (San Francisco: Jossey-Bass, 2005), 185–96.

28. See Sandra Shea, "A Public Forum on Casino Design," *Philadelphia Daily News*, 10 May 2006, 9; and "Public Forum on Casino Design" http://www.whyy.org/community/casino.html (accessed 4 October 2008).

29. The Penn's Landing Corporation, a public benefit corporation created in 1970 to plan and manage development of public land along the central Delaware, had lost the public's trust because it was plagued by a history of corruption and a lack of transparency and accountability. See "Former Penn's Landing Project Head Gets 30 Months in Corruption Case," *Philadelphia Business Journal*, 8 August 2006, http://philadelphia.bizjournals.com/philadelphia/stories/2006/08/07/daily24.html (accessed 4 October 2008).

30. See PlanPhilly, "Central Delaware Riverfront Planning Process," http://www.planphilly.com/node/277.

31. The Central Delaware Waterfront Planning Principles were drawn from the collective aspirations and values of more than 1,700 people who participated in facilitated public meetings between 11 December 2006 and 20 February 2007.

32. See Linda Harris, "The Hows and Whys of the Working Port Protest," http://www.planphilly.com/node/1052 (accessed 4 October 2008).

33. For information on the "Civic Vision for the Central Delaware," see http://www.planphilly.com/vision; for the "Action Plan for the Central Delaware: 2008 to 2018," see http://www.planphilly.com/actionplan. Also see Matt Blanchard, "Praxis' Year: Listening, Planning and Politics," http://www.planphilly.com/node/2217.

34. See Inga Saffron, "Developers Fight Plan to Extend Streets to the Riverfront," *Philadelphia Inquirer*, 5 October 2007, E1; and Sandra Shea, "Grid Is Good," *Philadelphia Daily News*, 30 October 2007, 18.

35. Altman and Hughes left their positions as this book was going to press.

36. In late 2008 Mayor Nutter announced a $1 billion budget shortfall over the next five years. Marcia Gelbart, "Budget Isn't Only Gap Vexing Nutter," *Philadelphia Inquirer,* 23 November 2008, B1.

37. The Brookings Institution, "MetroPolicy: Shaping a New Federal Partnership for a Metropolitan Nation," 12 June 2008, http://www.brookings.edu/reports/2008/06_metropolicy.aspx (accessed 22 August 2008).

38. A $700 billion federal bailout of the U.S. credit market was approved by Congress and signed by President George W. Bush on 3 October 2008. On 17 February 2009, President Barack Obama signed the $787 billion American Recovery and Reinvestment Act.

39. As of this writing, the owners of the Foxwoods casino have expressed interest in relocating from the riverfront to the Gallery shopping center on East Market Street. Governor Rendell announced the possible relocation on 10 September 2008 without public discussion, eliciting civic backlash from neighboring Chinatown.

40. On 1 March 2009, Mayor Nutter announced a $1 million grant from the William Penn Foundation that would match city funds for the creation of a public space on Pier 11 at the foot of Race Street and a master plan for the central Delaware.

41. Lincoln Steffens, *The Shame of the Cities* (New York: McClure, Philips, 1904), 1–18.

42. A PennDesign 2008 planning studio led by Jim Kise produced "Transportation Visioning Plan for the Philadelphia Region," which identified the R0 as a possible cross-county connecting rail line.

43. Should casinos come to East Market Street, one hopes that they will be integrated into the urban fabric with sound planning and urban design guidelines. American slot-machine casinos are typically "big boxes with neon," as a powerful real estate attorney told us during the creation of the "Civic Vision for the Central Delaware." Challenging that assumption and pushing the planning model toward an integrated urban paradigm based on sustainable planning and design principles are critical to the success of East Market Street.

44. Explore PAHistory.com, "William Penn's Prayer for Philadelphia, 1984," http://www.explorepahistory.com/odocument.php?docId = 12 (accessed 11 August 2008).

Afterword

1. Edmund Bacon, *Design of Cities* (New York: Viking, 1967), 297.

2. William Slayton, "State and Local Incentives and Techniques for Urban Renewal," *Law and Contemporary Problems* 25, 4 (1960): 793–812, 804.

3. U.S. Bureau of the Census, *Statistical Abstract* (Washington, D.C.: U.S. Government Printing Office, 1960).

4. Alice Sparberg Alexiou, *Jane Jacobs: Urban Visionary* (New Brunswick, N.J.: Rutgers University Press, 2006), 39–40.

5. Peter Laurence, "The Death and Life of Urban Design: Jane Jacobs, the Rockefeller Foundation and the New Research in Urbanism, 1955–1965," *Journal of Urban Design* 11 (2006): 145–71, 145.

Contributors

Eugenie L. Birch is Lawrence C. Nussdorf Chair of Urban Research and Education in the School of Design and co-director, Penn Institute for Urban Research, University of Pennsylvania.

Gregory L. Heller works as a planner at the Delaware Valley Regional Planning Commission in Philadelphia. He is currently writing a biography of Edmund N. Bacon.

Scott Gabriel Knowles is an assistant professor of history and director of the Great Works Symposium, Drexel University.

Guian McKee is an associate professor at the University of Virginia Miller Center of Public Affairs, and is the author of *The Problem of Jobs: Liberalism, Race, and Deindustrialization in Philadelphia*.

Harris M. Steinberg, FAIA, is director of PennPraxis.

Index

Acknowledgments

If you want to get a conversation started in Philadelphia, just start asking questions about Edmund Bacon and his legacy, his imprint on the city—people have strong opinions. I entered the conversation in 2006 while doing research for an article about cold war disaster preparedness in Philadelphia. While working one afternoon at the University of Pennsylvania Architectural Archives I came across an essay in Bacon's files, "Philadelphia in the Year 2009." I copied it and slipped it into a folder, and over the next couple of years I passed it around to friends and used it in the classroom to drive discussion, at which it never failed. With 2009 drawing nearer, it occurred to me that the time was right to assemble a team of authors who could contextualize, interpret, and even improvise new ideas using Bacon's vision for the city of the future—the Philadelphia of today. Sincere thanks go to the Bacon family for permission to reprint Ed Bacon's "2009" essay.

Each author will thank individuals critical to his or her own chapter, but here I wish to acknowledge people who were instrumental to the entire project. Without archivists and librarians this book would not exist. Thanks go to Bill Whittaker and Nancy Thorne and the staff at the Architectural Archives of the University of Pennsylvania, where we were opening boxes and reading documents before they had even been catalogued! Thanks to David Baugh and the staff of the Philadelphia City Archives—they have more information on the Bicentennial Corporation than anyone. Thanks to Brenda Galloway-Wright and the staff of the Temple University Urban Archives; also to staff of the Cornell University Libraries, the University of Pennsylvania Libraries, and the Philadelphia Free Library.

The research effort would not have been possible without two programs at Drexel University, and two outstanding research assistants. The College of Arts and Sciences Humanities Fellows program facilitated a summer research fellowship for Madison Eggert-Crowe, who also compiled the index; and the STAR program in the Pennoni Honors College facilitated a summer research fellowship for Michael Hess. The Drexel Engineering Cities Initiative brown bag series provided a forum for discussion of the book at a key stage. Thanks to Julie Thompson for fact-checking work, and to PennPraxis for making this and additional administrative support available. Each of the authors—Eugenie L. Birch, Gregory Heller, Guian McKee, and Harris M. Steinberg—provided research assistance and editorial support that strengthened the entire book. Jeffrey A. Knowles provided intellectual support throughout, and performed a heroic edit and fact-check in the eleventh hour. Thanks also to Julia Meurling and Susan Meurling for preparation of the Bacon manuscript essay.

Barbara Beach at *Philadelphia Magazine* helped arrange article reproduction permission, and assisted with tracking down the name of the artist whose extraordinary work provides the cover and several images in the book, William Barron. James Balga helped arrange permission to reproduce I. M. Pei's drawing of Society Hill Towers. Thanks to Don Springer for allowing us to use his photograph of Ed Bacon at Pennypack Creek.

Two anonymous reviewers provided useful critiques of this volume. Sincere thanks also to Ashley Nelson and Alison Anderson at University of Pennsylvania Press. Bob Lockhart rallied around this rather unconventional project, and provided needed advice, critique, and support throughout—he is a gem of an editor.

9 780812 220780